The High-Status Track

SUNY Series
FRONTIERS IN EDUCATION
Philip G. Altbach, Editor
*In cooperation with the Graduate School of Education,
State University of New York at Buffalo.*

The Frontiers in Education Series features and draws
upon a range of disciplines and approaches in the
analysis of educational issues and concerns, helping to
reinterpret established fields of scholarship in education
by encouraging the latest synthesis and research.

Other books in this series include:

The High-Status Track

Studies of Elite Schools
and Stratification

Paul William Kingston
Lionel S. Lewis
Editors

State University of New York Press

Published by
State University of New York Press, Albany

© 1990 State University of New York

For information, address State University of New York
Press, State University Plaza, Albany, NY 12246

Library of Congress Cataloging-in-Publication Data

The High-status track: studies of elite schools and stratification/
    edited by Paul William Kingston, Lionel S. Lewis.
        p.   cm.— (SUNY series. frontiers in education)
    Bibliography: p.
    Includes index.
    ISBN 0-7914-0010-7.—ISBN 0-7914-0011-5 (pbk.)
    1. Upper classes—Education—United States. 2. Social status—
United States. 3. Power (Social sciences) I. Kingston, Paul W.
II. Lewis, Lionel S. (Lionel Stanley) III. Series.
LC4941.H54   1990
371.96'2'0973—dc20   89-31600
                                                                  CIP

10 9 8 7 6 5 4 3 2

Contents

PART III
PROFESSIONAL SCHOOLS

Tables and Figures

TABLES

FIGURES

PAUL WILLIAM KINGSTON
LIONEL S. LEWIS

Introduction

Studying Elite Schools in America

Our title, *The High-Status Track*, refers to the small sets of schools—private secondary schools, the most prestigious undergraduate institutions (overwhelmingly private), and the top-ranked professional schools of business and law—that disproportionately channel their graduates into eventual positions of economic and cultural privilege.[1] Within the huge American system of secondary and higher education, these are the elite schools. Their academic reputations are unsurpassed; their facilities and their students are frequently the best. Yet their elite stature involves much more than academic quality. These schools are socially elite, largely enrolling offspring of the upper middle and upper classes. Moreover, their graduates are prepared for privilege and enjoy disproportionate access to high status occupations.

Even if their place in the stratification system has not been systematically assessed, the distinctiveness of these schools and colleges is readily evident:

- A few years ago, when median family income in the United States was less than $24,000, not quite half of the students at twenty of the most prestigious prep schools came from families with yearly incomes of more than $100,000. The parental income of about two-thirds of the students exceeded $75,000.
- In 1983 sixteen prep schools had a total plant value of $382 million, and through the generous support of their alumni and wealthy benefactors, they had endowments totaling $381 million.

- In the 1930s and 1940s, graduates of the so-called Select Sixteen prep schools almost routinely (two-thirds) went on to Harvard, Yale, or Princeton. In the 1970s, after the widely touted broadening of access at these highly competitive universities, the rate was still one in five.
- Prep school graduates still have a significant edge in admission to Ivy League and other prestigious colleges over public school graduates with equal Standard Achievement Test scores (Cookson and Persell, 1985).
- In 1984, more than half of the entering freshmen at the twenty-eight private colleges and universities rated highly selective had family incomes exceeding $50,000, and more than a fifth were above $100,000. (The comparable figures for all freshmen were 13.7 percent and 4 percent, respectively.) (Astin et al., 1984.)
- More than half the 1961 class at Harvard reported incomes in excess of $100,000.
- Although there are indications of a glut of M.B.A.s, graduates of a few top schools in 1985-86 command impressive starting salaries, approximately $40,000 on the average.
- A survey of some 3,000 senior managers and directors of 208 large corporations showed that about one-third had graduated from one of eleven top undergraduate institutions, eleven master of business programs, or nine law schools. In addition, 12 percent had attended one of sixteen elite boarding schools (Useem and Karabel, Chapter 8).
- A detailed study of Chicago Bar Association leadership roles indicates that an Ivy League law school degree greatly enhanced the chances of having attained this prominence in the profession. About a quarter of all leaders of Chicago's bar went to an Ivy League law school, and another 35 percent went to the University of Chicago or Northwestern (Cappell and Halliday, 1983.)

The point of these examples is that elite schools have a strong, _current_ connection to the top of the social hierarchy. The historical reality of such a connection, especially before the huge expansion of higher education and the growth of the meritocratic ideal, is readily documented. Yet it may be tempting to dismiss the contemporary significance of these schools: Fitzgerald's Princeton of raccoon-coated bluebloods has been superseded in a contemporary meritocratic order—so the reasoning goes. It cannot be denied that the social function of these schools has evolved throughout the twentieth century, as has the general nature of the stratification system. However, the fact of change does not signify a loss of their significance, nor should the more sanguine visions of changes in the stratification system be uncritically accepted. This

volume will expand on the thesis that these schools continue to perpetu-
ate and create privilege.

WHERE YOU GO: DOES IT MATTER?

The underlying theme for this collection of essays and studies is
that elite schools are strongly linked to the top reaches of the stratification system and provide their graduates with distinctly favorable life
chances. Put another way, it matters *where* one goes to school, not just
how much schooling one receives. Our brief recital of facts to this effect
in the previous section lends some prima facie credence to this conclusion. However, with some notable exceptions, most scholarly research
has denied—explicitly or implicitly—that the prestige of a degree has
any economic consequence. It is worth noting that common sense and
conventional wisdom could not be more at odds with this scholarly
judgment.

Everyday language, especially in the corridors of affluence and
power, attests to the significance of where one was schooled: "Where
did he prep?"; "He is a Yalie"; "He's got that Ivy League style." Or
conversely: "What do you expect from someone from Podunk?" Credentials from elite schools are cultural markers, defining their possessor
as the right sort. The Dartmouth graduate in charge of a corporate department knows that the job applicant from Princeton is one of them, that
he belongs. The competing applicant from State College is a less certain
commodity and may be excluded from the competition simply for that
reason. Thus many aspiring to top occupational positions make great
efforts to go to what most agree are the right schools. They believe that
this certification will have a pay-off in their eventual careers.

That many attach great significance to the prestige of degrees is
readily evident in patterns of application for college admission. At a
time when overall college attendance rates are dropping and many institutions have been forced into elaborate marketing efforts just to survive,
applications at many Ivy League schools are at record levels. Although
total costs amount to more than $15,000 a year, Harvard received 13,200
applications for 1,600 freshman slots in 1984. Princeton received almost
1,000 more applicants in 1984 than in the previous year (Maeroff, 1984).
Admission rates at these and some other prestigious institutions (e.g.,
Stanford, Amherst, and Yale) are less than one out of five (Fiske, 1985).

After some downturn in the early 1970s, applications to very expensive prep schools are also strong. A 1984 survey of a large number of
these schools showed that at almost three-quarters of them, applications

had increased over the previous year (Boarding Schools, 1984). In recent years some of the larger prominent New England schools such as Exeter and Choate received more than 500 applications; Woodberry Forest, perhaps the leading Southern school, received more than 300. Costs at a school of this caliber are about $10,000 a year. Admission is quite competitive at the best schools—less than a fifth are accepted at Groton, to cite an extreme case (*Peterson's Annual Guide, 1983*).

Why make such an investment? Parents sending their children to prep school expect that this will enhance the childrens' chances of getting into one of the elite colleges. These colleges are valued because they help open doors in the career world and to the most prestigious professional schools. Because of their financial pay-off, admission to these prestigious professional institutions is also very forthrightly coveted. The essays and studies in this volume indicate that this folk wisdom is valid: for the status maximizer, investment in attending an elite school is highly rational.

Nonetheless, since the first Coleman report, educational researchers have mostly ignored the significance of internal differentiation among schools in affecting life chances. Some have even argued that this lack of significance is a defining feature of the American system. In a prominent and well-received theoretical essay, "Education as an Institution," John Meyer (1977: 60) contends: "Since for many personnel assignment purposes all American schools have similar 'status rights,' variations in their effects should be small." Meyer's view is consistent with Ralph Turner's (1960) characterization of American society as being dominated by contest rather than sponsored mobility: individuals with broadly similar levels of education are thought to compete for desirable positions in a generally open contest on the basis of their own attributes; those who get these positions are presumed to have won them. The point of contrast is the British system of sponsored mobility, whereby "the elite or their agents, deemed to be best qualified to judge merit, choose individuals for elite status who have the appropriate qualities" (Turner, 1960: 857). The British elites are especially attracted to the presumed qualities of public school graduates (the English public school is private) who receive the added imprimatur of an Oxford or Cambridge degree. Once students enter these elite schools, their chances of subsequent induction into the elite are considerable. In British society, then, the right degree in itself creates highly favorable life chances.

Status attainment research, at first look, appears to support these claims. In a recent, elaborate study, *Who Gets Ahead?*, Christopher Jencks and his collaborators (1979) succinctly conclude that the answer is the more educated. Their answer is based on regression-based analyses designed to explain variance in occupational status and income. Confirming what many others have shown, their analyses indicate that *years* of education is the best single predictor of occupational status and income, and the additional explanatory power of degree prestige appears to be small or nonexistent. The direct effects of family background are comparatively weak.

The relevance of this sort of research for analyzing the top reaches of the social hierarchy is more thoroughly considered in Chapter 7. At this point, suffice it to say that distinctive elite-level processes can be hidden or overlooked in attempts to describe the "larger picture"—the general effects of education on the course of a career. The coefficients for education represent its *average* impact on all strata, the top, middle, and bottom. Obviously any pattern that has a bearing on small elite groups will contribute little to calculations of average impact. The possibility that a very small number of schools can create relatively great chances for attaining privilege (and the fact that those attending these schools are largely the children of the already privileged) is not taken into account by the status attainment perspective that has so dominated sociological analyses of the relationship between education and the stratification system.[2]

Although the neglect of elite schools and schooling reflects a theoretical concern to characterize the predominant, general processes involved in social mobility or what is now called "status attainment," the emphasis on years of education as an indicator of educational attainment also seems to involve some elements of the methodological tail wagging the substantive dog. Variables such as years of schooling and scales of occupational prestige are readily measured in large national surveys and lend themselves to the linear assumptions of regression-based analytical techniques. Results are deemed rigorous and hence are highly valued in the discipline and by those who distribute research money.

Involving so few, elite schools and their graduates generally escape the scrutiny of survey researchers and are thus largely missing from the social science literature. Though by no means impenetrable, the world of the elite is not readily available to the sociological observer—certainly less so than most computer tapes with survey data about the general population. To study elite-level processes, researchers must consider diverse methodologies, explore many less-than-perfect data sources, and proceed with unusual subtlety and sense of nuance. The study of elite education, in short, does not promise fully conclusive analyses readily summarized in a few statistical measures. This leaves such work outside the mainstream of contemporary sociological research.

In sum, whether out of theoretical conviction or methodological myopia, elite education at all levels has received little systematic attention. What Peter Cookson and Caroline Persell write about secondary boarding schools seems to apply as well to elite institutions of higher education: "If silence can be interpreted as an opinion then it is fair to say that most observers of the educational scene either consider the schools too specialized or snobbish to be relevant in the larger context" (1985: 15). Indeed, as Cookson and Persell note in their recent *Preparing for Power*, the last prominent sociological analysis of the impact of prep schools was in E. Digby Baltzell's (1964) insightful though largely impressionistic study, *The Protestant Establishment*, now more than twenty years old.

Research on colleges and professional schools has been at least equally sparse. As detailed in Chapter 7, some research has looked to the financial return of so-called college quality, a factor which has generally been viewed as a continuous variable. This, of course, implies that no set of schools such as the Ivy League has distinctive consequences. On the face of it, such an assumption seems problematic. Because sociologists have only very infrequently turned their attention to the specific institutional practices and social effects of the most prestigious institutions, analyses such as Jerome Karabel's (1984) historical study of admissions policies at Harvard, Yale, and Princeton is theoretically and empirically valuable, though noteworthy for its rarity.

At the professional school level, there seems to have been a recent obsession in developing (and debating) the rankings of institutions, and the popular press widely touts the spectacular salaries received by the graduates of the leading schools. Yet despite some notice of the disproportionate concentration of elite school graduates in prominent law firms (Smigel, 1964) and top managerial positions (Pierson, 1969), professional school practices and the ramifications of attending them have also not been systematically assessed.

DEFINING THE ELITE

If getting the right credential really does matter, the obvious question is: What schools are the best, the elite? Correlatively, what does it mean to be the best or most elite? Yet as obvious and directly relevant as these questions are to the concerns of this volume, it must be noted from the outset that there are no unambiguous answers. Determining what is the best or most elite involves both subjective and objective elements. In thinking about secondary schools, many in the upper class, as well as readers of Baltzell's sociological studies or Stephen Birmingham's (1968) journalistic accounts of life at this level may reply, "St. Grottesex." This is a coinage referring to exclusive private boarding schools. More widely recognized is the distinctive cachet of an Ivy League education—and possibly that at the "Little Three" (Amherst, Wesleyan, and Williams) and a small number of other private colleges and universities. And at the professional school level, the latest rankings are avidly discussed. Both aspirants and existing professional elites are keenly aware of the top echelon—Stanford, Harvard, etc., (or perhaps Harvard, Stanford, etc.). The fact that disparate observers arrive at basically similar rankings suggests that there is a recognizable, and recognized, top echelon at each level. The meaning of *best is* open to diverse interpretations, but popular answers show a remarkable consistency. Nonetheless, these lists do not reflect any conceptual precision in addressing the question, nor is there any authoritative membership list to cite.

This lack of precision is entirely understandable given the organization of American education. Different institutions do not have distinctive, formal rights and privileges that define their status as elite. Hence all graduates of any four-year college or university are eligible to apply for any occupational position that stipulates a bachelor's degree as a job requirement or to enter any post-B.A. educational program (though specific coursework may be required for some). In a formal sense, institutions at the same level confer equal certifications of academic achievement: a bachelor's degree is a bachelor's degree. American education, then, is not differentiated on an objective dimension that makes identification of the elite clear.

The elite status of certain American educational institutions rests on less tangible, less sharply demarcated subjective criteria—reputation and prestige (Trow, 1984). If a school is deemed an elite institution, that means that a sufficient number among its relevant constituencies—academics, students (and their parents) and occupational gatekeepers—consider it one of the best of its kind. Of course, these constituencies may emphasize different criteria in making their judgments, but as discussed later, these collective evaluations in large part rest on an institution's ability to generate favorable life chances for its graduates. However, without formal distinctions to both reflect and reinforce these subjective judgments, the resulting prestige hierarchy is not firmly fixed into clearly defined levels of status. Many educational institutions and affiliated social groups struggle to establish the prestige of their school, but as a basis for social distinction, prestige has a somewhat amorphous quality. A considerable number of schools can lay some claim to it: "They say it's the Harvard of the West"; "In a few years we'll be the

Princeton of the South"; "Everyone knows that they are the Williams of the Midwest." Distinctions among schools thus become blurred, not sharp; they mainly reflect the varying degrees of success that institutions have in convincing significant constituencies that they are the best.

The diversity of American society, the sheer size of the educational system, and the lack of detailed governmental control all combine to undercut the emergence of a sharply demarcated prestige hierarchy. Whatever the distinctive role Harvard and Yale may have had or presently have in our society, their preeminent standing as academic institutions is by no means as unchallenged as, say, that of Cambridge and Oxford in Britain, the *grandes ecoles* of France, or the universities of Tokyo and Kyoto in Japan. In these smaller, less diverse, and more traditional societies a consensus on prestige ratings has been more readily developed and has become reinforced through specific policies, especially recruitment patterns to top government and economic positions. On the other hand, Italy and to a lesser extent West Germany have relatively flat prestige hierarchies in higher education (even with the notable exceptions of the University of Rome and the University of Berlin). The governments of these countries have deliberately attempted to forge a unified system with minimal status distinctions. Comparatively, then, the American prestige educational hierarchy is less pronounced and delineated than in some societies but more so than in others. Nevertheless, the United States, proud of the ideal of one best system at *lower* levels, has significant and widely acknowledged differences in the social standing of institutions of *higher* learning. Indeed, noting the consequence of having so many private institutions of higher learning, Martin Trow (1984: 134) points to "the American interest in, indeed almost obsession with, relative prestige rankings among universities."

Although the degree of academic hierarchy and the distinctiveness of elite schools vary across societies, the underlying basis for judgments of esteem is remarkably similar. As Burton Clark (1983: 63) perceives:

> Institutions that place their graduates differentially are assigned different levels of prestige. What in comparative higher education is referred to as "institutional hierarchy" is a prestige ranking of institutions and sectors based primarily on perceived social value of graduation. Where are graduates placed in the labor force, and otherwise in social circles, that might shape life chances?

Thus the prestige of Princeton, Cambridge, and Kyoto reflects the career advantages enjoyed by their graduates. Similarly, Eton and Harrow in Great Britain as well as St. Paul's and Exeter in America have great prestige because so many of their graduates go on to highly esteemed colleges and universities and subsequent positions of economic privilege.

At first glance, this explanation of the basis for judgments of esteem may appear too simple. After all, isn't it a fact that faculty, students, and academic programs at Princeton are intellectually superior to those at State College or St. Theresa on the Hill? Isn't the same true for Groton by comparison to Anyplace High School? And wouldn't this hold true for schools at the top compared with those at the bottom of the hierarchies in other countries as well? Various academic and social indicators of quality appear to be closely interwined, so that the best or top schools on one dimension are also the best or top on others. This reinforcement of esteem from both academic and nonacademic quarters partly explains the consistency and the continuity of prestige hierarchies. Yet in the genesis of these rankings, the nature of an institution's connections to the stratification system is paramount. Those institutions with greater social value had the economic and cultural wherewithal to acquire academic value. With some notable exceptions, elite reputations in intellectual matters were built on the foundations of social elite connections. Moreover, schools with the highest academic esteem generally maintain these elite social connections, a fact that ensures their ongoing general prestige. In or by itself, a reputation for academic quality does not seem to have been sufficient for a school to gain a reputation as one of the best.

With the blurred contours of the prestige hierarchy, then, it is not really possible to specify with exact precision particular sets of schools as the elite institutions. Concretely, however, the essays and studies in this volume proceed with a rough but shared sense of which institutions are at the top and which generate the best life chances.

For secondary schools, these are private institutions—the prep schools. Most notable among them are a small number of boarding schools, predominantly located in rural areas of New England. Groton, Andover, Exeter, St. Paul's, Hotchkiss, Deerfield, and Woodberry Forest are prominent examples of these schools with national reputations. A somewhat larger number of private day schools are also distinctly connected to local elites—for example, Nichols in Buffalo, Kingswood in Hartford, Haverford in Philadelphia, Collegiate in Richmond, and St. Mark's in Dallas. Some wealthy suburban public schools (e.g., New Trier in Winnetka) or selective urban public schools (e.g., Bronx School of Science) can undoubtedly claim at least comparable academic quality, but none of the studies here considers whether these schools have consequences comparable to their prestigious private counterparts.

At the college or university level, these studies focus on a small set of schools with certain common characteristics: they are old (and frequently draped with ivy vines); they are expensive, largely Eastern, and with a few possible exceptions, private; and they have distinctly affluent and academically talented student bodies and alumni. Most prominent among these are the schools in the Ivy League (a well-known group of eight schools that banded together to form an athletic conference). Other private schools share these traits—e.g., the Little Three, Stanford, Swarthmore, Johns Hopkins, MIT, and the Seven Sisters (Mt. Holyoke, Smith, Wellesley, etc.). By some reckonings, a few public universities may also have some national elite status—e.g., the University of California at Berkeley, the University of Michigan, and the University of Virginia. And a few other institutions have regional reputations of the highest rank—e.g., Duke, Vanderbilt, Northwestern, Rice, and the University of North Carolina.

To reiterate: there is not a distinctive list of colleges and universities that have unambiguous elite stature; prestige is a somewhat amorphous asset. Yet for all the shadings of eliteness, there is remarkable continuity and consistency—among raters and over time—in the rankings of undergraduate schools. One evaluation of the 1940 status of colleges and universities (Coleman, 1973) listed eleven institutions at the top. Every one of them is included in the highest category of Astin et al.'s (1984) widely used "Selectivity Index" (based on the difficulty of admission) as well as in the highest categories in all prominent guidebooks for prospective students that employ somewhat more subjective rating criteria (see, for example, Cass and Birnbaum, 1984; Barron's, 1984). Ranking schemes employing very different methodologies (e.g., objective indicators of student body quality vs. reputations among a sample of putative experts) come up with essentially similar results. A few institutions may fare better or worse in particular rankings, but there is considerable consensus as to which ones are the best. The point to be drawn here is that researchers interested in studying the top of the collegiate hierarchy have a good sense of which institutions to include, even if the scope of their vision is not specifically defined.

A similar point holds for professional schools of law and business. The top schools are not clearly differentiated from those of somewhat lesser prestige, but those at the top in one scheme are at the top in others. Researchers readily know what dozen or so schools have the greatest prestige. Most of the debate about rankings seems to hinge on which is "really" number one—or the question may be, Is number four truly better than five? It is never about the broad contours of the top echelon. Notably, the elite professional schools are generally affiliated with institutions that also enjoy elite reputations at the undergraduate level. However, the prominence of a few public universities (California,

Michigan, and Virginia) at this level may be more established than at the undergraduate level.

A brief word should be interjected here to explain why this discussion of elite institutions at the professional level is restricted to law and business schools. Along with medical schools, they are the prime launching pads of high-income professional careers. With relatively few exceptions, those with other professional or graduate degrees do not become rich. A medical degree of any kind is a virtual ticket to the top reaches of the income hierarchy. In considerable measure this fact reflects the medical profession's power to limit the number of entrants into its ranks. Accordingly, given this ability to restrict supply, the prestige of physicians' degrees is relatively unimportant in determining income. Neither those in the legal profession nor those in business management have been so able to restrict supply. Consequently, with the great growth in the numbers of law and business school graduates, there is good reason to believe that the prestige ranking of these schools has acquired significance in affecting career chances.

For all the similarity in prestige rankings—and, indeed, their stability over time—there seems to be little value in striving for definitional precision in categorizing institutions as elite or not. On the other hand, how certain institutions acquire an elite reputation and how the meaning of *elite* has changed over time remain fruitful topics for investigation. It is also worthwhile to study the consequences of attending different schools that may have some claim to elite status. For example, does attending Harvard or Yale confer more advantages than attending other Ivy League institutions, other elite private colleges, or top-ranked public universities?

It is important to note that there is a danger in portraying the differentiation of the educational system at each level as simply a matter of varying degrees of quality or prestige on some multi-rung ladder. As several contributions in this volume make evident, there is good reason to believe that not all differences on some hierarchy are equally consequential in affecting life chances. Put another way, the effects of prestige or quality are not linear. Thresholds exist so that a relatively small number of institutions at the top distinctly enhance life chances, whereas a degree from a school of middling rank may not confer better chances than one from a school at the bottom of the prestige hierarchy. What we are saying here is that going to Yale or Stanford instead of State University has more consequence than going to State University instead of Northeast State College. If prestige is simply treated as a continuous variable with linear effects, the distinct impacts of institutions at the top of the hierarchy get lost and may well be overlooked.

THE NUMBERS INVOLVED

Whatever the disputes about what specific schools have elite status, it should be recognized that few students enjoy the benefits of being educated at an institution with any conceivable claim of this stature. Not only do these schools represent the tip of the academic iceberg, they are indeed a very small tip.

Consider, for example, the size of the tiny minority who go to the nation's most prestigious prep schools. Total enrollments at the Select Sixteen (Baltzell, 1958; Cookson and Persell, 1985) were less than 9,000 in recent years—not even 1 percent of all private secondary enrollments, and just a tiny fraction of total secondary enrollments. Private school enrollments account for about a tenth of secondary enrollments, but most of these schools are sectarian (primarily Roman Catholic and, increasingly, fundamentalist Protestant) and have no distinctive academic quality or social cachet. It is difficult to say reliably how many students attend a private secondary school that is not a local, religiously defined institution, but the numbers are few. *Peterson's Annual Guide to Independent Secondary Schools* (1983)—the most prominent collation of information for prospective applicants and their families—lists only about 1,200 schools. Prominent boarding schools as well as lesser day schools are included in this listing.

Attendance at an elite college is also rare. As a group, the Ivy League schools enroll about 0.5 percent of all undergraduates. More inclusive definitions of elite only slightly expand this percentage. Thus, the twenty-six schools (excluding the military academies) in the top category of *Barrons' Profiles of America Colleges* account for approximately 1 percent of total enrollments. And the seventy-four most selective private colleges and universities in Astin et al.'s widely noted selectivity index (1984) enrolled less than 3 percent of all full-time freshmen.

The college graduates who go on to get professional degrees in law, business, and medicine are a small minority, and those who go on to elite professional schools of business and law are a small percentage of this already select group. Just to give one indication of this latter group's size, consider the numbers who went to the top schools as identified in *Change* magazine (based on the assessments of a large number of "knowledgeable" scholars). In recent years, the top eleven business schools enrolled less than 11,000 students, about 5 percent of total graduate business enrollment. The top fifteen schools of law enrolled about 4,300 students in the first year, just more than a tenth of all first-year enrollments.

The case for studying elite schools, then, can hardly rest on the fact that they affect the life chances of many people. Indeed, with the general expansion of education, they have come to account for an even smaller proportion of enrollments at each level: that is, the size of these institutions has not grown in pace with the huge expansion of higher education. The democratization of higher education has largely meant expansion on the lower rungs of the prestige hierarchy, and thus elite schools have come to enroll a smaller proportion at each level. The reason for studying these schools is that their connections to the top reaches of the stratification system are distinctive. They thus affect the lives of many who have disproportionate social influence.

EMPIRICAL ISSUES

To establish the analytical framework for the concerns of this collection, it is useful to see the high-status track as an educational and occupational career path that provides highly favored life chances. The operating assumptions here are as follows: (1) the acquisition of a privileged economic position is strongly facilitated by passage through an interconnected system of prestigious educational institutions (and certain entry-level occupational positions); (2) this track is disproportionately travelled by the offspring of economically advantaged families; and (3) generally those who reach one step of this track in their educational and occupational career have a significant advantage in reaching each subsequent step—and eventually the highest-status positions.

In broad terms, this track includes several main steps. The first step is composed of private secondary schools or perhaps class-segregated, wealthy suburban high schools. With this experience, the chances of attending a selective, prestigious college—the second step—are greatly enhanced. In turn, the collegiate upper trackers have increased opportunities of meeting elite professional school requirements and of subsequently gaining access to lucrative entry-level positions (top law firms, certain corporate positions, or almost any medical practice) from which the next generation of the privileged will rise. Figure I.1 on page xxiv schematically represents this high-status track.

To be sure, many of the privileged did not travel on all or even any of the track, nor did even a large share of those who started on the track continue all the way. However, as analyses in this volume show, those who got on this track enjoyed unparalleled career success, and it was indeed disproportionately travelled by those with high-status backgrounds. The boxes and arrows of Figure 1.1 reflect a complex reality and point to a rich agenda for research. Here we indicate important topics that, to varying degrees, are addressed in the research reported in this volume.

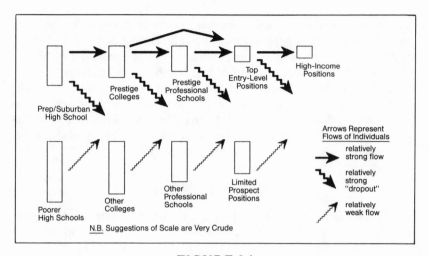

FIGURE I.1
The High-Income Track

The Emergence of Elite Schools

That a prestige hierarchy exists in American education is a popularly noted fact. At the same time, there has been only a limited amount of detailed research indicating how certain schools came to acquire an elite stature, and how various social conditions shaped the nature and functioning of this hierarchy. In short, research has not adequately analyzed organizational differentiation within education from a historical perspective.

The Content

Many have rightly criticized the practice (perhaps recently less evident) in the sociology of education of treating schools as black boxes that somehow produce outcomes (e.g., scores on standardized tests or aspirations to attend college). Sociologists must get inside these boxes and study the processes involved in generating these results. If schools actually do have such important consequences as the reproduction of social hierarchy, it is necessary to analyze how this process of reproduction takes place. This means examining what goes on in schools—what is taught (both in overt and hidden curricula), how it is taught, how students react to school efforts, and the extent to which learning is internalized and used as the basis for action. For the study of elite institutions, the analysis of content must particularly consider whether they have a distinctive emphasis on (and ability to instill) the cultural values, capacities, and skills that facilitate life within privileged circles. Quite clearly, those who pass through elite schools enjoy favorable life chances, but it is not evident that they do so because of what is taught or learned in these schools. To what extent do these schools *make* the right sort, and to what extent do these schools merely *mark* individuals as the right sort?

Links

As Figure 1.1 indicates, elite secondary, undergraduate, and professional schools may be seen as part of an interconnected track. However, the imagery of this figure lacks empirical documentation. A significant task of social arithmetic remains:

- To what extent do students at one stage of this track pass on to subsequent stages?
- How do the chances of students on the track at any one stage compare with those previously not on the track?
- To what extent does attendance at an elite institution, holding constant indicators of personal merit, enhance an individual's chances of staying on the track?
- How does elite school attendance in combination with other factors (especially family status and academic performance) work to affect subsequent academic attainment?
- What institutional practices (e.g., admission procedures and selection criteria) confer advantages on graduates of elite institutions?

Connection to the Stratification System

To understand the social role of elite institutions, it is necessary to consider both the social backgrounds of the prestigiously credentialled and how graduation from an elite institution is translated into a position of economic privilege. Even if the disproportionate concentration of the affluent at these institutions, as well as the relatively good life chances of their graduates, is reasonably plain, these general tendencies should be systematically documented with precise data. Moreover, they should be carefully examined for particular connections between certain elite institutions and specific segments of the top of the economic hierarchy.

Again, there is a formidable amount of social arithmetic to be done:

- How do the chances of acquiring prestigious, economically rewarded degrees vary by social status?
- To what extent do the prestigiously credentialled have better life chances than their less prestigiously credentialled counterparts? How are the benefits of elite institutions changed or conditioned by the

social status of their graduates? Do advantages vary by economic sector and region?

To the extent that these elite educational institutions disproportionately enroll the affluent and channel them into positions of privilege, they are involved in social reproduction. Yet beyond documenting the size and scope of advantages that accrue to the attainment of the right degree, researchers must also turn to the analysis of how this channelling occurs in the labor markets for top-level managerial and professional positions. What procedures are used to identify suitable candidates, who makes hiring decisions, and what evaluative criteria are used? The structure and function of labor markets, especially at the top of the occupational hierarchy, must be considered in analyzing the connection between elite schools and the stratification system.

THEORETICAL ISSUES

The empirical study of elite academic institutions and their connection to the stratification system presents its own challenges, but it is essential to recognize that this research has direct relevance to larger analytical questions in the sociology of education. Here we simply highlight a few key theoretical issues that are raised throughout this volume.

Achievement-Ascription

Analysis of social stratification, as Judah Matras writes (1975: 9), begins with the study of the "set of rules governing access to different social positions and to incumbency of the different social roles." From this starting point, our initial problem is to characterize this process in theoretically fruitful terms, especially as it involves educational institutions.

Various theorists (e.g., Linton, 1936; Parsons, 1951; Blau and Duncan, 1967) have quite similarly emphasized the distinction between ascribed (i.e., predominantly kinship-based) and achieved (i.e., individual merit) attributes as central to the analysis of stratification systems. At an empirical level this orientation has encouraged numerous attempts to assess the relative impact of each in affecting the distribution of power and privilege. (This analytical concern has been closely intertwined with an ideology which posits that ascription is bad and achievement criteria are just. This is in accord with the twentieth century liberal prescription to reward individual merit.) Thus, in their, pioneering study of the process of stratification, Blau and Duncan (1967) show that an achieved attribute, educational attainment, has the largest statistically independent effect on occupational attainment. As noted earlier, this finding has been replicated countless times. Educational attainment, however, has been found to be significantly affected by a number of ascribed characteristics. In fact, the major finding in the status attainment research since Blau and Duncan is that occupational prestige (and also income) is affected by a rather complex concatenation of factors, both achieved and ascribed.

At issue, however, is whether such a categorization of these factors accurately represents their true sociological meaning. There seems to be particular reason to question this meaning in regard to how top positions in the society are allocated and how education affects this allocation. Consider, for example, the case of a male Yale Law School graduate with a typical Anglo-Saxon name. In all likelihood he would have very high measured intelligence, and his graduation from such a prominent institution clearly represents a widely recognized achievement. After a series of interviews with prominent law firms, it can be expected that he would have a number of promising offers. A high-paying career would seem almost assured. However, an adequate sociological explanation of the facts of this career would have to recognize that ascribed characteristics—more specifically, particularistic criteria—may well be integral to this seemingly meritocratic selection process.[3]

To potential employers, graduation from Yale Law School does not simply represent some abstract ability at legal reasoning. Employers have neither the inclination nor the time to interview all law school graduates to find the most competent person available to, say, register securities. Technical competence is not their only concern, and, in any case, many skills will be learned on the job, not in school. Instead, it seems reasonable to suppose that credentials are used as a screening device: graduates from institutions like Yale are presumed relatively intelligent and more likely than others to have acquired through blood and training, or at least the latter, the appropriate elite cultural dispositions to fit in. As a consequence, certain elite institutions become the effective recruiting pool for top firms. These employers are personally comfortable with recruits who reflect the background and outlook of other employees, clients, and friends. Moreover, junior associates with a prestigious degree can reinforce the firm's standing.

On the other hand, a Catholic ethnic from St. John's Law School may also have the requisite skills to register securities, but neither he or any of his classmates are considered by the same set of firms that interview the Yale graduate. In short, a process that relies on ascription rather than achievement operates to the advantage of the Yale graduate and to the disadvantage of the St. John's graduate. Their individual merit is not directly compared, nor will it ever be. Although the interviewers may not have previously known the Yale graduate, his institutional affiliation provides access to the selection process. This example reflects what Matras (1975) calls "credential cronyism." Needless to say, the workings of more direct cronyism (friendship and family ties) may also predominantly benefit the offspring of wealthy families in gaining access to positions with high-income potential.

More generally, we suggest that certain important factors affecting occupational attainment or income do not necessarily reflect social processes connoted by the commonly affixed achievement label. In other occupations besides law, educational credentials may be the basis for substantially particularistic, ascriptive, not achievement-oriented selection processes. Indeed, Collins (1971), Bourdieu (1977), and others argue that schools predominantly teach different status cultures. They further contend that educational requirements are designed to restrict entry into elite positions and to ensure that only those with the elite culture have access. Although these analyses have their critics and are not conclusive, they do at least suggest that the significant effect of educational attainment on occupational career does not simply reflect the workings of an achievement-oriented process as that term is commonly understood.

That education explains the largest proportion of variance in occupational prestige or income does not mean that the stratification system is predominantly universalistic. Nominally achievement-oriented criteria can be part of relatively subtle particularistic modes of access to social position. To the extent that schools, most particularly elite schools, both inculcate and certify economically valued cultural capital, and that processes of credential cronyism are at work, educational attainment must be viewed as more than an achievement.

Human Capital, Cultural Capital, and Screening Perspectives

Complementary to the view that education is rewarded as an achievement, human capital theorists (e.g., Becker, 1964) assume that workers are paid a (real) wage rate proportional to their marginal product (subtracting costs for general training). Those with the highest rates of pay are presumably the most productive. In this view the labor market closely approximates the conditions of the free and efficient market that is integral to microeconomics. Human capital theorists explain the fact that education has a positive return—educational costs are an investment in oneself—on the supposition that better-educated workers are more productive and are in short supply (Blaug, 1972). The better educated are thus relatively well paid, and graduates of certain schools enjoy particularly good prospects simply because they are particularly well trained and are scarce relative to demand.

Especially in relation to managerial and professional positions, however, other analysts have charged that education primarily serves a credentialling or screening function (Miller and Reisman, 1969; Griliches and Mason, 1972, Thurow, 1975; Bowles and Gintis, 1976; Collins, 1971). The argument here is that entry into occupational positions is not open as the free competition model of the human capital theory suggests. Rather, these critics commonly contend, access to many positions "generally requires that a person of a given skill level also possess a minimun level of educational attainment" (Taubman and Wales, 1974: 153). Thus, in part, the better educated earn relatively high income because only this group is considered for the top jobs. In this view, the better educated are the beneficiaries of a system of restricted entry: they do not compete with equally deserving though lesser-educated individuals. The latter are in effect largely barred from certain high-paying positions. Attainment of the desired credentials has become recognized as a key market signal that distinguishes some applicants from the larger pool of aspirants (Spence, 1974).

Yet if education is a screen, the issue remains as to what the gatekeepers are looking for—that is, what is education signalling? Employers may seek out job applicants with certain credentials for reasons of economic rationality, as a wide range of economists such as Thurow and Taubman and Wales emphasize, or for reasons related to social discrimination, as sociologists such as Collins and Bourdieu argue—or perhaps some combination of both reasons.[4] In the former view, educational credentials are used to screen for human capital—skills and capacities that are directly productive in a technical sense. Quite differently, in the latter view, educational credentials are markers of cultural capital—the personal style, social outlooks and values, and aesthetic tastes that suit one for socially valued positions.

Much of the related debate on this question has been carried out on a very general level: what is *the* social meaning of educational credentials, or why does investment in education *typically* pay off? As argued in Chapter 10, however, "different sorts of education may have different impacts in different contexts—and, by implication, may do so for different reasons." A fine-grained analysis of what happens at the elite and nonelite levels is necessary for a full understanding of how educational and occupational careers are connected.

The School System and Rewards

The central role of education in the system of stratification raises other theoretical questions. As we noted, a prevalent scholarly view is that American education is essentially homogeneous—that is, for the most part, all schools at a certain level have similar career consequences (Turner, 1960; Treiman and Terrell, 1975). Although college graduates are thus presumed to have greater career chances than those with lesser education, the college graduates themselves are primarily distinguished by their personal qualities—especially ability, intelligence, and personality. Given roughly comparable educational attainment, individuals in American society openly compete on the basis of their own attributes for high positions.

Is Turner's ideal type of contest mobility as defined above consistent with the reality of American society? To the extent that the graduates of certain elite schools enjoy better chances than their equally talented but less prestigiously credentialled counterparts, there is reason to call into question this characterization of the American system. Again, one should be open to the possibility that distinct processes operate at the elite level; it may well be that some elements of sponsorship to elite positions are embedded in a general system of contest mobility.

Also at issue is how to theoretically characterize the educational system's allocative role. At the risk of oversimplification, the question is this: Do educational institutions generate opportunity and social mobility or do they serve to reproduce the stratification system? Of course the former view has been an article of faith in popular thought and much scholarly analysis. However, critics of this view have increasingly made the case that schools work to maintain intergenerational inheritance of status under the guise of a seemingly fair process (see, e.g., Bowles and Gintis, 1976). This latter argument rests on the contention that the offspring of high-status families are indirectly transmitted privilege because they are likely to attain the right credentials. Entrance to the schools that confer these credentials may well be largely governed by considerations of merit, but since the children of high-status families have had greater opportunity to become meritorious, they disproportionately gain admittance. And of course their families can more readily bear the considerable expense of acquiring the right degrees.

Any optimistic view that schools foster mobility is undercut by the simple fact that the extent of intergenerational circulation mobility has remained fairly constant throughout the century even as access to the educational system has expanded enormously. However, such negative evidence against the optimistic vision does not in itself make the case for the critics. If schools do not create mobility, that does not mean that they are the active agents of social reproduction, that they are central to a scheme that ensures the status quo. To make the case for a reproductive role, it is necessary to clarify, theoretically and empirically, the processes by which schools are involved in channelling the offspring of various strata into occupational positions similar to their origins.

FINAL COMMENTS

The purpose of this chapter has been to highlight an empirical and theoretical agenda for the study of elite schools. These institutions are important to study for the simple fact that they are so obviously connected to privileged social circles, strata with great societal influence. Moreover, an analysis of these institutions is crucial to developing a full, nuanced understanding of how and why education affects individual life chances as well as the structure of the stratification system.

No single collection could possibly address all the concerns which we have raised here. Our hope is that the papers in this volume will provide intriguing, worthwhile insights into specific aspects of the general topic and, collectively, underscore its importance. Toward that end, we have included contributions with diverse empirical concerns, methodological approaches, and theoretical commitments. We hope that our prefatory notes to each section will indicate their thematic relationships, but we should emphasize that these essays and studies do not reflect scholarly consensus among the contributors.

Because a concern for social stratification runs through all these contributions, it is especially relevant to note that they do not explicitly share a particular theoretical perspective of the stratification system. Our introductory comments are implicitly premised on a neo-Weberian model. This view focuses on the structured distribution of life chances of multiple-status groups defined by economic *and* cultural similarities, including educational affiliation. Thus we speak loosely of overlapping yet partially different groups—the privileged, the affluent, the economic elite, and top-status groups. For the most part, the contributions here seem generally compatible with this perspective, but a prior theoretical commitment to a neo-Weberian model is not necessary for the profitable study of elite schools. Indeed, the study of elite schools may be an important basis for refining the social theory of what Anthony Giddens calls the "structuration of society."

What these essays and studies share is very general: an awareness that elite schools play an important role in affecting who acquires positions of privilege and influence. Together, they are valuable in advancing our understanding of this process.

NOTES

1. As explained below, at the secondary level the focus is on independent college preparatory schools ("prep schools"), not on the much more numerous parochial schools.

2. This is the substantial body of research, following Blau and Duncan's (1967) pioneering work, that analyzes occupational attainment as a function of a complex concatenation of individual ascribed and achieved characteristics. Using various forms of the linear model, this research has documented the net and combined effects of such variables on occupational attainment. Clearly, for two decades this research has dominated social science efforts to understand the connection between educational and occupational attainments.

3. Particularistic attributes are those which enhance a person's access to certain statuses because of his or her membership in a particular group (Matras, 1975).

4. Such screening may be rational because certain credentials may be viewed as reasonable proxies for characteristics which are generally desired. Although it is difficult, if not impossible or prohibitively expensive, to acquire direct information on an applicant's intelligence and personality, employers may know from past experience that applicants with certain credentials tend to have certain desired characteristics. Of course, talented individuals with lesser credentials may lose out in this labelling process whereas mediocre persons with better credentials stand to benefit, but employers get an inexpensive way to sort out job applicants. Since there are generally no reliable indicators of subsequent job performance anyway, this low-cost way of obtaining information and selecting applicants may be considered rational for a profit-maximizing firm (Taubman and Wales, 1974).

REFERENCES

Astin, Alexander, et al. 1984. *The American Freshman: National Norms for Fall 1984.* Los Angeles: Cooperative Institutional Research Program. University of California, Los Angeles.

Baltzell, E. Digby. 1958. *Philadelphia Gentlemen: The Making of a National Upper Class.* New York: Free Press.

————. 1964. *The Protestant Establishment.* New York: Random House.

Barron's Educational Series, College Division, comp. and ed. 1984. *Barron's Profiles of American Colleges.* Woodberry, N.Y. Barron's Educational Series.

Becker, Gary. 1964. *Human Capital.* New York: National Bureau of Economic Research.

Birmingham, Stephen. 1968. *The Right People: A Portrait of the American Social Establishment.* Boston: Little Brown.

Blau, Peter, and Otis Duncan. 1967. *The American Occupational Structure.* New York: Wiley and Sons.

Blaug, Mark. 1972. "The Correlation between Education and Earnings: What Does It Signify?" *Higher Education* 1 (1972): 53-77.

Boarding Schools. 1984. "Boarding Schools' Admissions Outlook." Boston: National Association of Independent Schools.

Bourdieu, Pierre. 1977. "Cultural Reproduction and Social Reproduction." Pp. 487-511 in *Power and Ideology in Education,* edited by Jerome Karabel and A.H. Halsey. New York: Oxford University Press.

Bowles, Samuel, and Herbert Gintis. 1976. *Schooling in Capitalist America: Educational Reform and the Contradictions of Economic Life.* New York: Basic Books.

Cappell, Charles, and Terence Halliday. 1983. "Professional Projects of Elite Chicago Lawyers, 1950-1974." *American Bar Foundation Research Journal* 1983 (2): 291-340.

Cass, James, and M. Birnbaum. 1984. *Comparative Guide to American Colleges.* New York: Harper and Row.

Clark, Burton. 1983. *The Higher Educational System: Academic Organization in Cross-National Perspective.* Berkeley and Los Angeles: University of California Press.

Coleman, Richard. 1973. "Report on College Characteristics." Cambridge: MA: Harvard-MIT Joint Center for Urban Affairs.

Collins, Randall. 1971. "Functional and Conflict Theories of Educational Stratification." *American Sociological Review.* 36: 1002-1019.

Cookson, Peter, and Caroline Persell. 1985. *Preparing for Power: America's Elite Boarding Schools.* New York: Basic Books.

Fiske, Edward. 1985. *Selective Guide to Colleges.* New York: Times Books.

Griliches, Z.,and W. Mason. 1972. "Education, Income, and Ability." *Journal of Political Economy* 80 (3, Pt. 2): S74-S103.

Jencks, Christopher, et al. 1979. *Who Gets Ahead? Determinants of Economic Success in America.* New York: Basic Books.

Karabel, Jerome. 1984. "Status Group Struggle, Organizational Interests. and the Limits of Institutional Autonomy: The Transformation of Harvard, Yale, and Princeton 1918-1940." *Theory and Society* (January): 1-40.

Linton, Ralph. 1936. *The Study of Man.* New York: Appleton-Century Crafts.

Maeroff, Gene. 1984. "Top Eastern Colleges Report Unusual Rise in Applications." *New York Times,* February 21, 1984, A1, C10.

Matras, Judah. 1975. *Social Inequality, Stratification and Mobility.* Englewood Cliffs, N.J.: Prentice-Hall.

Meyer, John. 1977. "Education as an Institution." *American Journal of Sociology* 83: 55-77.

Miller, S., and Frank Reissman. 1969. "The Credential Trap." Pp. 69-77 in *Social Class and Social Policy,* edited by S. Miller and F. Reissman. New York: Basic Books.

Parsons, Talcott. 1951. *The Social System.* Glencoe, Ill.: Free Press.

Peterson's Annual Guide to Independent Secondary Schools. 1983. Princeton, N.J.: Peterson's Guides.

Pierson, George. 1969. *The Education of American Leaders.* New York: Praeger.

Smigel, Earwin. 1964. *The Wall Street Lawyer.* New York: Free Press.

Spence, A. Michael. 1974. *Market Signaling: Informational Transfer in Hiring and Related Screening Processes.* Cambridge: Harvard University Press.

Taubman, Paul, and Terence Wales. 1974. *Higher Education and Earnings.* New York: Carnegie Commission.

Thurow, Lester. 1975. *Generating Inequality.* Washington D.C.: Brookings Institute.

Treiman, Donald, and K. Terrell. 1975. "The Process of Status Attainment in the United States and Great Britain." *American Journal of Sociology* 81(3): 563-583.

Trow, Martin. 1984. "The Analysis of Status." Pp. 132-164 in *Perspectives on Higher Education,* edited by Burton Clark. Berkeley and Los Angeles: University of California Press.

Turner, Ralph. 1960. "Sponsored and Contest Mobility and the School System." *American Sociological Review* 25: 855-867.

Useem, Michael, and Jerome Karabel. 1985. "Pathways to Top Corporate Management." *American Sociological Review* 51: 184-200.

Part I

Preparatory Schools

INTRODUCTION

At the beginning of the high-status track (see Figure I.1, page xxiv in the Introduction) are private secondary schools—the training ground for few, but a crucial experience in many privileged lives. Yet although the affluence and power of their graduates should have commanded attention, social science has barely penetrated their world. In the popular imagination, they seem little more than a nice, nonessential accoutrement to a "preppy" life style, just as deck shoes, all-cotton khaki pants, and horn-rimmed glasses are the approved uniform.

While building on the efforts of a handful of previous scholars, the papers in this section clearly indicate that the general scholarly neglect of private schools is shortsighted and that the popularization of "preppydom" hardly represents their sociological significance. As these analyses collectively indicate, the educational experience at these schools has been distinctive in important ways, their graduates enjoy distinctive advantages in their careers, and these schools themselves have distinctive, ongoing ties to the upper class and its institutions.

Christopher Armstrong's chapter, "On the Making of Good Men: Character-Building in New England Boarding Schools," is appropriately historical. It traces how the present-day commitments of these schools are shaped by their Puritan roots and the cultural clashes of the developing modern American order. This historical perspective also suggests that these schools are not timeless in their commitments and practices and that Goffman's "total institution" metaphor cannot be uncritically used to describe current life at these schools. Belatedly and sometimes irresolutely, these schools and their students responded to changes in the larger society. Notwithstanding changes in efforts to build "character," Armstrong's largely implicit argument is that these socialization efforts had been successful, at least in the restricted sense of creating men to run the corporate world. Of course, it is difficult to rigorously demonstrate socialization effects for contemporary schools, much less for the schools of past eras. Yet if Armstrong's point about the declining emphasis on moral education at these schools is correct, one may be less inclined to conclude that any distinctive success of their current graduates is attributable to the actual content of their education.

Caroline Persell and Peter Cookson's analysis, "Chartering and Bartering: Elite Education and Social Reproduction," (Chapter 2) also takes us inside the operations of these elite schools. This paper came out of a larger project that resulted in their justly acclaimed (though controversial) book, Preparing for Power: America's Elite Boarding Schools. The particular value of this study is that it shows that these schools do not merely "pass on" already privileged students to subsequent privileged positions. Consciously and effectively, they work to create advantages for their students by adroitly manipulating their college placement: that is, the connections between elite secondary schools and elite institutions of higher education partly reflect institutionalized advantages that operate within the interstices of a sometimes meritocratic order.

Chapter One

On the Making of Good Men: Character-Building in the New England Boarding Schools

---

Character is higher than intellect.
—Ralph Waldo Emerson, "The American Scholar," August 31, 1837

In a very real sense, Phillips Academy was founded as a bulwark against change, an agency for maintaining the virtues of the past.
—The Bicentennial History of Phillips Academy, Andover

The last true autocrats of our society were the strong-minded, minister-headmasters of New England schools, fortified by traditions, motivated by a sense of righteousness, a conviction that they were acting under the will of God.
—Maitland Edey, Kent '28

PURITAN CHARACTER BUILDING: THE EARLY SCHOOLS

Character development has been the chief aim of the New England boarding schools over the past two centuries, even though the definition

3

and means of developing character have changed in the two hundred odd years since the founding of Phillips Academy in Andover, Massachusetts (1778). The concern with moral education and character has deep roots in New England's Puritan past. Much of boarding school history involves the attempt of old New England families to preserve the moral character of their Puritan heritage. Just how the attempt was made in the boarding schools they founded is the subject of this chapter.

Many of the schools were founded as conservative, reactionary responses to societal changes that were perceived as threatening to the preeminence of Puritan values. When Samuel Phillips, Jr., established Phillips Academy in 1778, he wanted to develop the moral character of Andover's boys by teaching them Puritan values.

Likewise, during the second half of the nineteenth century, when so many boarding schools were founded, the founders' concerns were with the corrupting influences of cities and the need to protect childhood innocence until proper moral character could be developed in sequestered, country settings. Most of the best-known New England boarding schools were started by moralists from old New England families desirous of maintaining the prominence of their virtues and values in a society that was becoming increasingly heterogeneous and urban.

Samuel Phillips sketched his ideas for his academy in a letter to his father in 1776. The letter not only outlined his ideas for his new school in Andover but also foreshadowed many of the concerns of old Puritan families. These concerns persisted throughout the nineteenth century leading them to found schools to teach and preserve their morality.

> In the first place one of the Best of Men to take Command ... who consequently will make it his first and chief concern to see to the regulation of their MORALS most attentively and vigorously to guard against the first Dawning of depraved Nature; to be early diligently painting in the purest simplicity the Deformity and Odiousness of VICE, the Comeliness and Amiableness of VIRTUE-who will spare no Pains to convince them of the indispensable Obligations they are under to abhor and avoid the former, and to love and practice the latter.[1]

The Phillips family also founded Phillips Exeter in Exeter, New Hampshire, in 1783. The two Phillips academies operated as academies, with scholars housed with families in town, until they became boarding schools in the late nineteenth century. Today, they are the largest, oldest, and most diverse in student population of all the boarding schools, and perhaps the most competitive academically.

Round Hill

The first true boarding school was Round Hill, founded by George Bancroft and Joseph Green Cogswell, an Exeter graduate, in 1823. Although Round Hill survived but eleven years, it established the precedent for most of the later schools by developing moral character in three ways—rigorous academics, required athletics, and daily devotionals that made religion a central focus of school life.

Round Hill's site on a hill overlooking the Connecticut River near Northampton, Massachusetts, was chosen because both schoolmasters believed that an unspoiled natural setting was a key to character development. Rural locations would become essential for most of Round Hill's successors. Endicott Peabody, Groton's founder, commented on the significance of the country location in 1925 when he said, "So long as people dwell in great cities, where the atmosphere, physical and moral, is in a large measure unwholesome, so long the boarding schools will continue to minister to the children of those who can afford to send them out of the towns."[2] Proximity to the natural world was necessary to maintain the uncorrupted innocence of young boys, and a country setting became increasingly attractive as cities became larger, dirtier, and more problem-filled during the last century.

More than that, Round Hill's schoolmasters saw the complete control of boys entrusted to their care as the key to character development. They intended to exercise the close parental supervision of demanding fathers: "If we would attempt to form the character as well as to cultivate the minds of the young, we must be able to control all their occupations. . . to have them under the same roof with ourselves, and we become responsible for their manners, habits, and morals."[3]

Sports were a crucial component of the curriculum. Boys learned to ride, skate, and swim. They played baseball, a primitive version of football, and wrestled. Often, instructors joined the games. Bancroft daily led the "morning mile," and Cogswell organized long and exhausting walking trips throughout New England.[4]

The Round Hill schedule controlled a boy's day from dawn to dusk, much as successor schools would. The day began at 6 a.m. A religious service preceded breakfast, and there were outside calisthenics between breakfast and morning classes. The main meal at noon was followed by another half hour of exercises and then classes all afternoon. A short exercise period separated the conclusion of afternoon classes and dinner at 5:30. Boys studied their languages (Spanish, French, German, and Italian) from 6:30 to 8:00 and, following evening prayers, retired at 8:15 p.m.

Other important precedents were set at the Northampton school. With its high tuition of $300 ($125 more than Harvard), it attracted sons from wealthy families. "The names of many great merchant families of the North, landed families of the South, and pioneers in industrialization appear on its list of alumni."[5] The Northampton school established a tradition among old and newly rich Protestant families of educating offspring in New England boarding schools where character was developed along traditional Puritan lines.

So famous did short-lived Round Hill become that de Tocqueville visited it when on his fact-finding trip that led to the writing of *Democracy in America*. Thomas Jefferson, perhaps aware of the school's attraction for America's evolving aristocracy of wealth rather than the "natural aristocracy" of character he sought, commented: "This will certainly prove a great blessing to the individuals who can obtain access to it. The only ground of regret is the small extent of its scale; in the few who can have its advantages, it will lay a solid foundation of virtue as well as learning."[6]

The practice of sending children away for proper moral training was an old Puritan practice. Puritans entrusted the disciplining of their children to others during the pubescent period to avoid friction between parents and child. Many Puritan sons were apprenticed to master craftsmen in neighboring towns, and daughters were "boarded out" with local families to learn their domestic duties. The New England practice of apprenticing a son to a craftsman had its variation among the privileged, who entrusted their sons to demanding schoolmasters to teach them properly. In the South, gentlemen often placed sons in families of fellow planters or even sent them abroad to be raised.

Most of the families who sent sons to Round Hill lived in rapidly growing cities, and many desired a more pastoral and quiet setting for their offsprings' education. Although America had only eleven cities in 1820 with more than 10,000 residents, 70 percent of Round Hill's students in 1829 lived in ten of those cities. Distrust of the city streets as a suitable environment for children was a concern of wealthy fathers who were spending more time on business and less time overseeing the raising of their sons. By entrusting them to the care of gentlemen schoolmen in the cloistered confines of a country school, they were assured of character training away from both urban blight and maternal coddling.

One of Round Hill's early graduates was George C. Shattuck, Jr., who had a long and successful career as professor and dean of the Medical School at Harvard. He married a sister of two Round Hill classmates, Anne Brune of Baltimore, and converted to her Episcopalian religion, a practice that became increasingly common among old New England families during the second half of the century. Shattuck's love of his new religion and his fond memories of Round Hill led him to found St. Paul's

School at Millville, his summer home outside Concord, New Hampshire. He hoped St. Paul's might provide his boys with the same character education he remembered at Round Hill.

St. Paul's: Cloistered Christianity

St. Paul's opened in 1856 and was modelled on the principles of Round Hill as George Shattuck had remembered: "The object [of the school] was to develop what was good in boys, to discourage & check what was evil [,] to train & educate all their powers mental physical and moral, & the Episcopal Church was selected as the most likely to accomplish these objects."[7]

To develop "what was good in boys," Shattuck chose Henry Augustus Coit, son of an Episcopal minister in an old Connecticut family, who had followed his father's example and had become an Episcopal clergyman after attending the University of Pennsylvania. Coit was an aloof and tightly controlled man, whose rigidity made him appear shy to adults and a distant Puritan father to his boys. His personal control set the tone for St. Paul's as well as successor clerics Peabody at Groton and Sill at Kent.

The Episcopal headmasters who ruled the church schools through the last half of the nineteenth and first half of the twentieth century were the last Puritan divines in this culture, although they preferred to think of themselves as proper Episcopal gentlemen. Their devotion to their clerical callings imposed such repressive regimens of rational self-control in their schools that boys more often feared than loved them. One student remarked of Coit that "he came as straight from the twelfth century as John Brown from the Old Testament."[8] Coit saw himself as the living embodiment of his boys' consciences. So powerful was his moral authority that boys recalled him appearing in their dreams thirty and forty years after leaving school. His personal restraint and self-denial set a decidedly Puritan tone in his Episcopal school.

St. Paul's schedule maintained the same tight control over boys' lives as the Round Hill schedule. After the rising bell at dawn (5:00 a.m. in the summer), prayers were said before breakfast. Classes lasted all morning until 1:30. The afternoons were for recreation, and initially sports were rather informal. By the 1890s, St. Paul's had football, but the school played its games intramurally and did not develop outside rivalries with other schools until later. With the increasing importance of organized sports in the afternoons, they became a significant component of character building. At St. Paul's none was more important than ice hockey during the winter, which St. Paul's claims to have introduced to this country from Canada.

The isolation of St. Paul's removed it even farther from the larger society than Round Hill. Frequently boys came from the Middle Atlantic states, a journey that took more than a day's travel from Philadelphia or New York. Many of the first students were relatives of Round Hill alumni: nearly 70 percent of the 136 families who had attended Round Hill educated sons at St. Paul's between 1856 and 1914.[9]

Coit sought to develop an explicit Episcopal version of the education at Round Hill, but the essential lesson remained the same: moral character development emphasizing personal integrity, honor, and justice and a respect for these qualities rather than wealth.

In Coit's words, the quality he most sought to develop in his charges was **Honour**:

> "The honour which you ought to show to one another here is just the same which you ought to show when you are full grown to your fellow men. Honour will be honour in the dealings with me here. Honour is real manliness, which is able to look everyone full in the face; not from the possession of vulgar brass, but from a free conscience that has nothing to fear because there is nothing to hide . . . Honour, boys, I say again is real manliness, and that is the tone I want to establish here.[10]

The Other Church Schools

St. Paul's is directly linked to several other schools founded in the second half of the nineteenth century. Joseph Burnett, a self-made millionaire and born-again Episcopalian, endowed St. Mark's in Southborough, Massachusetts, in 1865 at the instigation of Coit. Burnett had educated his oldest son at St. Paul's, and when he entered his second, Coit suggested he start his own school.

St. Mark's introduced a key change to boarding school life. The leaders in the sixth form (a term borrowed by the Episcopal schools from the British schools, which designated the senior class) were chosen by the faculty as "monitors" to act as liaisons between the faculty and boys. They presided over daily activities and helped enforce discipline in the lower forms. Monitors, or prefects, as they were known at other church schools, became powerful influences in the school. At times, they could be abusive of their power, as many had been in British schools, where young boys were often exploited for sexual favors and physically beaten by the prefects.

Another important school was established at Groton, Massachusetts. When Endicott Peabody began Groton with twenty-four boys from many of Boston's old families in 1884, he hoped to combine the Episcopal church influence of the earlier schools with the British aristocratic concern with leadership preparation. He had been educated at Cheltenham in England and sought to make his boys aware of obligations to lead that the English schools tried to inculcate. Groton's concern with developing a sense of noblesse oblige has been unique. Whereas most others wanted to educate boys to become gentlemen of character, Peabody wanted more: an aristocratic class of men whose moral strength would be validated by exercising responsible power. In the person of Franklin Delano Roosevelt, Peabody succeeded. Roosevelt, as one of only three boarding-school-educated presidents (Choate's John F. Kennedy and Andover's George Bush being the others), personified in his democratic policies the aristocratic sense of public service for the general good that Peabody hoped to instill.

Peabody's Groton was established to develop "manly Christian character" by toughening up boys to do battle as good, Christian soldiers. Groton's brand of Christianity was more aggressive and competitive than its predecessors. Boys were expected to prove themselves in sports, and the top performers were often chosen as school leaders because they showed through self-sacrifice, loyalty, and persistence the values that won victories in the battle of life.

That "the Rector's" (as Peabody was known) values were often in conflict with those of wealthy parents who sent boys to Groton was of little concern to Peabody. Severe, Spartan simplicity was the rule, exemplified in the small cubicles that the boys lived in, with bare walls and only a draw curtain for a door. Windows were left open at night all year round. The Spartan nature of Groton and the often severe power of the prefects made it more like the British schools than any other American school.

The Headmasters: Patrician Patriarchs and Moral Monarchs

It was a one-man school from start to finish, run by a peculiar but inspired man, one in which every boy had a personal relationship with that man. The relationship may not have been a good one. It may have been based on fear and avoidance—as mine was—but there was nothing phony or institutionalized or plastic about it. It was real."[1]

The memory of a 1928 Kent graduate of the school's founder and headmaster Rev. Frederick J. Sill, an Episcopal priest and member of the Order of the Holy Cross, was true for a great many boys educated under the authority of the great New England headmasters.

The heyday of the great New England schoolmasters extended from Groton's founding in 1884 through the sixty-four-year reign of Frank

Boyden at Deerfield (1902-66). The list of the great New England headmasters usually includes Alfred Stearns of Andover, Lewis Perry of Exeter,
Father Sill of Kent, George Van Santvoord of Hotchkiss, Samuel Drury
of St. Paul's, Horrace Dutton Taft of Taft, George St. John of Choate,
Endicott Peabody of Groton, Lawrence Terry of Middlesex, and Deerfield's Boyden. The list is invariably lengthened or shortened by alumni
from other schools, yet these men were most responsible for building
the reputations of the schools and setting the high standards of character they hoped to teach their charges.

   Sill and Peabody, as Coit had before them, often terrorized young
boys with their tirades against rule infractions. When a boy at Kent or
Groton was reported to the headmaster by a prefect for a serious violation, he was sent to the headmaster's study after dinner for a personal
confrontation with "the Old Man" (as Sill was known) or "the Rector"
(as Groton boys referred to Peabody). These could be devastating verbal whippings, as boys were made to feel that failing the trust of the
head was equivalent to deceiving an unmerciful God.

   At Groton, boys confronted "the Rector" in his study only for a
serious rule infraction or to be told of the death of a relative. So great
was Peabody's temper that boys, when told they were to be seen in his
study, usually hoped it was to be told of a relative's death rather than a
scolding for improper conduct.[12] Ironically, the headmasters who worked
hardest to develop stern self-control in surrogate sons demonstrated a
lack of it themselves in their emotional outbursts against their boys.
Sill's temper was as frightening as Peabody's, and his outbursts of right-
eous indignation as memorable:

> Father Sill's rampages were an important element in the emotional cli-
> mate of the school. They were partly calculated and partly the result of
> an ungovernable temper. . . . He had a complex and turbulent nature.
> He wrestled with himself, he wrestled with God, and he wrestled with
> the school. When anything went wrong with the latter he was apt to
> explode.[13]

   Episcopal ministers like Sill and Peabody derived the authority to
run their schools from the divine inspiration of the callings they pursued. Their callings to schoolmastering represented serious attempts to
inculcate sacred values in boys who, before and after school, had affluent lives with many temptations for self-indulgence. These men hoped
to impose a reverence for the restrictions, internalized as self-control
and denial, that they believed were crucial to good character. They saw
all violations of these restrictions as attacks on what was sacred and
absolute.

Headmasters at the nondenominational schools ruled with similar personal authority but without the moral sanctity of the Episcopal church. Even so, schools like Andover and Hotchkiss made daily chapel the cornerstone of moral education. Hotchkiss's Van Santvoord and Andover's Al Stearns, himself descended from a long line of Calvinist/Congregationalist clergymen, were devout men who saw chapel as the best way to teach boys moral lessons of Christianity. Indeed, when Stearns's alma mater Amherst College was considering abolishing compulsory daily chapel, he concluded a letter to the college's president in this way: "If we had to give up religion here, I should feel that we had knocked the bottom completely out of all that is of prime interest and concern to me in connection with the responsibilities and opportunities I face in my job as headmaster."[14]

Headmasters at nondenominational schools also imposed the code of Spartan simplicity and self-denial in their schools with their aloof and removed style. Most were rather cold and unfriendly to the boys, yet they often resented parents, especially mothers, interfering with their methods. None did so more than Hotchkiss's Van Santvoord, nicknamed the Duke, who presided over his Lakeville, Connecticut, fief for thirty years. His disdain for meddling mothers was well known, and his secretary was instructed to screen calls from doting mothers inquiring about a son's performance. He is reported to have once remarked to an intrusive mother, "Parents are the last people on earth who should have children." However, as changes in the world beyond their gates brought divorce and family fragmentation to parents of boarding school boys, he and other headmasters found it increasingly difficult to teach moral values that previously had been supported in the family.

A New Benevolence: Boyden and Terry

There was a crucial difference between the autocratic authoritarian Episcopal clerics with their Old Testament wrath and the more forgiving patriarchs of the nondenominational schools, like Boyden and Terry. The former imposed their absolute sovereignty on frightened boys with vengeful wrath, whereas the latter cared more for the peculiar differences of their surrogate sons. Such personal concerns enabled the last giants, Terry and Boyden, to cast the longest shadows.

Boyden and Terry were close friends who operated their schools on similar philosophies of benevolence. Boyden began his sixty-four-year tenure at Deerfield in August, 1902, two months after graduating from Amherst and a decade before Terry entered Groton in the first form.

Terry's life and leadership at Middlesex vividly illustrates the well-connected community of old eastern seaboard Protestant families responsible for the establishment and maintenance of the New England schools. He attended Groton because he was related to a master there. His best friend at Groton was John Crocker, who went to Princeton. After serving as Princeton's chaplain, Crocker returned to Groton to succeed Peabody as headmaster and to lead the school into the modern era (1942-65). Terry attended Harvard, where he met Freddy Windsor, the son of Frederick Windsor, the first headmaster of Middlesex and his predecessor in the post.

Terry had former Harvard football captain Walter Trumbull scout the country for boys of "good" character whose parents could not afford Middlesex, and the school developed a competitive exam that was administered by Harvard clubs around the country to academically qualified boys from modest backgrounds. This scholarship program eventually yielded more than 10 percent of the school's enrollment. He gave other school policies his democratic stamp. The daily devotional service that opened each day was not held in the chapel so that non-Protestant boys would feel less self-conscious. He made a special effort to invite diverse preachers for the Sunday chapel service, even including Father Flanagan, founder of Boy's Town, and posted a card in the chapel sacristy that listed the different denominations of boys in school for the visiting preacher.

Because Terry wished all the Middlesex boys to be treated equally, he did not have scholarship boys perform work as they were expected to do at other schools. He believed that any boy who could pass the school's entrance exam was a Middlesex student and should not be singled out because he was receiving scholarship aid.   Terry ran Middlesex like a warm and supportive family rather than like Christian army or football team; the boyish tyranny of athleticism he had experienced at Groton never gained a place. He kept enrollments under 250 boys so masters could know each boy well. At the end of each term there were faculty meetings in which every boy's progress in academics, athletics, and social life was discussed, and any individual problems were addressed. Reports were then sent home based on faculty decisions written by headmaster and advisor.[15]

Although the democratic innovations of Terry at Middlesex were later to be emulated at other schools, many of his ideas were borrowed from the littlest giant, 5'4" Frank Boyden, who transformed Deerfield from a dying academy of seven boys into one of America's most famous schools by teaching some simple lessons. Descended from an old New England family, Boyden was a classic Puritan, unpretentious and humble. Whereas many of the elder schools had tried to impose character on the boys by demanding conformity to rigid rules and a strict schedule,

Boyden preferred to draw it out of his boys by making them feel an important part of the Deerfield community. His philosophy was guided by Robert E. Lee's motto when he was president of Washington and Lee: "A boy is more important than any rule." Boyden tried to give his boys a sense of security through a feeling of belonging to a cooperative community that needed everyone's support. Character developed because boys felt their efforts were important, and they did not want to fail the trust they knew the headmaster had in them. A 1919 graduate recalled, "When you thought of doing something wrong, you would know that you would hurt him deeply, so you wouldn't do it." And a 1940 alumnus, "Whatever it was, you didn't do it, because you might drop a little in his eyes."[16]

Cases of discipline were handled by the headmaster personally, and frequently they were presented to the community for the judgment of the whole school. Boyden's Deerfield was clearly a shift away from the rigidity and austerity of the church schools, where the power of rules, prefects, and the priest or head imposed a regimen of threatened punishment rather than willful compliance.

When Boyden finally relinquished the reins at Deerfield in 1966 in his mid-eighties, the era of the "giants" was ended and with it the powerful presence of the Puritan character they had sought to develop in their boys since the opening of St. Paul's over a century earlier. The New England character represented by the quiet, reserved, cultured, and physically fit gentlemen that these schools had sent on to Yale, Harvard, and Princeton was greatly altered during the societal turbulence and change of the late 1960s and early 1970s. With the changes emerged a new character type, one that was not based on an inner-directed control and concealment but a more other-directed expressiveness that made personality rather than character development the implicit end, though not formal aim, of a boarding school education.

FROM CHARACTER TO PERSONALITY:
THE MODERN
CRUSADE FOR OPENNESS AND EXPRESSIVENESS

In the past two decades, the changes in the New England boarding schools have reflected changes in the world beyond their gates as they rarely did in the preceding century. The conservative, traditional Protestant values of the New England schools persisted for a century because of their moral and physical isolation, so that the upheavals of the late 1960s were unanticipated and far-reaching in scope.

Reforms initiated by the students at most of the schools in the late sixties called for a reexamination of the traditional methods by which moral character had been taught. For nearly four generations these schools had educated boys to become gentlemen by developing moral character through good habits of self-control, their minds through rigorous study of the liberal arts and Western culture, and their bodies through well-organized team sports that kept them physically fit and taught them to play by rules and cooperate with teammates. This three-pronged approach to character education had provided advantages to boys who went on to become successful members of the American elite and upper class.

Many graduates attributed much of their success to their boarding school education, which had taught them to excel and not be satisfied with less than their best effort. The schools had prepared boys for business careers, but, with few exceptions like Groton and St. George's, they had not been taught the inportance of public service or encouraged to pursue political careers. In their isolated cloisters, the schools had taught the time-worn habits of the Protestant gentleman (frugality, self-denial, hard work, and persistence). Their graduates had learned a style of living rather than the skills necessary to lead an increasingly diverse society of many peoples and cultures who lacked the privileges and prospects that graduates of these schools took for granted.

The protests of the late 1960s focused on three key points: loosening the rigid restrictions in the schools, both their rules and their tight daily schedule; increasing the flexibility in the curriculum to permit more current, socially relevant subjects and more independent work off campus for seniors; and sharing responsibility for discipline between faculty and students rather than autocratic control by the faculty. The springs of 1968 and 1969 brought student demonstrations that demanded changes, changes that drastically altered the century-old concern with manly Christian character.

The older idea of subjugation of self to community and self-control was challenged by an atmosphere that encouraged self-expression, flexible rules, and greater toleration of differences. The thrust was toward expanding one's potential by expressiveness rather than coercing the self into a rigid character mold of gentlemanly conduct. The older character type had been based on the Puritan's fear of the self as egocentric and corruptible; the new ideal glorified revelation and expression of the inner self, exemplified in the popular phrase "If it feels good, do it." Such indulgence was precisely the impulse to overcome in the Puritan character ideal.

Students saw their emotional development sacrificed on the altar of academic excellence and college preparation. They wanted their sensibilities developed rather than denounced, as they had been in the cold, austere cloisters of an earlier day. The *Exeter* Exonian of December 14, 1969 said the following: "Exeter quite simply fails to develop a boy emotionally so that he can handle situations outside the realm of academics in a reasonable and mature way."[17] A Groton senior in the spring 1969 Groton School Quarterly said this:

> "We have an increasing number of boys who are lonely, unsure of themselves, confused about their values, or about to give up all values. . . there is something curiously irrelevant about the escalation of intellectual power which has taken place. It doesn't seem to satisfy other, deeper needs. It seems emotionally deadening."[18]

Coupled with pressures to get into the best colleges, the stifling rigidity of rules and the unitary moral vision of these schools became intolerable to students increasingly aware and concerned with the changes beyond the school gates. This student challenge brought into high relief just how detached these schools were from the American mainstream. They had educated an upper class of Christian gentlemen who followed the footsteps of their fathers into corporate board rooms with little knowledge of all those Americans who lacked the privilege of a boarding school education. Their lives after school were lived in wealthy suburbs that kept them almost as isolated as they had been at school. They became successful businessmen in corporate America, but few had interest in or knowledge about America's problems.

Student reactions to Vietnam and the civil rights movement forced the boarding schools to recognize that they were out of touch with important societal concerns. In effect, students demanded changes that would prepare them for the current world rather than the long since vanished Puritan past. Their demands, at schools like Deerfield and St. Paul's, came in forcefully expressed petitions, entailing concerns for greater social engagement and more flexible and humane school policies.

THE RESPONSE TO CHANGE: REFORMATION AND COEDUCATION

The turmoil and confrontation of the late 1960s brought many of the desired changes, thus substantially altering the older structure and policies at the schools. With the coming of coeducation to most of the boys schools in the early 1970s, the schools became warmer, happier, and more open places. And certainly the students themselves rejected the Puritan emphasis on "character" as their defining goal. In a study of forty-two of the top boarding schools, Baird asked students what were the most important factors involved in popularity with the opposite sex. Eighty-three percent of the students thought having a good personality was very important, followed closely by 78 percent who believed it important to be an open, friendly person. Having a good, moral character was a distant third, deemed very important by only 35 percent of the students asked.[19]

The push to greater permissiveness corroded both the traditional conception of character and the importance of religion in the schools. Once obligatory, daily chapel became voluntary or was held only several days a week at most of the nondenominational schools. Even some of the Episcopal schools have made it voluntary. The demise of daily chapel represents the declining moral significance of the Protestant religion in character education in these schools as well as a shift away from a concern for the community to concern for the individual.

Also in response to student demands, the revision of the curriculum added more studies related to social changes and minorities, including courses on black history and literature, as well as more varied and serious courses in art, music, dance, and drama. The narrow intellectual vision that was joined to a narrow moral vision was thus significantly opened to broader vistas and alternative modes of expression.

At the same time, sports have continued to play the crucial role in the schools that they have had for over a century. The athletic facilities and diversity of sports offered in most of the schools are impressive, and the emphasis on physical education is obvious to any visitor. The reformist demands of the late sixties left athletics untouched, one of the few requirements to escape the demand for change. To many boarding school leaders, the lessons of sports have been at least as important as those of the classroom in developing character. As Lewis Perry said shortly after becoming Exeter's principal in 1914, "I am not one who thinks that the victories and defeats on the playing fields are soon forgotten in the victories and defeats of later life. The memories of some athletic victories and some athletic defeats will be vivid in your minds long after you have lost what skill you may have had with bat and ball."[20] Team games, school leaders believed, taught boys the desire to excel in competition and the accompanying belief that loyalty and cooperation were essential for the team's success. In playing by the rules, they were also to learn self-control and good sportsmanship. As Frank Boyden was fond of saying, "The consequences of poor sportsmanship is that you lose, somewhere along the line."[21] In a similar vein, Groton's 1981-82 catalogue mentioned the strong traditional lessons of sports: "The School holds to the traditional belief that much can be learned about cooperation, competition, and character through sports." The statement echoes the statement of founder Peabody that "athletics are of utmost important in establishing righteousness in the school."[22]

Other core components of character building have also not changed. Since nearly all schools expect students to be honest, lying, cheating, and stealing are immediate grounds for dismissal at nearly all schools. Indeed, integrity is seen as critical to the maintenance of community as well as a crucial component of individual character. "Offenses involving a student's integrity, social offenses that threaten the well-being of other individuals or the school community, and continued infractions that indicate an unwillingness to come to terms with the demands of the school—all render a student liable to dismissal," according to Andover's 1979-80 catalogue.[23] And similarly, at Groton, "the School expects all its students to offer to other students and to teachers, staff members, and their families both courtesy and respect. This expectation is one of the important characteristics of Groton."[24] Hotchkiss has historically claimed that "the School has always been run in the interests of trustworthy students."[25]

Although fundamental ethical precepts remain, behavioral restrictions are less stringent, suggesting a changed notion of how to develop character and a practical accommodation to student resistance. For example, many schools now permit smoking for upper-class students with home permission. All continue to prohibit alcohol and drugs. There have been serious and well-publicized problems with both substances in the last several decades, and most schools have had to alter their rules from immediate dismissal to less powerful punishments because of so many violations.

Peter Cookson and Caroline Persell perceptively describe the impact of the changes in their recent book, *Preparing for Power*:

> The schools made considerable concessions to youth culture in the late 1960s and early 1970s—coeducation, intervisitation, relaxed dress rules, greater freedom in room decoration, allowing stereos, increasing weekend leaves, eliminating mandatory chapel, allowing more choice of food and seating arrangements at meals, and so forth. The result has been an enormous transfusion of teen culture into the schools, reflected in the content of the student underlife—which no doubt always existed, but took different forms in earlier eras.[26]

The peer group culture of adolescent America has flowed into the boarding schools since students spend more time away from school and have greater opportunities to be influenced by that culture. In the cloisters of the past, the schools kept the outside world at bay and were isolated. No more. The current problems of drug and alcohol abuse are not merely a manifestation of greater permissiveness in society but reflect the inability of the schools to sustain their cloistered isolation in the electronic age of automated information. They were effective in promulgating a distinctive moral vision as long as they were separate and closed institutions, but they are no longer so and have had to accommodate themselves to the culture that their students experience before and while they are at school.

OF MORAL EDUCATION AND SOCIAL CHANGE: TOWARD AN UNCERTAIN FUTURE

The boarding school community once operated on powerful moral principles that were imposed by demanding authorities. The implicit and often explicit lesson was that to live in a community one had to obey its rules, whether one wished to or not. This "community" was narrowly delimited by the social world and interests of the upper class, but it nonetheless received precedence over individual desires. Furthermore, loyalty, especially loyalty to similar "moral" men, was placed before self; sacrifice rather than indulgence was demanded. This loyalty and attachment to others was molded in team sports, daily chapel, and dorm life. Disregard for the rules of the community was construed as rejection of this community, an unimaginable act. When Van Santvoord at Hotchkiss made all the students sign a nonsmoking pledge, he did so because he felt that once a boy had given him his word, he would not break it. Violation brought dismissal because it violated the trust between the boy and his headmaster.

The ethic of control, denial, and sacrifice that moral masters taught in the New England schools for nearly a century no longer dominates life at these institutions. Clearly, there are residues of that ethic in current practices, but the great practictioners of that ethic, the old New England headmasters whose own conduct so embodied that tradition, are no more. With them has vanished the claim to moral superiority that they hoped to maintain for those educated in their schools.

The schools tried to teach the class values of old Protestant New England, a sensible undertaking when all the students were drawn from that tradition and its cultural hegemony had not been greatly threatened in the larger society. Yet those very values bred an intolerant exclusiveness in this class. Although this moral education proved to be good training for business success in a WASP-dominated industrial order, it was inappropriate for an urban, polyglot world of many different, non-Protestant groups. Ironically, the schools were founded to develop Protestant virtues in the upper class, but they did so in a narrow, rigid form that prevented the development of tolerance or acceptance of those less fortunate or without similar character training. The schools succeeded in sequestering and training a class of very good businessmen with little sense of an obligation to understand or lead their society. Throughout their lives, they lived in the classbound isolation that they had first experienced in their schools, which were as isolated and separate as their founders could make them from the problems of urban society.

Yet while the evolving upper class in the late nineteenth century retreated from social problems, preferring to educate its children in cloistered private schools close to the Puritan values of New England, those problems eventually became too great for their grandchildren to ignore. Increasingly aware of other groups with different traditions, pasts, and problems than the WASP culture of New England, the younger members of the schools' constituency pushed for greater openness and freedom in the late 1960s. The schools were forced to take seriously the needs and demands of other less powerful groups. Although certainly not overthrown in toto, some class-bound traditions were significantly opened to accommodate recently mobile minorities and other groups in the schools. The awkwardness of the schools in responding to students' demands showed just how socially isolated and uninformed their schoolmasters were.

Important symbols of the old traditions became less compelling or even collapsed, undermining much of the substance of character training as it had been practiced. The greater openness of the schools was accompanied by an ethic of release rather than control: not restraint, but self-indulgence; not communal concerns, but self-seeking preoccupations. As moral austerity and certitude waned, rules became less stringent, and the schools' community weakened. In recent years, then, these schools have become beset by the prevailing attitudes of the larger society. No longer distinctive in vision, they, like their public counterparts, lack commitment to a guiding morality. Their previous emphasis on austere Protestant morality proved incompatible with modern demands, but their current practices represent an absence of a defining moral commitment, not a coherent alternative that successfully promotes an ethic of responsibility to others.

The graduates of the elite boarding schools are likely to continue to assume positions of power, but they may not be truly and adequately *prepared* for power unless the schools of the privileged classes develop a compelling new ethic of individual restraint and social concern. If

Emerson was correct, then the masters in the leading boarding schools might give more thought to developing character than intellect, and concern themselves more with teaching students how this society can be made better than with merely preparing them for college, and for their own financial advancement.

NOTES

1. Allis, *Youth from Every Quarter*, p. 47.

2. McLachlan, *American Boarding Schools*, p. 243.

3. Ibid., pp. 79-80.

4. Meisse, "The Round Hill School," p. 9.

5. McLachlan, *American Boarding Schools*, p. 90.

6. Meisse, "The Round Hill School," p.9.

7. McLachlan, *American Boarding Schools*, p. 143.

8. Ibid., p. 161.

9. Ibid., p. 158.

10. Ibid., p. 167.

11. Edey, "Some Recollections on Kent in the 1920s," p. 25.

12. Mentioned in interview with Laurence Terry, Groton '18, and Middlesex headmaster from 1938 to 1965 at Harvard, Mass., May, 1982.

13. Edey, "Some Recollections," p. 17.

14. Allis, *Youth from Every Quarter*, p. 336.

15. Material on Laurence Terry and Middlesex from personal interview with Mr. Terry in May, 1982.

16. McPhee, *The Headmaster*, p. 23.

17. *The Exonian*, December 14, 1969, n.p.

18. Sheerin, "Sixth Form Year—So What?" Groton School Quarterly, Spring 1969, n.p.

19. Baird, *The Elite Schools*, p. 98.

20. Williams, *The Story of Phillips Exeter Academy*, p. 103.

21. McPhee, *The Headmaster*, p. 31.

22. McLachlan, *American Boarding Schools*, p. 285.

23. Andover catalogue, 1979-80, p. 21.

24. Groton catalogue, 1981-82, p. 7.

25. Hotchkiss catalogue, 1986-87, p. 30.

26. Cookson and Persell, *Preparing for Power*, p. 206.

REFERENCES

Aldrich, Nelson W., Jr. Preppies—The Last Upper Class?" *Atlantic Monthly* (January 1979): 55-66.

Allis, Frederick S., Jr. *Youth from Every Quarter: A Bicentennial History of Phillips Academy, Andover.* University Press of New England: Hanover, New Hampshire, 1979.

Armstrong, Christopher F. "Privilege and Productivity: The Cases of Two Private Schools and Their Graduates." Ph.D. diss. University of Pennsylvania, 1974.

———."The Boarding School and Ruling Class Education, with particular reference to Great Britain and America." Paper presented at Southern Sociological Association annual meeting, Atlanta, 1979.

———."Boarding Schools: Sequestered Isolation and Elite Preparation." Paper presented at Eastern Sociological Society annual meeting, New York, 1979.

———."The Character of Christian Gentlemen: Victorian Educational Ideals in Old and New England Boarding Schools, 1875-1945." Unpublished paper, 1983.

———."The Lessons of Sports: Class Socialization in British and American Boarding Schools." *Sociology of Sport* (December 1984): 314-331.

Ashburn, Frank. *Peabody of Groton.* Coward McCann: New York, 1944.

Auchincloss, Louis. *The Rector of Justin.* Random House: New York, 1965.

Baird, Leonard L. *The Elite Schools.* Lexington Books: Lexington, Mass., 1977.

Baltzell, E. Digby. *Philadelphia Gentlemen: The Making of a National Upper Class.* The Free Press: Glencoe, Ill., 1958.

———*The Protestant Establishment: Aristocracy and Caste in America.* Random House: New York, 1964.

Berryman, Jack, and John Loy. "Secondary Schools and Ivy League Letters: A Comparative replication of Eggleston's 'Oxbridge Blues'." *British Journal of Sociology* (March 1976): 61-77.

Birnbach, Lisa, ed. *The Official Preppy Handbook*. Workman Publishing: New York, 1980.

Blackmer, Alan R. "An Inquiry into Student Unrest in Independent Secondary Schools." National Association of Independent Schools: Boston, 1970.

Boyd, David. *Elites and Their Education*. NFER Publishing: Slough, England, 1973.

Buell, Rev. William Ackermann. *My Life and St. George's School*. St. George's School Alumni Association: Newport, R.I., 1967.

Chamberlain, Ernest Barrett. *Our Independent Schools: The Private School in American Education*. American Book Company: New York, 1944.

Cole, Robert Danforth. *Private Secondary Schools for Boys in the United States*. University of Pennsylvania: Philadelphia, 1928.

Cookson, Peter. "Boarding Schools and the Moral Community." *Journal of Educational Thought* (August 1982): 89-97.

Cookson, Peter and Caroline Persell. *Preparing for Power*. Basic Books: New York, 1985.

Domhoff, G. William. *Who Rules America?* Prentice-Hall: Englewood Cliffs, N.J., 1967.

Drury, Roger W. *St. Paul's: The Scars of a Schoolmaster*. Little, Brown: Boston, 1964.

Durkheim, Emile. *Moral Education*. Translated by Everett K. Wilson and Herman Schnurer. Free Press: New York, 1961.

Eckland, Bruce K., and R.E. Peterson. " The Exeter Study: Technical Report and Compendium of Findings." Educational Testing Service: Princeton, N.J., 1969.

Edey, Maitland. "Some Recollections of Kent in the 1920's." *Kent Quarterly* (Winter 1983): 14-26.

Exeter School Archives.

Fraser, George MacDonald. *The World of the Public School*. St. Martin's Press: New York, 1977.

Gathorne-Hardy, Jonathan. *The Old School Tie*. Viking Press: New York, 1978.

Groton School Archives.

Groton School. *Views from the Circle.* Groton School Press: Groton, Mass., 1960.

Gutwillig, Robert. "The Select Seventeen: A Guide to Upper Class Education." *Esquire* (November 1960): 162-163.

Hecksher, August. *St. Paul's: The Life of a New England School.* Charles Scribner's Sons: New York, 1980.

Hotchkiss School Archives.

Konolige, Kit and Frederica. *The Power of Their Glory, America's Ruling Class: The Episcopalians.* Wyden: New York, 1978.

Kraushaar, Otto F. *American Nonpublic Schools: Patterns of Diversity.* Johns Hopkins University Press: Baltimore, Md., 1972.

Levine, Steven B. "The Rise of American Boarding Schools and the Development of a National Upper Class." *Social Problems* (October 1980): 63-94.

Maccoby, Michael. *The Gamesmen: The New Corporate Leaders.* Simon and Schuster:, New York, 1976.

McLachlan, James. *American Boarding Schools: A Historical Study.* Charles Scribner's Sons: New York, 1970.

McPhee, John. *The Headmaster: Frank L. Boyden of Deerfield.* Farrar, Straus, and Giroux: New York, 1966.

Mallery, David. "Independence and Community in Our Schools. National Association of Independent Schools: Boston, 1971.

Mangan, J.A. *Athleticism in the Victorian and Edwardian Public School.* Cambridge University Press: Cambridge, 1981.

Meisse, David K. "The Round Hill School: Once Famous, Now Forgotten." *Hampshire Life* (June 22, 1984): 8-9,23.

Mills, C. Wright. *The Power Elite.* Oxford University Press: New York, 1959.

Newsome, David. *Godliness and Good Learning.* John Murray: London, 1961.

Parkin, George. *Edward Thring, Headmaster of Uppingham School: Life, Diary, and Letters.* Macmillan: London, 1900.

Persell, Caroline Hodges. *Education and Inequality.* Free Press: New York, 1977.

Piaget, Jean. *The Moral Judgment of the Child.* Harcourt, Brace, Jovanovich: New York, 1932.

Prescott, Peter S. *A World of Our Own: Notes on Life and Learning in a Boys' Preparatory School.* Coward-McCann: New York, 1970.

St. George's School Archives.

St. John, George. *Forty Years at School*. Henry Holt and Company: New York, 1959.

St. Paul's School Archives.

Saltonstall , William G. *Lewis Perry of Exeter*. Atheneum: New York, 1980.

Strong, William S. "New England Prep Schools — Are They Still the ULTIMATE?" *Town and Country* (August 1980): 65-72.

Terry, Lawrence. Interviews in his home in Spring 1981 and Fall 1983.

Useem, Michael. "The Social Organization of the American Business Elite." *American Sociological Review* (August 1979): 553-572.

Wakeford, John. *The Cloistered Elite*. Praeger: New York, 1969.

Weinberg, Ian. *The English Public Schools: The Sociology of Elite Education*. Atherton Press: New York, 1967.

Wertenbaker, Lael Tuck, and Maude Basserman. *Hotchkiss School: A Portrait*. Hotchkiss School: Lakeville, Conn., 1966.

Wilkinson, Rupert. *Gentlemanly Power*. Oxford University Press: London, 1964.

Williams, Myron R. *The Story of Phillips Exeter Academy*. Harvard University Press: Cambridge, 1951.

CAROLINE HODGES PERSELL
PETER W. COOKSON, JR.

Chapter Two

Chartering and Bartering: Elite Education and Social Reproduction*

The continuation of power and privilege has been the subject of intense sociological debate. One recurring question is whether the system of mobility is open or whether relationships of power and privilege are reproduced from one generation to the next. If reproduction occurs, is it the reproduction of certain powerful and privileged families or groups (cf Robinson, 1984)? Or, does it involve the reproduction of a structure of power and privilege which allows for replacement of some members with new recruits while preserving the structure?

The role of education in these processes has been the subject of much dispute. Researchers in the status attainment tradition stress the importance for mobility of the knowledge and skills acquired through education, thereby emphasizing the meritocratic and open basis for mobility (e.g., Alexander and Eckland, 1975; Alexander et al., 1975; Blau and Duncan, 1967; Haller and Portes, 1973; Otto and Haller, 1970; Kerckhoff, 1984; Sewell et al., 1969, 1970; Wilson and Portes, 1975). On the other hand, theorists such as Bowles and Gintis (1976) suggest that education inculates certain noncognitive personality traits which serve to reproduce the social relations within a class structure; thus they put more emphasis on nonmeritocratic features in the educational process.

Collins (1979) also deals with nonmeritocratic aspects when he suggests that educational institutions develop and fortify status groups, and that differently valued educational credentials protect desired market positions such as those of the professions. In a related vein, Meyer (1977) notes that certain organizational "charters" serve as "selection criteria" in an educational or occupational marketplace. Meyer defines "charter" as "the social definition of the products of [an] organization" (Meyer, 1970:577). Charters do not need to be recognized formally or legally to operate in social life. If they exist, they would create structural limitations within a presumably open market by making some people eligible for certain sets of rights that are denied to other people.

Social observers have long noted that one particular set of schools is central to the reproduction and solidarity of a national upper class, specifically elite secondary boarding schools (Baltzell, 1958, 1964; Domhoff, 1967, 1970, 1983; Mills, 1956). As well as preparing their students for socially desirable colleges and universities, traditionally such schools have been thought to build social networks among upper class scions from various regions, leading to adult business deals and marriages. Although less than 1 percent of the American population attends such schools, that 1 percent represents a strategic segment of American life that is seldom directly studied. Recently, Useem and Karabel reported that graduates of 14 elite boarding schools were much more likely than nongraduates to become part of the "inner circle" of Fortune 500 business leaders. This evidence suggests that elite schools may play a role in class reproduction.

Few researchers have gained direct access to these schools to study social processes bearing on social reproduction. The research reported here represents the first systematic study of elite secondary boarding schools and their social relations with another important institution, namely colleges and universities.

The results of this research illustrate Collins' view that stratification involves networks of "persons making bargains and threats . . . [and that] the key resource of powerful individuals is their ability to impress and manipulate a network of social contacts" (1979:26). If such were the case, we would expect to find that upper class institutions actively develop social networks for the purpose of advancing the interests of their constituencies.

By focusing on the processes of social reproduction rather than individual attributes or the results of intergenerational mobility, our research differs from the approaches taken in both the status attainment and status allocation literature. Status attainment models focus on individual attributes and achievements, and allocation models examine structural supports or barriers to social mobility; yet neither approach explores the underlying processes. Status attainment models assume the existence of a relatively open contest system, while reproduction and allocation models stress that selection criteria and structural barriers create inequalities, limiting opportunities for one group while favoring another (Kerckhoff, 1976, 1984). Neither attainment nor allocation models show how class reproduction, selection criteria, or structural opportunities and impediments operate in practice.

Considerable evidence supports the view that structural limitations operate in the labor market (e.g., Beck et al., 1978; Bibb and Form, 1977; Stolzenberg, 1975), but, with the exception of tracking, little evidence has been found that similar structural limitations exist in education. Tracking systems create structural impediments in an open model of educational attainment (Oakes, 1985; Persell, 1977; Rosenbaum, 1976, 1980), although not all research supports this conclusion (e.g., Alexander et al., 1978; Heyns, 1974).

In this paper we suggest that there is an additional structural limitation in the key transition from high school to college. We explore the possibility that special organizational "charters" exist for certain secondary schools and that a process of "bartering" occurs between representatives of selected secondary schools and some college admissions officers. These processes have not been clearly identified by prior research on education and stratification, although there has been some previous research which leads in this direction.

EMPIRICAL LITERATURE

Researchers of various orientations concur that differences between schools seem to have little bearing on student attainment (Averch et al., 1972; Jencks et al., 1972; Meyer, 1970, 1977). Indeed, Meyer (1977) suggests the most puzzling paradox in the sociology of American education is that while schools differ in structure and resources, they vary little in their effects because all secondary schools are assumed to have similar "charters." Meyer believes that no American high school is specially chartered by selective colleges in the way, for instance, that certain British Public Schools have been chartered by Oxford and Cambridge Universities. Instead, he suggests that "all American high schools have similar status rights, (and therefore) variations in their effects should be small" (Meyer, 1977:60).

Kamens (1977:217-18), on the other hand, argues that "schools symbolically redefine people and make them eligible for membership in societal categories to which specific sets of rights are assigned." The work of Alexander and Eckland (1977) is consistent with this view. These researchers found that students who attended high schools where the social status of the student body was high also attended selective colleges at a greater rate that did students at other high schools, even when individual student academic ability and family background were held constant (Alexander and Eckland, 1977). Their research and other work finding a relationship between curricular track placement and college attendance (Alexander et al., 1978; Alexander and McDill, 1976; Jaffe and Adams, 1970; Rosenbaum, 1976, 1980) suggest that differences between schools may affect stratification outcomes.

Research has shown that graduation from a private school is related to attending a four-year (rather than a two-year) college (Falsey and Heyns, 1984), attending a highly selective college (Hammack and Cookson, 1980), and earning high income in adult life (Lewis and Wanner, 1979). Moreover, Cookson (1981) found that graduates of private boarding schools attended more selective colleges that did their public school counterparts, even when family background and Scholastic Aptitude Test (SAT) scores were held constant. Furthermore, some private college acknowledge the distinctive nature of certain secondary schools. Klitgaard (1985: Table 2.2) reports that students from private secondary schools generally had an advantage for admission to Harvard over public school graduates, even when their academic ratings were comparable. Karen (1985) notes that applications to Harvard from certain private boarding schools were placed in special colored dockets, or folders, to set them apart from other applications. Thus, they were considered a distinct group. Not only did Harvard acknowledge the special status of certain schools by color-coding their applicants' folders, but attendance at one of those schools provided an advantage for acceptance, even when parental background, grades, SATs, and other characteristics were controlled (Karen, 1985).

NETWORKS AND THE TRANSMISSION OF PRIVILEGE

For these reasons we believe it is worth investigating whether certain secondary schools have special organizational charters, at least in relation to certain colleges. If they do, the question arises, how do organizational charters operate? Network analysts suggest that "the pattern of ties in a network provides significant opportunities and constraints because it affects the relative access of people and institutions to such resources as information, wealth and power" (Wellman, 1981:3). Furthermore, "because of their structural location, members of a social system differ greatly in their access to these resources" (Wellman, 1981:30). Moreover, network analysts have suggested that class-structured networks work to preserve upper class ideology, consciousness, and life style (see for example Laumann, 1966:132-36).

We expect that colleges and secondary schools have much closer ties than has previously been documented. Close networks of personal relationships between officials at certain private schools and some elite colleges transform what is for many students a relatively standardized, bureaucratic procedure into a process of negotiation. As a result, they are able to communicate more vital information about their respective needs, giving selected secondary school students an inside track to gaining acceptance to desired colleges. We call this process "bartering."

SAMPLE AND DATA

Baltzell (1958, 1964) noted the importance of elite secondary boarding schools for upper class solidarity. However, he was careful to distinguish between those boarding schools that were truly socially elite and those that had historically served somewhat less affluent and less powerful families. He indicates that there is a core group of eastern Protestant schools that "set the pace and bore the brunt of criticism received by private schools for their so-called 'snobbish,' 'undemocratic' and even 'un-American' values" (Baltzell, 1958:307-08). These 16 schools are: Phillips (Andover) Academy (MA), Phillips Exeter Academy (NH), St. Paul's School (NH), St. Mark's School (MA), Groton School (MA), St. George's School (RI), Kent School (CT), The Taft School (CT), The Hotchkiss School (CT), Choate Rosemary Hall (CT), Middlesex School (MA), Deerfield Academy (MA), The Lawrenceville School (NJ), The Hill School (PA), The Episcopal High School (VA), and Woodberry Forest School (VA). We refer to the schools on Baltzell's list as the "select 16."[1]

In 1982 and 1983, we visited a representative sample of 12 of the select 16 schools. These 12 schools reflect the geographic distribution of the select 16 schools. In this time period we also visited 30 other "leading" secondary boarding schools drawn from the 1981 *Handbook of Private Schools'* list of 289 "leading" secondary boarding schools. This sample is representative of leading secondary boarding schools nationally in location, religious affiliation, size, and the sex composition of the student body. These schools are organizationally similar to the select 16 schools in offering only a college preparatory curriculum, in being incorporated as nonprofit organizations, in their faculty/student ratios, and in the percent of boarders who receive financial aid. They differ somewhat with respect to sex composition, average size, the sex of their heads, and number of advanced placement courses (see Table 2.1). However, the key difference between the select 16 schools and the other "leading" schools is that the former are more socially elite than the latter. For instance, in one of the select 16 boarding schools in 1982, 40 percent of the current students' parents were listed in *Social Register*.[2]

TABLE 2.1
Comparison of Population and Two Samples of Boarding Schools[a]

	Total Population (N=289)	Other Boarding School Sample (N=30)	Select 16 Sample (N=12)
Percent with College Preparatory Cuuriculum	100	100	100
Percent with No Religious Affiliation	65	70	67
Percent Incorporated, Not-for-profit	83	90	83
Average Faculty/Student Ratio	0.17	0.15	0.15
Average Percent of Boaders Aided	15	16	18
Percent of Schools which are All-Boys	28	17	33
Percent of Schools which are All-Girls	17	28	0
Percent Coeducational Schools	55	55	67
Percent with Male Heads	92	73	100
Average Number of Advanced Courses	3.5	4.8	6.7
Average Size	311	322	612

a. Computed from data published in the Handbook of Private Schools (1981).

All 42 schools were visited by one or both of the authors. Visits lasted between one and five days and included interviews with administrators, teachers and students. Most relevant to this study were the lengthy interviews with the schools' college advisers. These interviews explored all aspects of the college counseling process, including the nature and content of the advisers' relationships with admissions officers at various colleges. At a representative sample of six of the select 16 schools and a representative sample of 13 of the other "leading" schools a questionnaire was administered to seniors during our visits. The questionnaire contained more than 50 items and included questions on parental education, occupation, income, number of books in the home, family travel, educational legacies as well as many questions on boarding school life and how students felt about their experiences in school. Overall, student survey and school record data were collected on 687 seniors from the six select 16 schools and 658 seniors from other leading schools. Although not every piece of data was available for every student, we did obtain 578 complete cases from six select 16 schools and 457 cases from ten leading schools.[4] School record data included student grade point averages, Scholastic Aptitude Test (SAT) scores, class rank, names of colleges to which students applied, names of colleges to which students were accepted, and names of colleges students will attend. This material was supplied by the schools after the seniors graduated, in the summer or fall of 1982 and 1983. With this population actual enrollment matches school reports with high reliabilty. The record data have been linked with questionnaire data from the seniors and with various characteristics of the college. The colleges students planned to attend were coded as to academic selectivity, Ivy League, and other characteristics not analyzed here.[5]

CHARTERING

Historical evidence shows that the select 16 schools have had special charters in relation to Ivy League colleges in general, and Harvard, Yale, and Princeton in particular. In the 1930s and 1940s, two-thirds of all graduates of 12 of the select 16 boarding schools attended Harvard, Yale, or Princeton (Karabel, 1984). But, by 1973, this share had slipped noticeably to an average of 21 percent, although the rate of acceptance between schools ranged from 51 percent to 8 percent (Cookson and Persell, 1978: Table 4). In the last half century, then, the proportion of select 16 school graduates who attended Harvard, Yale or Princeton dropped substantially.

This decrease was paralleled by an increase in the competition for admission to Ivy League colleges. According to several college advisors at select 16 boarding schools, 90 percent of all applicants to Harvard in the 1940s were accepted as were about half of those in the early 1950s. In 1982, the national acceptance rate for the eight Ivy League schools was 26 percent, although it was 20 percent or less at Harvard, Yale and Princeton (*National College Data Bank, 1984*).

The pattern of Ivy League college admissions has changed during this time. Ivy League colleges have begun to admit more public school graduates. Before World War II at Princeton, for example, about 80 percent of the entering freshman came from private secondary schools (Blumberg and Paul, 1975:70). In 1982, 34 percent of the freshman class at Harvard, 40 percent of Yale freshmen, and 40 percent of Princeton freshmen were from nonpublic high schools (*National College Data Bank,* 1984).

This shift in college admissions policy, combined with increased financial aid and an inflationary trend in higher education that puts increased emphasis on which college one attends, contributes to the large number of applications to certain colleges nationally. Thus, while in the past decade the number of college age students has declined, the number of students applying to Ivy League colleges has increased (Mackay-Smith, 1985; Maeroff, 1984; Winerip, 1984).

In view of these historical changes, is there any evidence that the select 16 schools still retain special charters in relation to college admissions? When four pools of applications to the Ivy League colleges are compared, the acceptance rate is highest at select 16 schools, followed by a highly selective public high school, other leading boarding schools, and finally the entire national pool of applications (Table 2.2).[6]

TABLE 2.2
Percent of Applications That Were Accepted at Ivy League Colleges
from Four Pools of Applications

College Name	Select 16 Boarding Schools[a] (1982-1983)	Other Leading Boarding Schools[b] (1982-83)	Selective Public High School[c] (1984)	National Group of Applicants[d] (1982)
Brown University				
Percent Accepted	35	20	28	22
Number of Applications	95	45	114	11,854
Columbia University				
Percent Accepted	66	29	32	41
Number of Applications	35	7	170	3,650
Cornell University				
Percent Accepted	57	36	55	31
Number of Applications	65	25	112	17,927
Dartmouth				
Percent Accepted	41	21	41	22
Number of Applications	79	33	37	8,313
Harvard University				
Percent Accepted	38	28	20	17
Number of Applications	104	29	127	13,341
Princeton University				
Percent Accepted	40	28	18	18
Number of Applications	103	40	109	11,804
University of Pennsylvania				
Percent Accepted	45	32	33	36
Number of Applications	40	19	167	11,000
Yale University				
Percent Accepted	40	32	15	20
Number of Applications	92	25	124	11,023
Overall Percent Accepted	42	27	30	26
Total Number of Applications	613	223	960	88,912

a. Based on school record data on the applications of 578 seniors.
b. Based on school record data on the applications of 457 seniors.
c. Based on data published in the school newspaper.
d. Based on data published in the National College Data Bank (1984).

While we do not have comparable background data on all the applicants from these various pools, we do know that the students in the highly selective public high school have among the highest academic qualifications in the country.[7] Their combined SAT scores, for example, average at least 150 points higher than those of students at the leading boarding schools. On that basis they might be expected to do considerably better than applicants from boarding schools: which they do at some colleges, but not at Harvard, Yale or Princeton.

TABLE 2.3
Boarding School Students' College Application, Chances of Acceptance,
and Plans to Attend

A. Percent of Boarding School Samples Who Applied		Ivy League Colleges	Highly Selective Colleges
Select 16 Boarding Schools	% =	61	87
	N =	(353)	(502)
Other Leading Boarding Schools	% =	28	61
	N =	(129)	(279)
B. Percent of Applicants Who Were Accepted		Ivy League Colleges	Highly Selective Colleges
Select 16 Boarding Schools	% =	54	84
	N =	(191)	(420)
Other Leading Boarding Schools	% =	36	64
	N =	(47)	(178)
C. Percent of Acceptees Who Plan to Attend		Ivy League Colleges	Highly Selective Colleges
Select 16 Boarding Schools	% =	79	81
	N =	(151)	(340)
Other Leading Boarding Schools	% =	53	77
	N =	(25)	(137)

The most revealing insights into the operation of special charters, however, are provided by a comparison between select 16 boarding schools and other leading boarding schools—the most similar schools and the ones on which we have the most detailed data.

Students from select 16 schools apply to somewhat different colleges than do students from other leading boarding schools. Select 16 school students were much more likely to apply to one or more of the eight Ivy League and at least one of the other highly selective colleges than were students from other leading boarding schools (Table 2.3). Among those who applied, select 16 students were more likely to be accepted than were students from other boarding schools, and, if accepted, they were slightly more likely to attend.

Before we can conclude that these differences are due to a school charter, we need to control for parental SES[8] and student SAT scores.[9] This analysis is shown in Table 2.4. One striking finding here is the high rate of success enjoyed by boarding school students in general. At least one-third and as many as 92 percent of the students in each cell of Table 2.4 are accepted. Given that the average freshmen combined SAT score is more than 1175 at these colleges and universities, it is particularly notable that such a large proportion of those with combined SAT scores of 1050 or less are accepted.

In general, high SAT scores increase chances of acceptance, but the relationship is somewhat attenuated under certain conditions. Students with low SAT scores are more likely to be accepted at highly selective colleges if they have higher SES backgrounds, especially if they attend a select 16 school. These students seem to have relatively high "floors" placed under them, since two-thirds of those from select 16 schools and more than half of those from other schools were accepted by one of the most selective colleges. [10]

TABLE 2.4
Percent of Students Who Applied to the Most Highly Selective Colleges
Who Were Accepted, with SAT Scores, SES, and School Type Held Constant[a]

| | | Student Combined SAT Scores | | | | |
| | | High (1580-1220) | | Medium (1216-1060) | | Low (1050-540) | |
		Select 16 Schools	Other Leading Boarding Schools	Select 16 Schools	Other Leading Boarding Schools	Select 16 Schools	Other Leading Boarding Schools
Student Socioeconomic Status							
High	% =	87	70	80	64	65	53
	N =	(93)	(33)	(73)	(36)	(34)	(30)
Medium	% =	89	71	85	76	44	35
	N =	(100)	(28)	(66)	(46)	(18)	(51)
Low	% =	92	72	78	69	55	33
	N =	(72)	(25)	(51)	(32)	(33)	(49)

a. Based on student questionnaires and school record data on 1035 seniors from whom complete data were available.

The most successful ones of all are relatively low SES students with the highest SATs attending select 16 schools—92 percent of whom were accepted. Students from relatively modest backgrounds appear to receive a "knighting effect" by attending a select 16 school. Thus, select 16 schools provide mobility for some individuals from relatively less privileged backgrounds. To a considerable degree all students with high SATs, regardless of their SES, appear to be "turbocharged" by attending a select 16 school compared to their counterparts at other leading schools.

At every level of SATs and SES, students' chances of acceptance increase if they attend a select 16 school. Such a finding is consistent with the argument that a chartering effect continues to operate among elite educational institutions. The historical shifts toward admitting more public school students on the part of Ivy League colleges and the increased competition for entry, described above, have meant that more effort has been required on the part of select 16 schools to retain an advantage for their students. We believe that certain private boarding schools have buttressed their charters by an increasingly active bartering operation.

BARTERING

Normally, we do not think of the college admissions process as an arena for bartering. It is assumed that colleges simply choose students according to their own criteria and needs. Few students and no high schools are thought to have any special "leverage" in admissions decisions. Our research revealed, however, that select 16 boarding schools— perhaps because of their perennial supply of academically able and affluent students—can negotiate admissions cases with colleges. The colleges are aware that select 16 schools attract excellent college prospects and devote considerable attention to maintaining close relationships with these schools, especially through the college admissions officers. Secondary school college advisors actively "market" their students within a context of tremendous parental pressure and increasing competition for admission to elite colleges.

SELECT 16 COLLEGE ADVISORS AND IVY LEAGUE ADMISSIONS DIRECTORS: THE OLD SCHOOL TIE

Of the 11 select 16 school college advisors on whom data were available, 10 were graduates of Harvard, Yale, or Princeton. Of the 23 other leading boarding school college advisors on whom data were available, only three were Ivy League graduates, and none of them was from Harvard, Yale, or Princeton. College advisors are overwhelmingly white men. At the select 16 schools only one (an acting director) was a woman, and at other schools five were women. Some college advisors have previously worked as college admissions officers. Their educational and social similarity to college admissions officers may facilitate the creation of social ties and the sharing of useful information. Research shows that the exchange of ideas most frequently occurs between people who share certain social attributes (Rogers and Kincaid, 1981).

College advisors at select 16 schools tend to have long tenures—15 or more years is not unusual. On the other hand, college advisors at other schools are more likely to have assumed the job recently. A college advisor at one select 16 school stressed the "importance of continuity on both sides of the relationship." Thus, it is not surprising that select 16 schools hold on to their college advisors.

Select 16 college advisors have close social relationships with each other and with elite college admissions officers that are cemented through numerous face-to-face meetings each year. All of the select 16 schools are on the east coast, whereas only 70 percent of the other leading boarding schools are in that region. However, even those leading boarding schools on the east coast lack the close relationships with colleges that characterize the select 16 schools. Thus, geography alone does not explain these relationships.

The college advisors at most of the boarding schools we studied have personally visited a number of colleges around the country. Boarding schools often provide college advisors with summer support for systematic visits, and a number of geographically removed colleges offer attractive incentives, or fully paid trips to their region (e.g., Southern California). These trips often take place during bitter New England winters, and include elegant food and lodging as well as a chance to see colleges and meet admissions officers.

However, the college advisors at select 16 schools are likely to have visited far more schools (several mentioned that they had personally visited 60 or 70 schools) than college advisors at other schools (some of whom had not visited any). They are also much more likely to visit regularly the most selective and prestigious colleges.[11]

Numerous college admissions officers also travel to those boarding schools to interview students and meet the college advisors. The select 16 schools have more college admissions officers visit than do other schools; more than 100 in any given academic year is not unusual. College advisors have drinks and dinner with selected admissions officers, who often stay overnight on campus. As one college advisor noted, "We get to establish a personal relationship with each other." Moreover, Ivy League colleges bring students from select 16 schools to their campus to visit for weekends.

By knowing each other personally, college advisors and admissions officers "develop a relationship of trust," so that they can evaluate the source as well as the content of phone calls and letters. We observed phone calls beteen college advisors and admissions officers when we were in their offices. Several college advisors mentioned, "It helps to know personally the individual you are speaking or writing to," and one college advisor at a select 16 school said, "I have built up a track record with the private colleges over the years."

Virtually all of the select 16 school college advisors indicated that in the spring—before colleges have finished making their admissions decisions—they take their application files and drive to elite colleges to discuss "their list." They often sit in on the admissions deliberations while they are there. In contrast, the other schools' college advisors generally did not make such trips. Such actions suggest the existence of strong social networks between select 16 school college advisors and elite college admissions officers.

HOW THE SYSTEM WORKS:
"FINE TUNING" THE ADMISSIONS PROCESS

Bartering implies a reciprocal relationship, and select 16 schools and elite colleges have a well-developed system of information exchange. Both sides have learned to cooperate to their mutual benefit. College advisors try to provide admissions officers with as much information about their students as possible to help justify the acceptance of a particular applicant. Select 16 schools have institutionalized this process more than other schools. The most professional operation we found was in a select 16 school where about half the graduating class goes to Harvard, Yale, or Princeton. There, the college advisor interviews the entire faculty on each member of the senior class. He tape records all their comments and has them transcribed. This produces a "huge confidential dossier which gives a very good sense of where each student is." In addition, housemasters and coaches write reports. Then the college advisor interviews each senior, dictating notes after each interview. After assimilating all of these comments on each student, the college advisor writes his letter of recommendation, which he is able to pack with corroborative details illustrating a candidate's strengths. The thoroughness, thought, and care that goes into this process insures that anything and everything positive that could be said about a student is included, thereby maximizing his or her chances for a favorable reception at a college.[12]

Information also flows from colleges to the secondary schools. By sitting in on the admissions process at colleges like Harvard, Princeton, and Yale, select 16 school college advisors say they "see the wealth and breadth of the applicant pool." They get a first-hand view of the competition their students face. They also obtain a sense of how a college "puts its class together," which helps them to learn strategies for putting forward their own applicants.

By observing and participating in the admissions process, select 16 school college advisors gain an insider's view of a college's selection process. This insider's knowledge is reflected in the specific figures select 16 advisors mentioned in our conversations with them. One select 16 school college advisor said that a student has "two and one half times as good a chance for admission to Harvard if his father went there than if he did not." Another said, "While 22 percent in general are admitted to Ivy League colleges, 45 percent of legacies are admitted to Ivy League colleges." In both cases, they mentioned a specific, quantified statement about how being a legacy affected their students' admissions probabilities.[13] Similarly, several select 16 school college advisors mentioned the percentages of the freshman class at Harvard and Yale that were from public and private schools, and one even mentioned how those percentages have changed since 1957. College advisors at other schools do not lace their conversations with as many specific figures nor do they belong to the special organization that some of the select 16 schools have formed to share information and strategies.

The special interest group these schools have formed is able to negotiate with the colleges to their students' advantage. For instance, the college advisors explained that select 16 school students face greater competition than the average high school student and carry a more rigorous course load.[14] Therefore, this group persuaded the colleges that their students should not receive an absolute class rank, but simply an indication of where the students stand by decile or quintile. Colleges may then put such students in a "not ranked" category or report the decile or quintile rank. No entering student from such a secondary school is clearly labeled as the bottom person in the class. To our knowledge, only select 16 schools have made this arrangement.

Armed with an insider's knowledge of a college's desires, select 16 school college advisors seek to present colleges with the most appropriate candidates. As one select 16 school college advisor said, "I try to shape up different applicant pools for different colleges," a process that has several components. First, college advisors try to screen out hopeless prospects, or as one tactfully phrased it, "I try to discourage unproductive leads." This is not always easy because, as one said, "Certain dreams die hard." College advisors in other schools were more likely to say that they never told students where they should or should not apply.

One select 16 school requires students to write a "trial college essay" that helps the college advisor ascertain "what kind of a student this is."

From the essay he can tell how well students write, determine whether they follow through and do what they need to do on time, and learn something about their personal and family background. With faculty and student comments in hand, college advisors can begin to assemble their applicant pools. One thing they always want to learn is which college is a student's first choice, and why. This is useful information when bartering with colleges.

Some college advisors are quite frank when bartering, for example, the select 16 college advisor who stressed, "I am candid about a student to the colleges, something that is not true at a lot of schools where they take an advocacy position in relation to their students . . . We don't sell damaged goods to the colleges." College advisors at other schools did not define their role as one of weeding out candidates prior to presenting them to colleges, although they may do this as well. It would seem then that part of the gate-keeping process of admission to college is occurring in select 16 secondary schools. College advisors, particularly those with long tenures at select 16 schools, seem quite aware of the importance of maintaining long-term credibility with colleges, since credibility influences how effectively they can work for their school in the future.

While the children of certain big donors (so-called "development cases") may be counseled with special care, in general the college advisors have organizational concerns that are more important than the fate of a particular student. Several select 16 school college advisors spoke with scorn about parents who see a rejection as the "first step in the negotiation." Such parents threaten to disrupt a delicate network of social relationships that link elite institutions over a considerable time span.

At the same time, college advisors try to do everything they can to help their students jump the admissions hurdle. One select 16 school advisor said,

> I don't see our students as having an advantage (in college admissions). We have to make the situation unequal. We do this by writing full summary reports on the students, by reviewing the applicants with the colleges several times during the year, and by traveling to the top six colleges in the spring. . . [Those visits] are an advocacy proceeding on the side of the students. The colleges make their best decisions on our students and those from [another select 16 school] because they have the most information on these students.

Another select 16 college advisor said, "We want to be sure they are reading the applications of our students fairly, and we lobby for our students." A third select 16 college advisor made a similar statement, "When I drive to the [Ivy League] colleges, I give them a reading on our applicants. I let them know if I think they are making a mistake. There is a lobbying component here."

Select 16 college advisors do not stop with simply asking elite college admissions officers to reconsider a decision, however. They try to barter, and the colleges show they are open to this possibility when the college admissions officer says, "Let's talk about your group." One select 16 college advisor said he stresses to colleges that if his school recommends someone and he or she is accepted, that student will come. While not all colleges heed this warranty, some do.

One select 16 college advisor said, "It is getting harder than it used to be to say to an admissions officer 'take a chance on this one,' especially at Harvard which now has so many more applications." But it is significant that he did not say that it was not impossible. If all else fails in a negotiation, a select 16 college advisor said, "We lobby for the college to make them their absolute first choice on the waiting list." Such a compromise represents a chance for both parties to save face.

Most public high school counselors are at a distinct disadvantage in the bartering process because they are not part of the interpersonal network, do not have strategic information, and are thus unable to lobby effectively for their students. One select 16 advisor told us about a counselor from the Midwest who came to an Ivy League college to sit in on the admissions committee decision for his truly outstanding candidate—SATs in the 700s, top in his class, class president, and star athlete. The select 16 college advisor was also there, lobbying on behalf of his candidate—a nice undistinguished fellow (in the words of his advisor, "A good kid,") with SATs in the 500s, middle of his class, average athlete, and no strong signs of leadership. After hearing both the counselors, the Ivy League college chose the candidate from the select 16 school. The outraged public school counselor walked out in disgust. Afterwards, the Ivy League college admissions officer said to the select 16 college advisor, "We may not be able to have these open meetings anymore." Even in the unusual case where a public school counselor did everything that a select 16 boarding school college advisor did, it was not enough to secure the applicant's admission. Despite the competitive environment that currently surrounds admission to elite colleges, the admissions officers apparently listen more closely to advisors from select 16 boarding schools than to public school counselors.

CONCLUSIONS AND IMPLICATIONS

The graduates of certain private schools are at a distinct advantage when it comes to admission to highly selective colleges because of the special charters and highly developed social networks these schools possess. Of course, other factors are operating as well. Parental wealth (which is not fully tapped by a measure of SES based on education, occupation, and income), preference for the children of alumni, Advanced Placement (AP) coursework, sports ability especially in such scarce areas as ice hockey, crew or squash, and many other factors also influence the process of college admission. Elite boarding schools are part of a larger process whereby more privileged members of society transmit their advantages to their children. Attendance at a select 16 boarding school signals admissions committees that an applicant may have certain valuable educational and social characteristics.

Significantly, neither the families nor the secondary schools leave the college admissions process to chance or to formal bureacratic procedures. Instead, they use personal connections to smooth the process, and there is reason to believe that those efforts affect the outcomes. The "knighting effect" of select 16 schools helps a few low SES, high SAT students gain admission to highly selective colleges, evidence of sponsored mobility for a few worthy youngsters of relatively humble origins. Our findings are consistent with Kamen's (1974) suggestion that certain schools make their students eligible for special social rights. Furthermore, the interaction between social background, SATs, and select 16 school attendance suggests that both individual ability and socially structured advantages operate in the school-college transition.

These results illustrate Collins' (1979) view that stratified systems are maintained through the manipulation of social contacts. They show one way that networks and stratification processes are interconnected. College access is only one aspect of the larger phenomenon of elite maintenance and reproduction. Elite boarding schools no doubt contribute as well to the social contact and marriage markets of their graduates. What this instance shows is that reproduction is not a simple process. It involves family and group reproduction as well as some structural replacement with carefully screened new members. There is active personal intervention in what is publicly presented as a meritocratic and open competition. The internal processes and external networks described here operate to construct class privileges as well as to transmit class advantages, thereby helping to reproduce structured stratification within society.

If this example is generalizable, we would expect that economically and culturally advantaged groups might regularly find or create specially chartered organizations and brokers with well-developed networks to help them successfully traverse critical junctures in their social histories. Such key switching points include the transition from secondary school to college, admission to an elite graduate or professional school, obtaining the right job, finding a mentor, gaining a medical residency at a choice hospital (Hall, 1947, 1948, 1949), getting a book manuscript published (Coser et al., 1982), having one's paintings exhibited at an art gallery or museum, obtaining a theatrical agent, having one's business considered for venture capital or bank support (Rogers and Larsen, 1984), being offered membership in an exclusive social club, or being asked to serve on a corporate or other board of directors (Useem, 1984).

In all of these instances, many qualified individuals seek desired, but scarce, social and/or economic opportunities. Truly open competition for highly desired outcomes leaves privileged groups vulnerable. Because the socially desired positions are finite at any given moment, processes that give an advantage to the members of certain groups work to limit the opportunities of individuals from other groups.[15] In these ways, dominant groups enhance their chances, at the same time that a few worthy newcomers are advanced, a process which serves to reproduce and legitimate a structure of social inequality.

NOTES

*We wish to thank E. Digby Baltzell, Steven Brint, Kevin Dougherty, Eliot Freidson, Kathleen Gerson, David Greenberg, Wolf Heydebrand, Herbert Menzel, John Meyer, Karen Miller, Richard R. Peterson, Edwin Schur, Susan Shapiro, Beth Stevens, and a number of anonymous reviewers for their thoughtful reactions to this paper. Needless to say, they cannot be held responsible for the way we have utilized their comments. Correspondence to: Persell, Department of Sociology, New York University, 269 Mercer Street, New York, NY 10003.

1. Others besides Baltzell have developed lists of elite private schools, including Baird (1977), Domhoff (1967, 1970, 1983), and McLachlan (1970).

2. We were not able to compute the percent of students in *Social Register* for every school because most schools do not publish the names of their students. Hence, we were not able to look their families up in the *Social Register*. We do know that less than .000265 percent of American families are listed in *Social Register*. See Levine (1980) for an historical discussion of the social backgrounds of students at several of the select 16 schools.

3. We asked to give the student questionnaires at nine of the 12 select 16 schools and six of those nine schools agreed. At the other leading schools, we asked to give the questionnaires at 15 and 13 schools agreed.

4. Three leading schools did not supply the college data.

5. Following Astin et al. (1981:7), we measured selectivity with the average SAT scores of entering freshmen.

6. The entire national applicant pool includes the relatively more successful subgroups within it. If they were excluded, the national acceptance rate would be even lower.

7. Students admitted to this selective public high school must be recommended by their junior high school to take a competitive exam, where they must score very well. The school was among the top five in the nation with respect to the number of National Merit Scholarships won by its students, and each year a number of students in the school win Westinghouse science prizes. This school was selected for purposes of comparison here because academically it is considered to be among the very top public schools in the nation. However, it does not have the social prestige of the select 16 boarding schools.

8. SES was measured by combining father's education, father's occupation, and family income into a composite SES score. These SES scores were then standardized for this population, and each student received a single standardized SES score.

9. The combined verbal and mathematics scores were used.

10. We performed separate analyses for boys and girls to see if sex was related to admission to a highly selective college when type of boarding school, SATs, and SES were held constant, and generally it was not. Girls who attend either select 16 or other leading boarding schools do as well or better in their admission to college as do their male counterparts, with the single exception of girls at select 16 schools in the top third on their SATs and SES. In that particular group, 92 percent of the boys but only 77 percent of the girls were accepted at the most highly selective colleges. Since that is the only exception, boys and girls are discussed together in the text of the paper.

11. Our field visits and interviews with college advisors at two highly selective public high schools and three open admissions public high schools show that college advisors at even the most selective public high schools generally do not personally know the admissions officers at colleges, particularly at the most selective and Ivy League colleges, nor do they talk with them over the phone or in person prior to their admissions decisions.

12. Such a procedure requires considerable financial and personnel resources. Select 16 schools have more capital-intensive and professional office services supporting their college admissions endeavor than other schools. Most

of them have word processors, considerable professional staff, and ample secretarial and clerical help.

13. We did not ask students what colleges their parents attended so we could not control for college legacy in our analysis. Future research on the admissions process should do so.

14. One way select 16 schools establish their reputations as rigorous schools is through the numbers of their students who succeed on the Advanced Placement (AP) Exams given by the College Entrance Examination Board. Compared to other secondary schools, select 16 schools offer larger numbers of advanced courses (Table 2.1), encourage more students to take them, coach students very effectively on how to take the test, and maintain contacts with the people who design and read AP exams so that they know what is expected and can guide students accordingly. (See Cookson and Persell, 1985, for more discussion of these processes.) Other schools are much less likely than select 16 ones to have teachers who have graded AP exams or to know people who have helped to write the tests.

15. See Parkin (1979) for a discussion of social closure as exclusion and usurpation.

REFERENCES

Alexander, Karl L., Martha Cook, and Edward McDill
1978 "Curriculum tracking and educational stratification:some further evidence." *American Sociological Review* 43:47-66.

Alexander, Karl L., and Bruce K. Eckland
1975 "Contexual effects in the high school attainment process." *American Sociological Review* 40:402-16.
1977 "High school context and college selectivity: institutional constraints in educational stratification." *Social Forces* 56:166-88.

Alexander, Karl L., Bruce K. Eckland, and Larry J. Griffin
1975 "The Wisconsin model of socioeconomic achievement: a replication." *American Journal of Sociology* 81:324-42.

Alexander, Karl L., and Edward L. McDill
1976 "Selection and allocation within schools: some causes and consequences of curriculum placement." *American Sociological Review* 41:963-80.

Astin, Alexander W., Margo R. King, and Gerald T. Richardson
1981 *The American Freshmen: National Norms for Fall 1981.* Los Angeles: Laboratory for Research in Higher Education, University of California.

Averch, Harvey A., Steven J. Carroll, Theodore S. Donaldson, Herbert J. Kiesling, and John Pincus
1972 *How Effective is Schooling? A Critical Review and Synthesis of Research Findings.* Santa Monica, CA: The Rand Corporation.

Baird, Leonard L.
1977 *The Elite Schools.* Lexington, MA: Lexington Books.

Baltzell, E. Digby
1958 *Philadelphia Gentlemen.* New York: Free Press.
1964 *The Protestant Establishment.* New York: Random House.

Beck, E.M., Patrick M. Horan, and Charles M. Tolbert II
1978 "Stratification in a dual economy." *American Sociological Review* 43:704-20.

Bibb, Robert C., and William Form
1977 "The effects of industrial, occupational and sex stratification on wages in blue-collar markets." *Social Forces* 55:974-96.

Blau, Peter, and Otis D. Duncan
1967 *The American Occupational Structure.* New York: Wiley

Blumberg, Paul M., and P.W. Paul
1975 "Continuities and discontinuities in upper-class marriages." *Journal of Marriage and the Family.* 37:63-77.

Bowles, Samuel, and Herbert Gintis
1976 *Schooling in Capitalist America.* New York: Basic Books.

Collins, Randall
1979 *The Credential Society.* New York: Academic Press.

Cookson, Peter Willis Jr.
1981 "Private secondary boarding school and public suburban high school graduation: an analysis of college attendance plans." Unpublished Ph.D. dissertation, New York University.

Cookson, Peter W.,Jr., and Caroline Hodges Persell
1978 "Social structure and educational programs: a comparison of elite boarding schools and public education in the United States." Paper presented at the annual meeting of the American Sociological Association, San Francisco.
1985 *Preparing for Power: America's Elite Boarding Schools.* New York: Basic Books.

Coser, Lewis A., Charles Kadushin, and Walter W. Powell
1982 *Books: The Culture & Commerce of Publishing.* New York: Basic Books.

Domhoff, G. William
1967 *Who Rules America?* Englewood Cliffs: Prentice-Hall.
1970 *The Higher Circles.* New York: Vintage.
1983 *Who Rules America Now?* Englewood Cliffs: Prentice-Hall.

Falsey, Barbara, and Barbara Heyns
1984 "The college channel: private and public schools reconsidered." *Sociology of Education* 57:111-22.

Hall, Oswald
1946 "The informal organization of the medical profession." *Canadian Journal of Economics and Political Science* 12:30-41.
1948 "The stages of a medical career." *American Journal of Sociology* 53:327-36.
1949 "Types of medical careers." *American Journal of Sociology* 55:243-53.

Haller, Archibald O., and Alejandro Portes
1973 "Status attainment process." *Sociology of Education* 46:51-91.

Hammack, Floyd M., and Peter W. Cookson, Jr.
1980 "Colleges attended by graduates of elite secondary schools." *The Educational Forum* 44:483-90.

Handbook of Private Schools
1981 Boston: Porter Sargent Publishers, Inc.

Heyns, Barbara
1974 "Social selection and stratification within schools." *American Journal of Sociology* 79:1434-51.

Jaffe, Abraham, and Walter Adams
1970 "Academic and socio-economic factors related to entrance and retention at two- and four-year colleges in the late 1960s." New York: Bureau of Applied Social Research, Columbia University.

Jencks, Christopher, Marshall Smith, Henry Acland, Mary Jo Bane, David Cohen, Herbert Gintis, Barbara Heyns, and Stephan Michelson
1972 *Inequality*. New York: Basic Books.

Kamens, David
1974 "Colleges and elite formation: the case of prestigious American colleges." *Sociology of Education* 47:354-78.
1977 "Legitimating myths and educational organization: the relationship between organizational ideology and formal structure." *American Sociological Review* 42:208-19.

Karabel, Jerome
1984 "Status-group struggle, organizational interests, and the limits of institutional autonomy: the transformation of Harvard, Yale, and Princeton 1918-1940." *Theory and Society* 13:1-40.

Karen, David
1985 "Who Gets into Harvard? Selection and Exclusion." Unpublished Ph.D. Dissertation, Department of Sociology, Harvard University.

Kerchoff, Alan C.
1976 "The status attainment process: socialization or allocation?" *Social Forces* 55:368-81.

1984 "The current state of social mobility research." *Sociological Quarterly* 25:139-53.

Klitgaard, Robert
1985 *Choosing Elites*. New York: Basic Books.

Laumann, Edward O.
1966 *Prestige and Association in an Urban Community: An Analysis of an Urban Stratification System*. Indianapolis: Bobbs-Merrill.

Levine, Steven B.
1980 "The rise of American boarding schools and the development of a national upper class." *Social Problems* 28:63-94.

Lewis, Lionel S., and Richard A. Wanner
1979 "Private schooling and the status attainment process." *Sociology of Education* 52:99-112.

Mackay-Smith, Anne
1985 "Admissions crunch:top colleges remain awash in applicants despite a smaller pool." *Wall Street Journal* (April 2):1,14.

McLachlan, James
1970 *American Boarding Schools: A Historical Study*. New York: Charles Scribner's Sons.

Maeroff, Gene I.
1984 "Top Eastern colleges report unusual rise in applications." *New York Times* (February 21):A1,C10.

Meyer, John
1970 "The charter: conditions of diffuse socialization in school." Pp. 564-78 in W. Richard Scott (ed.), *Social Processes and Social Structure*. New York: Holt, Rinehart.
1977 "Education as an institution." *American Journal of Sociology* 83:55-77.

Mills, C. Wright
1956 *The Power Elite*. London: Oxford University Press.

National College Data Bank
1984 Princeton: Peterson's Guides, Inc.

Oakes, Jeannie
1985 *Keeping Track: How Schools Structure Inequality*. New Haven: Yale University Press.

Otto, Luther B., and Archibald O. Haller
1979 "Evidence for a social psychological view of the status attainment process: four studies compared." *Social Forces* 57:887-914.

Parkin, Frank
  1979 *Marxism and Class Theory: A Bourgeois Critique.* New York: Columbia University Press.

Persell, Caroline Hodges
  1977 *Education and Inequality.* New York: Free Press.

Robinson, Robert V.
  1984 "Reproducing class relations in industrial capitalism." *American Sociological Review* 49:182-96.

Rogers, Everett M., and D. Lawrence Kincaid
  1981 *Communications Networks: Toward a New Paradigm for Research.* New York: Free Press.

Rogers, Everett M., and Judith K. Larsen
  1984 *Silicon Valley Fever: The Growth of High-Tech Culture.* New York: Basic Books.

Rosenbaum, James E.
  1976 *Making Inequality: The Hidden Curriculum of High School Tracking.* New York: Wiley.
  1980 "Track misperceptions and frustrated college plans: an analysis of the effects of tracks and track perceptions in the national longitudinal survey." *Sociology of Education* 53:74-88.

Sewell, William H., Archibald O. Haller, and Alejandro Portes
  1969 "The educational and early occupational attainment process." *American Sociological Review* 34:82-91.

Sewell, William H., Archibald O. Haller, and George W. Ohlendorf
  1970 "The educational and early occupational status achievement process: replication and revision." *American Sociological Review* 35:1014-27.

Social Register
  1984 New York: Social Register Association.

Stolzenberg, Ross M.
  1975 "Occupations, labor markets and the process of wage attainment." *American Sociological Review* 40:645-65.

Useem, Michael
  1984 *The Inner Circle: Large Corporations and the Rise of Business Political Activity in the U.S. and U.K.* New York: Oxford University Press.

Wellman, Barry
  1981 "Network analysis from method and metaphor to theory and substance." Working Paper Series 1B, Structural Analysis Programme, University of Toronto.

Wilson, Kenneth L. and Alejandro Portes
  1975 "The educational attainment process: results from a national sample."
  American Journal of Sociology 81:343-63.

Winerip, Michael
  1984 "Hot colleges and how they got that way." *New York Times Magazine*
  (November 18):68ff.

Part II

Elite Undergraduate Institutions

INTRODUCTION

As our introductory chapter indicated, the broad contours of the hierarchy in American higher education are widely recognized, though the reasons why it emerged as it has, its changing relationship to the stratification system, especially in our putative meritocratic era, and its consequences for life chances are all less well understood. One collective message of the chapters in this section is that these issues are complex and far from being settled. Yet an equally clear collective message is that the elite colleges and universities have been distinctive and consequential.

At a very general level, these chapters tell a unified story: high social status begets academic prestige; status and academic prestige have long gone hand-in-hand, though less certainly and directly; and academic prestige fosters high social status. The value of these chapters is that they add subtlety, nuance, detail, and even some disclaimers to this rough plot line.

As in Part I, we start with historical studies. In Chapter 3, "Patterns of Upper-Class Higher Education in Four American Cities: 1875-1975," Richard Farnum examines the college attendance patterns of four local upper classes with special attention to their allegiance to their local prestigious institution, their enrollments at institutions of the national upper class, and their coherence as a class. His careful study extends and complements E. Digby Baltzell's pioneering work on the changing centrality of educational institutions in upper-class life. In Chapter 4, "Prestige in the Ivy League," Farnum goes on to show that institutional connections to high-status groups, especially at particular historical junctures, have been vital to the development and maintenance of prestige. The "mismanagement" of these connections at Penn and Columbia is an interesting story of educational history with larger implications for understanding the basis of the academic hierarchy as a whole.

In Chapter 5, "Undergraduates at Elite Institutions," we analyze the current connection between family income and enrollments at elite institutions. This simple social arithmetic establishes the highly affluent composition of these schools, a characteristic that appears to be becoming more pronounced in recent years.

In a complementary study, in Chapter 6, "Pathways to Attendance at the Elite Colleges," James Hearn uses sophisticated multivariate techniques to explore how these attendance patterns emerged. Although academic factors predominate, as might be expected, the allocation of students within the academic hierarchy is far from the full triumph of meritocratic principles.

Not only do the affluent disproportionately go to elite institutions, but their graduates have done disproportionately well—a fact confirmed in Kingston and John Smart's study, "The Economic Pay-off of Prestigious Colleges" (Chapter 7). Here they address the question of whether elite institutions, per se, confer advantages or are merely the educational way stations for those who would do well in any case because of their individual characteristics and talents.

The disproportionate success of the elite college graduates is also confirmed in Michael Useem and Jerome Karabel's study, "Pathways to Top Corporate Management" (Chapter 8), a detailed look at the educational and class backgrounds of the managers at the pinnacle of the corporate world. Useem and Karabel insightfully examine the mutually supportive interaction of prestigious credentials and advantaged family background in the organization of the corporate economy.

Richard Farnum

Chapter Three

Patterns of Upper-Class Education in Four American Cities: 1875-1975*

INTRODUCTION

This paper develops several issues raised by E. Digby Baltzell's work on higher education and the upper class. Although primarily concerned with examining the structures, functions, and value orientations of the upper class in American society, he has specifically considered the relationship between the upper class and institutions of higher education— both the colleges and universities which members of the upper class have attended and the contributions these schools have made to the coherence and maintenance of the upper class (1958, 1964, 1979). A Philadelphian, Baltzell has focussed on the upper class of his native city, but he has supplemented this analysis with a comparative study of Boston and generalizations about the national American upper class at large. This study will systematically extend his work by examining patterns of college attendance of the upper classes of Philadelphia, Boston, New York, and Baltimore from 1880 to 1970.

What has been the history of higher-educational attendance of the Philadelphia upper class since the late nineteenth century? Baltzell found that upper-class Philadelphians typically attended the local university, the University of Pennsylvania (Penn), until around 1900, when it reached the zenith of its prestige as a Proper Philadelphia institution. But during the twentieth century, and particularly after World War I, local fidelity was eroded and eventually eclipsed as a majority went away to Harvard,

53

Yale, and Princeton (hereafter referred to as HYP), the national upper-class colleges. The precise timing of this pattern will be examined systematically and extended beyond World War II.

How does the Philadelphia pattern compare with those of other metropolitan upper classes in the East? Baltzell's work on Boston suggested that Harvard's national eminence is significantly attributable to the great support and fidelity that the Boston upper class gave to its local college. Yet further comparisons are in order. New York is of particular relevance because, like both Boston and Philadelphia, it has a local higher educational institution of colonial vintage (Columbia, 1754). Did the attachment of the New York upper class to its local college resemble the pattern in Philadelphia or Boston? Baltzell has observed that the rise of a national associational upper class began in the 1880s in New York where the first *Social Register* was published in 1886. This might suggest that the New York upper class is more cosmopolitan, even less given to local pride and attachments than the Philadelphian upper class. To add another point of comparison, Baltimore will be examined, though it did not acquire a local college of repute until the late nineteenth century (Johns Hopkins, 1876).

How have the patterns of upper-class college attendance changed since World War II? Much of Baltzell's work has been confined to the prewar period, though in *The Protestant Establishment* (1964) he did briefly extend his analysis into the post-war era. There he charted the rise of the achievement principle as both faculty appointments and student admissions became based increasingly on meritocratic criteria. Whereas during the 1930s and 1940s very few Jews received tenure at HYP, by the 1960s these faculties were quite heterogeneous ethnically. Before World War II "good character and adequate preparation" (read "WASP and boarding school") were sufficient to gain admission, but by the 1960s SAT scores of 625 were average, and public school graduates outnumbered those from private schools. Such chances had important consequences for upper-class college attendance and elite college functions.[1]

In answering these questions, this paper details differences between urban upper classes and suggests the changing significance of higher education for the upper class and society as a whole. Baltzell has described the importance of the socialization and status-ascribing functions of HYP for the maintenance of an authoritative establishment up to 1940. Does the evidence from other cities indicate that HYP became national upper-class institutions as Baltzell has suggested? Have these institutions continued to perform these functions in the postwar era? Do other colleges belong in this category? How and when did these institutions acquire national prominence, and does such prominence still exist?

These questions bear on the issues of the functions of elite higher education, as well as on the institutional hierarchy within higher education and its connection to the class structure.

Data for this study were collected from the *Social Registers* of Boston, New York, Philadelphia, and Baltimore at decade intervals from the 1880s through the 1960s.[2] Two general types of information are summarized in tabular form for each city. The first indicates the extent of concentration of these upper classes within the system of higher education. Here are presented the number of colleges from which upper-class members graduated during a given decade, as well as the percentage of upper-class graduates in each decade who received their degrees from one of the five most frequently attended colleges (top five). This information directly relates to issues raised by Baltzell: (1) the extent to which the upper class of a particular city is unified in its conception of desirable institutions of higher education, (2) the extent to which the members of an upper class share a common socialization and status-ascribing experience, and (3) the extent to which the particularistic association of an upper class with specific institutions has been disrupted since World War II, thereby "democratizing" the upper class with respect to higher education. Each of these conditions bears on the cohesion and integrity of the relevant upper class. For example, it might be expected that those upper classes that have a relatively low percentage in the "top five" category would tend to be less cohesive than others.

Also considered is the particular schools most attended by an upper class from 1880 to 1970—specifically, the proportion of these classes accounted for by the five most commonly attended colleges, the proportion attending HYP as a group, and the proportion going to the preferred local institution. These percentages, calculated for each decade of the period under study, suggest the degree of localism or cosmopolitanism in an upper class, the extent of the hegemony exerted by HYP, and changes in these phenomena over time.

BOSTON

The first and most obvious measure of upper-class concentration in higher education is simply the number of schools mentioned in the *Social Registers* by decades from which members of the upper class graduated (see Table 3.1). The overall trend here for the Boston upper class from 1880 to 1970 was a nearly fivefold increase in the number of schools chosen—from 6 to 35. This expansion began in the twenties and proceeded in two spurts. The first sustained increase, embracing the twenties and thirties, represented a doubling of the relatively constant levels that marked the 1880s to the 1910s. This was very likely the result of World War I. As David Levine (1981) has pointed out in his study of higher education during the interwar years, World War I initiated the modern era of increased and more democratized college attendance. Martin Trow (1972) has dubbed this the beginning of the shift from elite to mass higher education. The second expansion, starting in the 1940s and 1950s and accelerating in the 1960s, was the result of the even greater democratization of higher education that followed World War II. This development involved the institutionalization of increasingly universalistic, meritocratic standards at elite colleges and universities. Faced with such less directly ascriptive admissions criteria, members of the upper class found themselves less able to enter the prestige colleges of choice and were forced to be more "democratic" in their selection of schools.

TABLE 3.1
Boston—Colleges Graduating Social Registrants, by Decade (N)

1880s	1890s	1900s	1910s	1920s	1930s	1940s	1950s	1960s
6	11	5	6	12	11	18	20	35

In a related fashion, the percentage of the upper class attending one of the five most selected schools declined by nearly 50 percent (see Table 3.2). In the earliest period from the 1880s until World War I, more than 90 percent of the upper class attended one of the top five schools, with the single anomaly of the 1890s, when the number sunk to 84 percent. This exception might reflect the more democratic and professional orientation that President Eliot tried to establish at Harvard at the time. After World War I, for two decades, the percentage attending the top five dropped slightly to 86 percent. After World War II, however, during the 1940s and 1950s, upper-class concentration dropped to three-quarters, and in the 1960s to just more than half.

TABLE 3.2
Boston—Colleges of Social Registrants, by Decade of Graduation (%)

	1880s	1890s	1900s	1910s	1920s	1930s	1940s	1950s	1960s
Top Five	93	84	96	98	86	86	75	74	51
Other	7	16	4	2	14	14	25	26	49
Total	100	100	100	100	100	100	100	100	100

Clearly, then, over these nine decades, the Boston upper class sent its offspring to a much wider set of colleges. This increasing dispersion reflected both an educational "democratization" of the upper class and a sociological democratization of the most preferred schools. Even so, the fact that as late as 1970 more than half of the upper class attended one of the top five schools indicates that the Boston upper class, largely through disproportionate admission to prestigious institutions, maintained very considerable coherence in its pattern of college attendance.

Harvard, Yale, Princeton, Williams, and MIT remained throughout the ninety-year period the five most chosen schools, in that order, based on an overall average representation (see Table 3.3). Together they accounted for 80 percent of the upper-class graduates on average. Yet Harvard was far and away the top choice of the Boston upper class, accounting for two-thirds of the social registrants on average. None of the other four ever accounted for more than 11 percent (Princeton in the 1950s); on average, none was above 5 percent.

TABLE 3.3
Boston—Social Registrants Graduating from Top Five Colleges, by Decade of Graduation (%)

	1880s	*1890s*	*1900s*	*1910s*	*1920s*	*1930s*	*1940s*	*1950s*	*1960s*	*Ave.*
Harvard	78	72	92	85	70	78	61	54	38	67
Yale	5	2	0	6	4	8	7	5	4	5
Princeton	0	0	2	2	9	0	1	11	7	4
Williams	3	4	2	3	2	0	4	3	1	2
MIT	7	6	0	2	1	0	2	1	1	2
Total	93	84	96	98	86	86	75	74	51	80

Harvard's attraction was a compound of at least two elements: it was both the first and premier local Boston college, and it, along with Yale and Princeton, had a long-standing reputation as one of the three most prestigious national undergraduate institutions. Yale and Princeton were among the top five for this latter reason alone. To Bostonians, Williams and MIT also represented "local" institutions of high standing. Although Williams is not exactly local to Boston, it is in Massachusetts and has long enjoyed a reputation as perhaps the finest New England liberal arts college.

Nonetheless, the predominance of Harvard graduates did significantly decline, with some fluctuations, in this time—from a high of 92 percent in the 1900s to a low of 38 percent by 1970. Harvard's share of the upper class began to wane sometime in the 1900s, was arrested and actually increased during the 1930s, but sharply descended again beginning in the 1940s. The latter decline may be attributable to the democratizing trends mentioned above. The earlier decline, however, is difficult to interpret in this way, especially because admittance to any of the Big Three during the 1920s and 1930s was not all that difficult (cf. Bloomgarden, 1960).

More plausibly, the Boston upper class may have seen Harvard as having become too radically democratized under Charles Eliot, the president of Harvard in this era. In concrete terms, to the upper class this meant that there were too any Jews and other non-WASPs. Eliot had attempted to institutionalize a more rigorously universalistic orientation at Harvard and let the sociological chips fall where they might. This had resulted in a rather naked and invidious system of social stratification within the college. Many members of the upper class reacted by sending their children away from the city altogether to smaller and more protected liberal arts colleges (Synnott, 1979).

This explanation makes sense because the Boston upper class "returned" to Harvard in the late 1920s and early 1930s, a time of very different admissions policies. Eliot's successor in 1909 was A. Lawrence Lowell, a man very much attuned to the sociology of the college and of the nation. An active member of the immigration restriction movement of the 1920s, Lowell began a policy of restricting the number of Jews at Harvard by the use of quotas in 1922. To the extent that attracting the Boston upper class back to Harvard was an objective, his policy apparently succeeded, at least temporarily. As the figures indicate, the percentage of the upper class at Harvard increased during his tenure.

Harvard's overall loss of the upper class from 1880 to 1970 was not compensated by increases in the other top five schools so that the Boston upper class became more dispersed throughout the higher-educational system (see Table 3.2). To an extent, however, the share attending Yale and Princeton, although small, increased over time (see Table 3.4). Thus, some of Harvard's losses were to the benefit of Yale and Princeton, especially the latter. During the 1920s Princeton's share of the Boston upper class increased dramatically, to almost a tenth. Princeton was of course the smallest, least urban, and, especially during Fitzgerald's era of gin and jazz, the most socially homogeneous of the Big Three. That Princeton would have drawn so many more proper Bostonians in the 1920s lends further support to the idea that they were disturbed by democratization at Harvard.

TABLE 3.4
Boston—Social Registrants Graduating from Harvard (H) and Yale-Princeton (YP), by Decade of Graduation (%)

	1880s	*1890s*	*1900s*	*1910s*	*1920s*	*1930s*	*1940s*	*1950s*	*1960s*
H	78	72	92	85	70	78	61	54	38
YP	5	2	2	8	13	8	8	15	11
Total	83	74	94	93	83	86	69	69	49

NEW YORK

The patterns of concentration and dispersion in college attendence of the New York upper class generally parallel the Boston findings. The number of schools increased fourfold over the ninety-year period (see Table 3.5). The number dramatically increased in the 1890s and remained fairly constant until the 1930s. At that time, the upper class became slightly more dispersed, but after World War II, significantly more so. The timing of the first major rise coincided with the influx of southern and eastern European migration to this country in the 1880s.

TABLE 3.5
New York—Colleges Graduating Social Registrants, by Decades (N)

1880s	*1890s*	*1900s*	*1910s*	*1920s*	*1930s*	*1940s*	*1950s*	*1960s*
13	22	23	21	24	31	30	58	66

Even as the New York upper class sent its offspring to a wider set of institutions, until the 1930s, the proportion attending the five most selected schools remained high, more than 80 percent (see Table 3.6). In later decades, however, this proportion dropped notably, to less than half in the 1960s. This growth in dispersion, somewhat greater than Boston's, again indicates the increasing democratization of higher education.

TABLE 3.6
New York—Colleges of Social Registrants, by Decade of Graduation (%)

	1880s	*1890s*	*1900s*	*1910s*	*1920s*	*1930s*	*1940s*	*1950s*	*1960s*
Top Five	81	82	80	81	89	69	69	70	45
Other	19	18	20	19	11	31	31	30	55
Total	100	100	100	100	100	100	100	100	100

As its counterpart in Boston, the New York upper class was frequently educated at Harvard, Yale, and Princeton (see Table 3.7). Columbia, the local elite institution, had a position somewhat similar to Harvard's in Boston. Williams, the fifth most common school, was attractive to the upper classes in both cities. Although local to neither, it is not too far away, and, as mentioned, had a reputation as a fashionable liberal arts college. Nonetheless, only a very small proportion ever graduated from there.

Strikingly, the most prestigious local college, Columbia, graduated on average only 7 percent of the New York upper class. More of the New York upper class went to Yale (28 percent), Harvard (22 percent), and Princeton (14 percent). Only in the 1880s was Columbia the first choice of New Yorker's and then just barely—25 percent to Yale's 24 percent. By the 1890s Columbia had begun its rather steep descent, arrested only briefly in the early 1900s and insignificantly after World War II. Yale, with the exceptions of 1890s and 1910s, when it was marginally surpassed by Harvard, has been the preferred choice of New Yorkers.

TABLE 3.7
New York—Social Registrants Graduating from Top Five Colleges,
by Decade of Graduation (%)

	1880s	*1890s*	*1900s*	*1910s*	*1920s*	*1930s*	*1940s*	*1950s*	*1960s*	*Ave.*
Yale	24	25	26	25	33	34	25	34	20	28
Harvard	15	27	25	32	32	15	20	21	9	22
Princeton	14	13	12	16	19	13	20	12	12	14
Columbia	25	15	16	6	4	3	1	3	3	7
Williams	3	2	1	2	1	4	3	0	1	2
Total	81	82	80	81	89	69	69	70	45	73

What is particularly interesting here is the timing of the exodus of the New York upper class from the local quality institution beginning as it did in the 1890s. Not unlike the situation in Boston, it seems related to increasing urban heterogeneity and what became known as the "Jewish problem." In the 1920s, under then President Nicholas Murray Butler, Columbia, like Harvard, instituted a quota against Jews, who by that time constituted more than 40 percent of the student body (Wechsler, 1977). This democratic trend may have occurred first, or at least became more apparent first, in New York, thus prompting the upper-class emigration. Whatever the cause, it is clear that Columbia was never able to halt the defection of its local upper class.

Until the 1930s, Columbia's loss was HYP's gain (see Table 3.8). The percentage of the upper class going to these four schools actually increased at the same time that Columbia's share declined. Thus, not only did HYP (especially Harvard) take away Columbia's prospects at this time, but they added others as well. It is not until the 1960s that the proportion educated at HYP dropped substantially. This willingness to leave their city for education may suggest a greater cosmopolitanism on the part of New York's upper class than Boston's. It almost certainly suggests less local filiation. At no time did Columbia's share of the upper class exceed that of the Big Three or even any combination of two of them. Harvard's role in the Boston upper class, on the other hand, dwarfed that of all other institutions, though it had the distinctive dual advantage of unparalleled national prestige and proximate location. Yale and Princeton, of course, have had no local urban upper class on which to draw.

TABLE 3.8

New York—Social Registrants Graduating from Columbia and
Harvard-Yale-Princeton (HYP), by Decade of Graduation (%)

	1880s	*1890s*	*1900s*	*1910s*	*1920s*	*1930s*	*1940s*	*1950s*	*1960s*
Columbia	25	15	16	6	4	3	1	3	3
HYP	53	65	63	73	84	62	65	67	41
Total	78	80	79	79	88	65	66	70	44

PHILADELPHIA

Very similar to the pattern for New York, the number of colleges attended by Philadelphians tripled from 1880 to 1970 (see Table 3.9). Unlike in New York, however, this increase did not happen until after World War II. Before the war the number hovered somewhere between 15 and 20. In the 1950s this figure rose to 30, and then doubled again in the 1960s. As for the upper classes in New York and Boston, it is likely that upper-class Philadelphians were forced away from their most preferred colleges by the advent of more strictly meritocratic admissions criteria that attended the great increase in college matriculation after the war.

TABLE 3.9

Philadelphia—Colleges Graduating Social Registrants, by Decade (N)

1880s	*1890s*	*1900s*	*1910s*	*1920s*	*1930s*	*1940s*	*1950s*	*1960s*
20	16	21	16	19	18	19	30	61

Further indicating the educational dispersion of this upper class, the percentage of proper Philadelphians graduating from one of the five most selected colleges dropped from a high of 89 percent in 1880 to a low of 32 percent by 1970 (see Table 3.10). The most radical shift occurred after World War II, when the percentage attending the preferred five colleges dropped by a quarter from 80 percent to 60 percent. In the 1960s this was cut nearly in half to 32 percent.

TABLE 3.10

Philadelphia—Colleges of Social Registrants, by Decade of Graduation (%)

	1880s	*1890s*	*1900s*	*1910s*	*1920s*	*1930s*	*1940s*	*1950s*	*1960s*
Top Five	89	68	83	73	74	78	78	60	32
Other	11	32	17	27	26	22	22	40	68
Total	100	100	100	100	100	100	100	100	100

Although these twentieth century patterns are not unexpected in light of the other cases, the sharp defection of the Philadelphia upper class in the 1890s from the five most preferred schools is peculiar and difficult to interpret. In the 1880s five schools accounted for 89 percent of the upper class but only 68 percent in the following decade. By the 1900s, this figure again rose to 83 percent. Some loss was experienced by all of the top five schools, though Princeton and Harvard remained relatively constant, but in absolute terms the greatest part of this decline reflected lesser attendance at the University of Pennsylvania, the local prestige college of Philadelphia (see Tables 3.11 and 3.12).

TABLE 3.11
Philadelphia—Social Registrants Graduating from Top Five Colleges, by Decade of Graduation (%)

	1880s	*1890s*	*1900s*	*1910s*	*1920s*	*1930s*	*1940s*	*1950s*	*1960s*	*Ave.*
Penn	49	39	51	52	14	23	24	18	14	29
Princeton	16	15	17	11	40	30	35	18	10	21
Yale	8	2	3	7	8	14	14	12	5	8
Harvard	8	7	4	1	7	8	2	6	2	5
Haverford	8	5	8	2	5	3	3	6	1	4
Total	89	68	83	73	74	78	78	60	32	67

TABLE 3.12
Philadelphia—Social Registrants Graduating from Penn and HYP, by Decade of Graduation (%)

	1880s	*1890s*	*1900s*	*1910s*	*1920s*	*1930s*	*1940s*	*1950s*	*1960s*
Penn	49	39	51	52	14	23	24	18	14
HYP	32	24	24	19	55	52	51	36	17
Total	81	63	75	71	69	75	75	54	31

Why the lesser attraction of Penn at the time? In the 1890s, the university began a policy of admitting local high school graduates without examination if their school was "certified" by Penn. This certification method of admission was adopted in an effort to secure greater numbers of students. From the point of view of the upper class, however, such a policy must have had disconcerting effects, attracting not just greater numbers but also a more socially heterogeneous student body drawn from the public high schools. Perhaps this discouraged the Philadelphia upper class from sending its children to Penn. Whatever the explanation, the precipitous drop was temporary and substantially restored to 1880s levels by the 1900s.

The Philadelphia upper class, like those in Boston and New York, was often educated at Harvard, Yale, and Princeton. Of the five most attended institutions, the other two were both local, Penn and Haverford. As the local institution of colonial pedigree and greatest prestige, Penn has had an analogous position to Harvard in Boston and Columbia in New York. Haverford has been much like Williams, a local liberal arts college, small and fashionable. On average two-thirds of the Philadelphia upper class have attended one of these five schools; in rank order they looked to Penn, Princeton, Yale, Harvard, and Haverford as their alma mater.

With many Penn degrees within its ranks (29 percent), the Philadelphia upper class has been neither as cosmopolitan as New Yorkers, who fled Columbia, nor as locally-oriented as Bostonians, who flocked to Harvard. As mentioned, this comparison is complicated by the fact that Harvard is simultaneously one of the Big Three and the local Boston upper-class college. Neither Columbia nor Penn has ever had Harvard's level of national prestige.

In the 1880s Penn graduates were about half of the upper class, but in the one decade from 1910 to 1920 they dropped from this level to 14 percent. Almost all of this decline corresponded to Princeton's ascent from 11 percent to 40 percent in the same decade.

This is the period in Penn's history when its undergraduate population was characterized as having the "democracy of the streetcar" (Slosson, 1910: 361-63). Upper-class alumni and trustees after World War I complained about its urban setting, a polite euphemism for the increasing admission of Jews and other non-WASPs. Various proposals were circulated, largely initiated by disgruntled alumni, to redress what was perceived as an unacceptable and increasing level of heterogeneity. "Education for leadership and character" was hailed as an antidote to mass education and the creeping control of the state. An unsuccessful effort was made to secure the services of General Leonard Wood, World War I hero and ardent advocate of immigration restriction, as Provost.[3] Perhaps the most ingenious and desperate attempt to rid the college of urban and "un-American" influences was the attempt to move the entire plant wholesale to the pastoral setting of Valley Forge (Cheyney, 1940), a move intended to discourage those without the means to reside on campus from bothering to attend at all. As this plan fell through, many upper-class members deserted the local university for the more socially homogeneous and environmentally congenial setting at Princeton.

Although Penn's fortunes rebounded somewhat between the wars from its nadir of the 1920s, its share of its own upper class never again exceeded a quarter. Only after World War II did it again surpass Princeton and reclaim its position as the preferred college of the Philadelphia upper class. Far from a triumph, this seems only to have been the result of

Princeton's precipitous drop after the war from 35 percent in the 1940s to 10 percent in the 1960s. Penn's decline was less sharp, probably because, with the great rush to higher education after World War II, it became far harder to gain admission to Princeton than to Penn on a meritocratic basis. The Philadelphia upper class was probably making the best of a difficult situation and attending Penn by default.

BALTIMORE

As in the other cities, the concentration and dispersion data for Baltimore show an unmistakable trend toward democratization. The number of colleges attended tripled from 17 in the 1880s to 53 in the 1960s, a general trend that may be broken into three major periods, bounded by the world wars (see Table 3.13). Before World War I the number of schools attended hovered around 20; during the 1920s-1950s it rose to about 30, after which it nearly doubled to 53 in the 1960s. However, the increase in the number of colleges did not substantially alter the concentration of the Baltimore upper class at preferred schools. With the single anomaly of the 1890s, 55 to 65 percent of the upper class attended a Top Five school. Only in the 1950s did this drop to less than half, but by 1960 it had declined to approximately a quarter (Table 3.14).

TABLE 3.13
Baltimore—Colleges Graduating Social Registrants, by Decade (N)

1880s	*1890s*	*1900s*	*1910s*	*1920s*	*1930s*	*1940s*	*1950s*	*1960s*
17	20	20	18	26	29	29	30	53

TABLE 3.14
Baltimore—Colleges of Social Registrants, by Decade of Graduation (%)

	1880s	*1890s*	*1900s*	*1910s*	*1920s*	*1930s*	*1940s*	*1950s*	*1960s*
Top Five	63	72	56	63	57	58	57	49	26
Other	37	28	44	37	43	42	43	51	74
Total	100	100	100	100	100	100	100	100	100

For the Baltimore upper class the five most popular schools were, in order, Princeton, Johns Hopkins, Virginia, Harvard, and Yale (see Table 3.15). Thus, once again, we find the influence of both cosmopolitan and local orientations. Princeton, Harvard, and Yale represented the cosmopolitan attractions of the national prestige colleges, and Johns Hopkins and Virginia embodied local filiation.As in the other cities, two schools had by far the greatest attraction, and the others accounted for much lesser numbers.

TABLE 3.15
Baltimore—Social Registrants Graduating from Top Five Colleges,
by Decade of Graduation (%)

	1880s	*1890s*	*1900s*	*1910s*	*1920s*	*1930s*	*1940s*	*1950s*	*1960s*	*Ave.*
Princeton	14	21	25	20	26	22	25	20	7	20
John Hopkins	37	34	22	24	22	16	10	8	5	18
Virginia	6	7	8	6	5	11	9	11	7	8
Harvard	3	3	0	4	3	7	9	7	5	5
Yale	3	7	1	9	1	2	4	3	2	3
Total	63	72	56	63	57	58	57	49	26	54

However, whereas in Philadelphia and Boston the local school held the highest allegiance, in Baltimore, Hopkins (18 percent) took second place to Princeton (20 percent). Johns Hopkins was not founded until 1876 and thus lacked deep roots in the local community. Moreover, from the outset it established the highest academic standards and focussed less on undergraduate than on graduate departments, taking as its model the German university rather than the English. If upper-class members selected colleges less on academic than on social or status grounds, then these two factors would militate against the selection of Hopkins over Princeton. Indeed, by the 1960s Hopkins graduates accounted for only 5 percent of the Baltimore upper class, third position behind Virginia and Princeton.

For the Baltimore upper class, Virginia seems to have had a position functionally analogous to Williams for Boston and New York and Haverford for Philadelphia; unlike those latter two schools, however, the local significance of the University of Virginia generally exceeded that of Harvard and Yale. Indeed, by 1970 it had even tied Princeton for first rank.. This suggests a somewhat greater local orientation by Baltimoreans, perhaps an inclination to view themselves as southerners. Harvard and Yale are decidedly New England schools; Princeton, on the other hand, in the Middle Atlantic region has traditionally drawn a substantial conponent of its student body from the South. For Baltimoreans the "northernness" of Harvard and Yale may constitute a sufficient disincentive to lead them to prefer Virginia.

About 25 to 35 percent of the Baltimore upper class graduated from HYP until the 1960s, when only 14 percent did so (see Table 3.16). Hopkins exceeded HYP only in the 1880s and 1890s. From the 1900s until the 1930s the local college accounted for close to 23 percent, after which it commenced its long decline to 5 percent in the 1960s. Until that time Hopkins's post-World War I losses did not go to the more fashionable schools but to the more democratic process of dispersion to a large number of schools. Thus, the prestige of the Big Three remained fairly constant over time while the democratic process occurred at the expense of localism.

TABLE 3.16
Baltimore—Social Registrants Graduating from Johns Hopkins and HYP, by Decade of Graduation (%)

	1880s	*1890s*	*1900s*	*1910s*	*1920s*	*1930s*	*1940s*	*1950s*	*1960s*
John Hopkins	37	34	22	24	22	16	10	8	5
HYP	20	31	26	33	30	31	38	30	14
Total	57	65	48	57	52	47	48	38	19

CONCLUSION

The principal findings of this study generally corroborate Baltzell's work on the upper class and higher education. First, the upper classes in all four cities often patronized a local institution, especially before World War I. In every case at least one of the five most attended schools was a local college, and in some cases a second was at least proximate. In Baltzell's terms the local upper-class colleges for each of the four cities were Boston-Harvard, Philadelphia-Penn, Baltimore-Johns Hopkins, New York-Columbia. Nonetheless, this "localism" declined over time, and sharply so. Localism was at its highest in the 1880s, the earliest period in this study, when almost half of these upper classes graduated from "their" school. Baltzell's analysis (1958) suggests even this notable localism constitutes a decline from an earlier period, probably prior to the Civil War, after which a *national* upper class started to develop. Localism dropped sharply in the 1920s, the period when the attraction of the national upper-class institutions, Harvard, Yale, and Princeton, was at its zenith, and dropped sharply again in the 1960s. At that time only a small minority (15 percent) went to a local institution. The two world wars apparently eroded localism considerably.

The localism of these upper classes also diverged sharply. When the four cities are compared (the average percentage of each upper class attending its premier local institution for the entire time period), they rank as follows: Boston (67 percent), Philadelphia (29 percent), Baltimore (18 percent), New York (7 percent). The most striking finding here is the magnitude by which the Boston upper class exceeded all others in its fidelity to its local college. Although it is true that Harvard is both a local *and* a national upper-class institution, Baltzell would argue that this dual status directly reflects Boston's distinctive cultural heritage.

The Puritan faith in education and fidelity to local institutions was precisely the reason for Harvard's accession to national prominence.

That the New York upper class demonstrated the least local loyalty reflected their greater cosmopolitanism. Indeed, they were probably the first to shift their orientation to the national level. As early as the 1890s Columbia had fallen behind Yale and Harvard, and it was eclipsed by Princeton as well in the 1910s and 1920s. Somewhat similarly, in Baltimore Johns Hopkins fell behind Princeton around World War I, never to recover. Philadelphians, interestingly, were closest to Bostonians in local fidelity. With the single exception of the interwar period, when Princeton was their first choice, they have attended Penn in greater numbers than any other college.

For all of these cities World War I constituted a watershed in the shift from local to national upper-class colleges. Overall, Baltzell's thesis about the loss of local pride and the development of a national upper class is confirmed. The apparent exception of Boston is only in keeping with the perspective developed in *Puritan Boston and Quaker Philadelphia*.

The second major finding is that the nationally most prestigious colleges, HYP, attracted the offspring of the upper classes in all four cities. These institutions constituted three of the top five colleges for all of the upper classes studied. The only other institution to appear in the top five for more than one city was Williams, often attended both by New Yorkers and Bostonians. Although somewhat local to both New York and Boston, the fashionability that Williams developed, especially in the 1920s, may suggest that it became something of a national upper-class liberal arts college. Its Puritan origins and Massachusetts location probably helped foster this reputation.

The average percentage attending HYP from all four cities, however, makes clear that their influence rose and then fell. In the 1880s about half (47 percent) graduated from one of the Big Three, again suggesting that a national upper class was well into the process of formation. This figure rose to a peak of 63 percent in the 1920s, the "Anglo-Saxon decade," descended slowly to about half again in the 1950s, and then dropped sharply to 30 percent in the 1960s. In all likelihood, this latter decline is attributable to increasingly strong commitments to meritocratic standards as well as more intense competition that made it harder for members of any upper class to gain admission.

At the same time the four upper classes differed in enrollments at the Big Three: Boston (76 percent), New York (64 percent), Philadelphia (34 percent), Baltimore (28 percent). Boston led the others primarily because Harvard has been both a local and a national upper-class school. The strong attraction of New Yorkers to HYP is a mirrored reflection of its exceedingly small local orientation. In a sense, it might even be argued that New York was the most national in its orientation since it was almost completely unalloyed with any localism, unlike the situation in Boston. Both the local school and the national ones held more attraction in Philadelphia than in Baltimore. The attendance patterns among the Baltimore upper class may reflect some southern regionalism, which deterred them from being so well integrated into a northeast upper class.

The third major finding of this study is that in each of the four cities the percentage of the upper class attending the most chosen schools declined, and the overall number of colleges attended increased over time. In other words, there is a general trend toward greater dispersion in the higher education of each upper class. This trend is pronounced in the period following World War II. On average, the total number of colleges attended by all upper classes rises from a low of 14 in the 1880s to a high of 54 in the 1960s. The sharpest increases occurred in the 1930s and 1960s. Correlatively, the average percentage attending the five preferred colleges for all cities declined from a high of 82 perent in the 1880s to a low of 39 percent by the 1960s. Again, the decline is fairly gradual until after World War II.

Yet this educational dispersion within the upper class was much less marked in some cities than in others. The average percentage of the upper class for each city graduating from one of the five preferred schools was Boston (80 percent), New York (73 percent), Philadelphia (67 percent), and Baltimore (53 percent). This pattern perfectly matches the findings above on both "localism" and "cosmopolitanism." Once again, the Boston upper class was the most concentrated in its pattern of educational attendance, thus perhaps having the most common socialization experience and coherence as a class.

The dispersion of the upper classes throughout greater numbers of colleges and universities largely seems to be the result of the upgrading of selection criteria that attended the great surge in college applicants after 1945. From 1945 to 1970 the percentage of the eighteen- to twenty-one-year-old age cohort attending college expanded fron 15 percent to 50 percent, in real terms from 1.5 million to 6.5 million (Trow, 1972). The system of higher education responded in a variety of ways to this influx, perhaps especially by expansion of the numbers and types of institutions. At the highest levels of the system, however, the principal response has been to restrict entrance by meritocratic selection. This procedure excluded many of the members of the upper class who were previously admitted on more particularistic grounds. They were thus forced to seek higher education elsewhere. The upper-class "monopolization" of places in preferred colleges has clearly declined, especially in the post-war years.

By the 1960s only 51 percent of the Bostonians, 45 percent of the New Yorkers, 32 percent of Philadelphians, and 26 percent of Baltimoreans graduated from one of the five colleges preferred by their upper classes. By no means is this level of concentration insubstantial, but it was far less than that of previous eras.

These findings about local upper-class colleges, national upper-class colleges, and the decline of ascription both complement and support Baltzell's work on the upper class and higher education. The findings about how local upper classes differed in their orientations also corroborate his views. Boston, the home of Puritanism, hierarchy, and authority, had the greatest local fidelity as well as the greatest national influence among its upper-class members. Philadelphia, on the other hand, was inferior in both these regards. Indeed, the attendance patterns within these four upper classes suggest that hierarchy, authority, and upper-class coherence in educational experience have been inversely related to distance from the Puritan Jerusalem. For most of the measures of educational concentration, Boston was the leader, followed in order by New York, Philadelphia, and Baltimore. Only in the case of local loyalty were New Yorkers inferior to all others, reflecting the greater cosmopolitanism and commercial emphasis of that city.

Not only did these upper classes differ in *where* they educated their children, but they also varied in their commitment to education. One indication of their value orientations to education is the percentage of the upper class listed as college graduates in the *Social Registers*. The overall averages for each city were Boston (55 percent), New York (50 percent), Philadelphia (44 percent), Baltimore (27 percent). The spread among the four was greatest in 1910 (the earliest years in which data were available for all four cities):[4] Boston (58 percent), New York (43 percent), Philadelphia (33 percent), Baltimore (16 percent). However, thereafter their commitments to higher education became more similar, especially among the first three. By 1960 Boston, New York, and Philadelphia were all around a half, and Baltimore had risen to only a third. Once again Baltimore seens to have operated by some different standards from the other three. The general convergence, however, probably reflects the fact that education became understood by all as essential to status attainment and occupational placement. The differential influence of the religious ethics toward education in each city became both secularized and diluted.

What, finally, is to be made of the socialization and status-ascribing functions that Baltzell found to be essential to the national upper-class colleges in sustaining a national upper class, especially in view of the increased dispersion of all four of the upper classes among a variety of colleges since World War II? As the upper classes became dispersed among more colleges and universities, their socialization experience at a crucial time of life became less coherent. In recent decades none of the upper-class colleges, not even Harvard, Yale, and Princeton, reached the proportion of the upper class that they had in the past. With the shift to universalistic and meritocratic principles , especially since World War II, these colleges have perhaps ceased to function in the status-ascribing terms that Baltzell argued they had before the war.

From one perspective this change is both deplorable and dangerous. Insofar as the upper class is a repository of responsible values, and insofar as it is unable to sustain its coherence through the common socialization experience at elite colleges and universities, it becomes incapable of exercising its authoritative and leadership functions in the society. It may simply withdraw to a world of private privilege and social irresponsibility. At the same time it is supplanted by an atomized, egoistic, and acquisitve elite unregulated by the disciplines and unmotivated by the ideals of a moral ethic. In this view elite colleges and universities are performing a "liberal-democratic" but not an "authoritative-aristocratic" function, to borrow the terms of *The Protestant Establishment.* They are assisting in the attainment of individual mobility and equal opportunity without assimilating new elite members into any authoritative communal value orientation. In functional terms they have shifted from status ascription to status creation at the very time that they have undermined the structural underpinnings of moral education. Under such circumstances the prospects for a coherent and secure upper class must seem dim.

But from another point of view our judgment may be more sanguine. Insofar as it is the elite colleges and universities themselves that are the fiduciaries of the moral orientations essential to communal solidarity and authoritative leadership, and insofar as more talented and motivated young adults are being exposed to them as a consequence of meritocratic selection, then in Shils's terms the periphery is being drawn closer to the center, central cultural orientations are being diffused throughout larger segments of society, solidarity is enhanced, and authoritative and responsible leadership will be sustained.

Which side one comes down on hinges very greatly on the extent to which elite colleges and universities are sensitive to and responsible in acquitting themselves of this important charge. Having arrogated to themselves the task of selecting and creating the elite of the society, a function once largely discharged through the ascriptive solidarities of family and class, they must also embrace the more diffuse socialization function performed by those agencies. Whether they are successful in this effort, or can be, is a vital matter for the future of American society.

NOTES

*An earlier version of the paper by Richard Farnum appeared in *Studies in American Democracy: A Volume in Honor of E. Digby Baltzell, edited by Harold Bershady,* University of Pennsylvania Press, 1988. Used by permission.

1. The term *elite* is used here not in Baltzell's sense but rather to suggest those colleges and universities that are most "selective." The criteria for selectivity have of course shifted over time from particularistic to universalistic orientations. In general, in this paper I follow Baltzell's usage for the terms *elite* and *upper class*, a distinction which has been given insufficient attention in the sociological literature. "The elite concept refers to those individuals in any social system who hold the top positions in their chosen careers, occupations, or professions ... An upper class is a sociological and historical, rather than a natural, aristocracy. It is a group of consanguine families whose ancestors were elite members and family founders one or more generations earlier. Whereas elites are formed anew in each generation and according to contemporary criteria, upper classes are always the product of two or more generations" (1979: 24-25).

2. Although the *Social Register* is an index of the upper class and must not be mistaken for the real thing, it has been used by sociologists as divergent in their orientations as E. Digby Baltzell and C. Wright Mills. It is "the nearest thing to an official status center that this country, with no aristocratic past, no court society, no truly capital city, possesses" (Mills, 1956: 57). It emerged in the industrial era of the late nineteenth century as a response to the onslaught of newly created plutocratic fortunes on the citadel of society. With the coming of the centralization of the economy at this time, the upper class itself became more national in scope and more associational in character as it assimilated the new families of great wealth (Baltzell, 1958: 17-20). Although the exact criteria for inclusion are unclear, the *Social Register* provides a convenient, if imperfect, guide to families of status, as opposed to the individuals of high functional class position recorded in *Who's Who*. "In any individual case admission may be unpredictable or even arbitrary, but as a group the people in the *Social Register* have been chosen for their money, their family, and their style of life. Accordingly, the names contained in these twelve magic volumes do stand for a certain type of person" (Mills, 1956: p. 57).

3. Penn is the only higher-educational institution in the country to have had a provost rather than a president as its leader. Not until 1930 did Penn have a president in name, and not until the 1950s did it have one in fact. The relative impotence of the provost as against the trustees, symbolized by the anomalous title, is taken by Baltzell as evidence of the traditional distrust of leadership in Philadelphia.

4. The exact dates of the *Social Register*s used for each city are noted in the references. For Boston, New York, and Philadelphia a 10 percent sample was taken, whereas for Baltimore a 25 percent sample was used because it is so much smaller in population.

REFERENCES

Baltzell, E. Digby. *Philadelphia Gentlemen: The Making of a National Upper Class.* Glencoe, Ill.: The Free Press, 1958.

_____. *The Protestant Establishment: Aristocracy and Caste in America.* New York: Random House, 1964.

_____. *Puritan Boston and Quaker Philadelphia: Two Protestant Ethics and the Spirit of Class Authority and Leadership.* New York: The Free Press, 1979.

Bloomgarden, Lawrence. "Our Changing Elite Colleges." *Commentary*, February 1960: 150-54.

Cheyney, Edward P. *History of the University of Pennsylvania, 1740-1940.* Philadelphia: University of Pennsylvania Press, 1940.

Coon, Horace. *Columbia: Colossus on the Hudson.* New York: Dutton, 1947.

Earnest, Ernest. *Academic Procession: An Informal History of the American College 1636-1953.* New York: Bobbs Merrill Company, Inc., 1953.

Farnum, Richard. "Prestige in the Ivy League: Democratization and Discrimination at Penn and Columbia, 1890-1970." Unpublished paper, Department of Sociology, University of Pennsylvania, 1980.

Goddard, David R., and Linda C. Koons. "A Profile of the University of Pennsylvania," pp. 225-48 in David Riesman and Verne Stadtman, eds. , *Academic Transformation: Seventeen Institutions Under Pressure.* New York: McGraw-Hill, 1973.

Higham, John. *Strangers in the Land: Patterns of American Nativism, 1860-1925.* New York: Atheneum, 1968.

Jencks, Christopher, and David Riesman. *The Academic Revolution.* New York: Doubleday, 1968.

Karabel, Jerome. "Status-Group Struggle, Organizational Interests, and the Limits of Institutional Autonomy: The Transformation of Harvard, Yale, and Princeton 1918-1940." *Theory and Society* (January 1984): 1-40.

Levine, David. "The Functions of Higher Education In American Society Between World War I and World War II." Ph.D. Dissertation, Department of History, Harvard University, 1981.

Lipset, Seymour Martin, and David Riesman. *Education and Politics at Harvard.* New York: McGraw-Hill, 1975.

Mills, C. Wright. *The Power Elite.* New York: Oxford University Press.

Morison, Samuel Eliot. *Three Centuries of Harvard, 1636-1936.* Cambridge: Harvard University Press, 1936.

Pierson, George W. *The Education of American Leaders: Comparative Contributions of U.S. Colleges and Universities.* New York: Praeger, 1969.

Slosson, Edwin E. *Great American Universities.* New York: Macmillan, 1910.

Social Register. New York: The Social Register Association. Baltimore, 1899, 1912, 1922, 1929, 1940, 1950, 1960, 1974. Boston, 1899, 1910, 1920, 1930, 1940, 1950, 1960, 1975. New York, 1900, 1918, 1930, 1940, 1950, 1960, 1973. Philadelphia, 1910, 1920, 1930, 1941, 1950, 1958, 1965, 1975.

Steinberg, Stephen. *The Academic Melting Pot: Catholics and Jews in American Higher Education.* New York: McGraw-Hill, 1974.

Synnott, Marcia Graham. *The Half-Opened Door: Discrimination and Admissions at Harvard, Yale, and Princeton, 1900-1970.* Westport, Conn.: Greenwood Press, 1979.

Trow, Martin. "The Expansion and Transformation of Higher Education." *International Review of Education* 18, No. 1 (1972): 61-84.

_____. "The Second Transformation of American Secondary Education." *International Journal of Comparative Sociology* 2 (1961): 144-65.

Useem, Michael, and S. M. Miller. "Privilege and Domination: The Role of the Upper Class in American Higher Education." *Social Science Information* 14, No. 6 (1975): 115-45.

Veysey, Laurence R. *The Emergence of the American University.* Chicago: University of Chicago Press, 1965.

Wechsler, Harold S. *The Qualified Student: A History of Selective College Admission in America.* New York: John Wiley and Sons, 1977.

Richard Farnum

Chapter Four

Prestige in the Ivy League: Democratization and Discrimination at Penn and Columbia, 1890-1970

Although American colleges and universities are loosely organized into a hierarchy of institutional prestige, the origins of this hierarchy and the criteria by which it is organized are less well understood. The Ivy League colleges are usually regarded as the pinnacle of the academic system, conferring on their graduates privileged access to the most rewarding social positions. Entrance to these elite colleges and universities is largely contingent on the manifestly universalistic grounds of scholastic performance or other achievements, and their differential ranking is to a large extent governed by precisely such criteria. The best colleges are inhabited by the best scholars and attract the best students, who are admitted mostly according to their academic merits.[1] Within the Ivy League itself, however, member schools are ranked in a hierarchy. Thus, within this group of academically elite colleges and universities there exists a further system of stratification reflecting fundamental differences of prestige. What is the nature of this hierarchy, and how are we to account for it?

At the top of the Ivy League stands the Big Three, Harvard, Yale, and Princeton, perhaps the premier American undergraduate institutions. Ironically, the name *Big Three* has its origins in the football domination enjoyed by these schools in the late nineteenth century.

Graduates of the Big Three are disproportionately and overwhelmingly represented among the elites of this society (Pierson, 1969).

75

Much lower in the Ivy League hierarchy, perhaps even at the bottom, is the University of Pennsylvania (Penn). A *New York Times* feature article for October 22, 1977, entitled "The University of Pennsylvania Is Suffering From An Identity Crisis," explained that many people tend to confuse Penn with Penn State, unaware that Penn is in fact a member of the "prestigious Ivy League." As early as 1911, in his panoramic tour of the "great American universities," the journalist Edwin Slosson (1910) was disconcerted at his inability to divine a distinctive ethos at Penn in contrast to Harvard, Yale, and Princeton, each of which demonstrated some sort of constitutive character. More recently, in his *Selective Guide to Colleges,* Times education editor Edward B. Fiske claims that "University of Pennsylvania faculty members and students consider their school the ugly duckling of the Ivy League and not without reason" (Fiske, 1982: 295). Expatriate Philadelphian Nathaniel Burt has succinctly posed the perennial questions that vex the members of his native city.

> Boston has its Harvard, New York has its Columbia, what is the matter with Philadelphia? Why is the University of Pennsylvania neither the Harvard nor Columbia of Philadelphia? Any Philadelphian, even the most rabid devotee of the University, will agree that the University of Pennsylvania is not either Harvard or Columbia, but nobody knows just why. (Burt, 1963: 80)

Of the search for the origins of Penn's inferior reputation there may be no end. (And, counter to Burt, the same search may be directed to Columbia, an institution of far lesser prestige than Harvard.) Former university president Martin Meyerson claims that Penn's lack of self-regard is just one manifestation of a more general tendency among Philadelphians to self-derision. Burt suggests that Penn is no Harvard because its trustees have historically been more interested in their own prestige than in educational leadership, its student body is socially declasse, and Princeton's proximity provides overwhelming competition. Bicentennial historian Edward Potts Cheyney stressed both poor administration and the failure to adequately support the undergraduate college (Cheyney, 1940).[2] More recently, sociologist E.D. Baltzell has attempted to organize all of the more concrete causes of Penn's inferior position and explain them in terms of the Quaker religious orientations of Philadelphia's upper-class founders. These orientations evolved into a secular value complex characterized by attitudes both anti-intellectual and suspicious of authority and leadership.[3] In contrast, Harvard's success, as well as that of its sister schools, Yale and Princeton, is ascribed to the values of a secularized Calvinism which emphasized erudition, hierarchy, and authority (Baltzell, 1979).

However valid Baltzell's argument about the cultural origins of these prestige distinctions, the bearing of more recent institutional practices on prestige warrants attention. Here I historically compare the fates of Penn, Columbia, and the Big Three with a particular emphasis on the social composition of their student bodies, especially from 1890 to 1940, a time that was crucial to the development of their subsequent institutional reputations.

In another analysis of the higher-educational patterns of the upper classes in New York, Philadelphia, Boston, and Baltimore from 1870 to 1970 (see Chapter 3 in this volume), I showed that the upper classes of all four cities preferred to attend certain local institutions as well as Harvard, Yale, and Princeton.[4] Although the top local universities were generally the most preferred prior to World War I, between the world wars at least one of the Big Three emerged as the most preferred college in each city. By no later than World War I, Harvard, Yale, and Princeton had emerged as the preferred colleges of a national upper class.[5]

At least two questions are suggested by these results. First, why did the preferred local colleges in New York and Philadelphia, Columbia and Penn,[6] never develop national prestige? Second, why were Columbia and Penn unable to retain the affections of even their local upper classes? An institution would seem hard-pressed to develop a national reputation if its own upper class deserts it. Both social reputation and material resources are importantly affected by high-status constituencies; indeed, the social composition of the undergraduate student body seems to constitute at least one element in the prestige or "quality" of the college (see Chapter 3 of this volume). If so, one possible explanation for the upper-class desertion of Penn and Columbia is that their student bodies became more heterogeneous, more democratic, more open to members of the community not previously present and regarded as socially undesirable. Similarly, if Harvard, Yale, and Princeton retained and enhanced their attraction for the upper classes, as well as rising elites, then their student bodies probably remained more homogeneous and less open to those of diverse backgrounds.

The period under consideration here, roughly from 1890 to 1940, coincides with two social movements of potential relevance. First, during the late nineteenth and early twentieth centuries the great migrations from eastern and southern Europe occurred, swelling the cities of the East Coast with Italians, Slavs, and Jews. Second, at the same time public secondary education became firmly institutionalized, extending previously unknown opportunities to the children of the immigrants. These trends taken in combination meant that more people of urban and immigrant backgrounds sought places in higher education. The general social response to the immigrant influx and their attempted inclusion into American society was one of hysteria, paranoia, and outbreaks of nativism, characterized by racial hostility, anti-Semitism, conspiracy theories, and legal restriction (Higham, 1978). How the colleges of interest here responded to these social currents is the subject of this study.

In the last decade sociological and historical research has taken up the issue of discrimination in admissions at elite colleges and universities during the 1920s and 1930s, especially against Jews (Wechsler, 1977; Synnott, 1979; Karabel, 1984; Karen, 1985; Oren, 1985; Levine, 1986). With the qualified exception of Wechsler, this literature has focussed primarily on those institutions which "successfully" imposed quotas and repelled the "Jewish problem," thereby sustaining their social prestige and maintaining their upper-class WASP constituencies. Karabel, for example, shows how Harvard, Yale, and Princeton succumbed to particularism in the 1920s and 1930s to close off scarce cultural capital to rising immigrant groups in order to preserve both their links to the upper class and their institutional prestige. In this status-group struggle organizational interest and limited institutional autonomy turned them away from greater democratization and meritocratic standards. In this paper I look at the same process but from the point of view of those institutions, such as Columbia and especially Penn, that took a more democratic course. Their early democratization, however laudable, may from another angle have constituted a mismanagement of their funds of institutional prestige, one that tells to this day.

The information for this paper was collected principally from archival sources at Columbia and Penn. I analyze four types of information, each of which bears on the issue of the social heterogeneity of the undergraduate student body: the formal admissions procedures and criteria as they are specified in the undergraduate announcements,[7] the geographic origins of the student body,[8] the proportion of the undergraduate college represented by graduates of public versus private secondary schools,[9] and the religious composition of the student bodies.[10] Taken together, these data indicate that student bodies at both Penn and Columbia became relatively heterogeneous and democratic places very early in the twentieth century.

COLUMBIA

Admissions

Prior to the late nineteenth century all college admissions were conducted on the basis of examinations administered at the college, usually involving Latin and Greek translations of particular authors and perhaps some mathematics based on a specific text (Broome, 1903). These exams were peculiar to each college, and because they were locally administered, restricted the college's clientele. Students decided on a college and then prepared for its particular exams. Beginning in the late nineteenth century, however, various educational entrepreneurs perceived the need for a better articulation between secondary and higher education. This was motivated variously by a desire to improve the efficiency of the system, a progressive impulse to make higher education more universally accessible, and an interest in improving their institutional finances by garnering more students. Several innovations were attempted to achieve these ends. Perhaps the most democratic, begun by the University of Michigan and soon adopted by most western schools, was the certificate. Under this system the college would examine the educational program of a secondary school, and if found acceptable, would certify it, so that any of its graduates recommended by the headmaster as being capable of college work would be accepted into the college. This effectively put the burden of selection in the hands of the secondary schools.[11]

In the East, however, where colleges had ties to both traditional feeder schools and traditional subjects, the certificate system was resisted, especially by the older and more prestigious institutions. Columbia was one of these, along with Harvard, Yale, and Princeton. At the same time, however, some administrators at these schools saw closer ties with the emerging public school system as desirable in order to draw large numbers of students, at that time a source of both income and prestige.

In the 1890s Nicholas Murray Butler, then dean at Columbia, realized that although Harvard, Yale, and Princeton could afford to wait for students to come to them, Columbia could not, and he began a series of innovations in admissions policies to improve connections with the growing public education system in New York. Since the faculty refused to accept a certificate system, he moved to standardize college admissions exams under the College Entrance Examination Board (CEEB), as well as the offerings of the secondary schools (Schudson, 1972; Wechsler, 1977). In 1901, this standardization was evident in Columbia's admissions requirements. The applicant had to have taken 15 points (1 point equalled one year of study) in English, math, science, modern languages, and ancient languages, with a prescribed number for each. Moreover, he had to take entrance exams in each of these subjects as well as furnish a statement of his good moral character from his principal or headmaster. The exams could be either those given by Columbia or the CEEB, and New York State Regents' Exams could be substituted.

By 1919 two methods of admission were developed. By the "old method" the student would take either Columbia or CEEB exams in 15 units of secondary work, or, for those with outstanding records, comprehensive exams in four subjects could be substituted. By the "new method," however, the student could show the minimum school record plus take an exam of "mental alertness and power." This was the first evidence of the IQ test being used in college admissions.[12] The background for the implementation of these exams was twofold. First, after the war many more students were applying to college, and the IQ test offered an efficient method of selecting among them. Second, according to Wechsler, Butler's efforts at gaining more students had been successful—too successful. By standardizing exams and forging ties with the New York public school system, Columbia had indeed gained more students. What had not been anticipated was that the social composition of New York would change so dramatically. Now many, "too many," of those students were from immigrant and Jewish families of the "undesirable sort" (Keppel, 1914). In 1922 Dean Herbert Hawkes explained that "most Jews, especially those of the more objectionable type, have not had the home experiences which enable them to pass these tests as successfully as the average native American boy" (Synnott, 1979: 18). Thus, the IQ test was implemented to screen out many of the "undesirables," who were alleged to be "destroying Columbia" (Slosson, 1910).

In addition to the IQ tests, new application forms asked for the candidate's place of birth, religious affiliation, and father's name, place of birth, and occupation. Students were also asked to submit photographs and to present themselves for a personal interview. Other information sought included leadership in school, leadership in the community, breadth of interests, and motivation and potential (Wechsler, 1977: 156). The obvious intent was to identify and favor the traditional constituency of the Protestant elite.

That the situation was not regarded as critical in 1919 is evidenced by the fact that the IQ test was optional. By 1929, however, these tests were required of all students in the form of either the Thorndike Intelligence Examination or the Scholastic Aptitude Test. Other admissions requirements were also becoming stricter. By 1939 the intelligence test requirement for all students had been dropped, and Columbia was back to substantially the same admissions plan that it had in 1919. By this time, according to Wechsler, the "Jewish invasion" had been repelled.

By 1949 there was no longer a formal unit requirement in coursework, but students were urged to be prepared in English, math, social studies, foreign languages, and laboratory science. All exams, the SAT and three achievement tests, were administered exclusively by the CEEB.

By then the SAT had been institutionalized across the country and could no longer be regarded as a veiled discrimination device. Since 1949 there have been no substantial changes in Columbia's admissions requirements.

Geographic Origins

Since 1870 Columbia has been predominantly a New York institution, though in more recent times it has become much less so (see Table 4.1). The overall trend was downward from 92 percent to 45 percent over the hundred-year period. The rising importance of other regions may have reflected Columbia's growing prestige throughout the nation. For this study the most interesting information is the contribution to Columbia from the New York metropolitan area. Fully 72 percent of the undergraduates in 1870 were from New York City, but their representation declined precipitously over the next hundred years.

TABLE 4.1
Geographic Origins of Columbia Undergraduates (%)

Region	1870	1880	1891	1900	1911	1920	1930	1940	1950	1960	1972
New York State	92	86	76	79	81	79	66	78	60	68	45
New York City	(72)	(57)	(56)		(59)	(54)	(23)	(23)	(17)	(26)	(7)
Mid-Atlantic	8	12	12	10	10	10	17	12	19	14	10
New England		1	1	3	1	3	4	4	8	5	15
Midwest			4	1	3	1	2	2	5	3	7
South				2	1	1	5	2	4	5	10
West			3	2	3	4	2	2	4	4	11
Foreign			3	3	1	3	4	2	0	1	2
Total	100	99	99	100	100	101	100	102	100	100	100

Note: Totals not equal to 100% are due to rounding.

The slight increase in both the overall New York contingent and that from the City between 1890 and 1910 probably reflected the effects of Butler's democratic reform efforts. From 1920 to 1930, however, the percentage coming from New York City dropped sharply from 54 percent to 23 percent; thereafter it remained in a fairly gradual downward slope to less than a tenth in 1970. The sharp drop in the 1920s paralleled the institutionalization of IQ tests in admissions. Whether the geographic shift was entirely an effect of the change in admissions policy or whether it also reflected the implementation of a strict geographic quota, the effect is undeniable. It was precisely at this time that Columbia was concerned with repelling the "invasion of the Jewish student," and whatever devices were used, they obviously had the intended effect. It was then that Dean Hawkes remarked to Yale's admissions director Corwin that "the proportion of Jews in Columbia has been reduced from about 40% to about 20%" (Synnott, 1979: 18). It is not possible to infer from Table 4.1 whether quotas persisted after 1930, but it appears possible since the New York City contingent never again reached its earlier magnitude.

Secondary School Backgrounds

Information on the secondary school backgrounds of Columbia undergraduates is presented in Table 4.2. The general trend was from a predominance of private school graduates to a predominance of those with public school backgrounds. This is only to be expected since in the late nineteenth century public secondary education was just becoming institutionalized.[13] What is important is the timing of the shift. Private school graduates accounted for 51 percent of Columbia's students in 1890 and stayed at about this level through 1911. By 1930, however, this figure was nearly halved to 28 percent and reached a low of 19 percent in 1940. After the war, the proportion of private school graduates slowly climbed back to 28 percent by 1972. The increase in public school graduates between 1886 and 1905 (19 percent to 53 percent) occurred during the precise period that Butler's democratic reforms were taking effect.[14] Thus by 1905 Columbia's public school students were the majority. This gives some indication of the timing of Columbia's democratization, since it can be assumed that the public school graduates were more heterogeneous than their private school classmates.

TABLE 4.2
Secondary School Backgrounds of Columbia Undergraduates (%)

Type	1886	1903	1905	1911	1930	1940	1962	1972
Private	51	57	47	49	28	19	23	28
Public	19	32	53	51	72	81	77	72
Transfer		10						
Tutor	30							
Total	100	99	100	100	100	100	100	100

Religious Backgrounds

From 1879 to 1911 students of Protestant faiths were dominant, though in decline (see Table 4.3). In 1879, 81 percent of the seniors were Protestants, whereas by 1911 only 64 percent claimed this designation. Over the same period the percentage of Catholics increased from 3 to 12 percent. The proportion claiming Jewish affiliation was 5 percent in 1879. This increased to 22 percent in 1903 but declined to 9 percent by 1911.

Such figures must be regarded with some suspicion since they are self-reported, and the stigma ascribed to non-Protestant faiths at this time probably discouraged many from stating any religious preference at all.[15]

TABLE 4.3
Religious Backgrounds of Columbia Undergraduates (%)

Religion	1879	1880	1889	1903	1905	1911
Protestant	81	82	78	64	55	64
Catholic	3	2		2	2	12
Jew	5	7		22	12	9
Other	11				2	4
None		9	22	11	29	11
Total	100	100	100	99	100	100

According to the *American Jewish Yearbook* (cited in Synott, 1979: 16), the overall percentage of Jews at Columbia in 1918-19 was 21.2 percent. It was in this immediate post-war period that the numbers of Jews became an obsession at Columbia. As early as 1914 Dean Keppel attempted to refute the prevailing conception that Columbia was "overrun with European Jews, who are most unpleasant persons socially," by averring that "Columbia is not overrun with Jews any more than it is with Roman Catholics or Episcopalians." He continued:

Columbia is open to any student of good moral character who can satisfy the entrance requirements, without limitation of race or creed. No questions are asked and no records kept of the race or religion of incoming students, but it is evident that the proportion of Jewish students is decreasing rather than increasing. (Keppel, 1914: 179)

Having apparently contradicted himself, Keppel concluded by pronouncing most of the Jews at Columbia "desirable students and fit companions."

During the 1920s agitation over the "Jewish problem" reached fever pitch, and the selective admissions policies described above were put in place to reduce the Jewish population to 22 percent in the college. It is arguable whether the proportion of Jews ever reached the 40 percent claimed by Keppel's successor Herbert E. Hawkes in 1922, but "figures on the nationality of the student body revealed that at all times through the mid-1920s at least 40 percent of the entering freshman class was from immigrant families" (Wechsler, 1977: 164). That the issue had not died by the 1930s is clear from Butler's comment to Hawkes in 1933: "I don't know whether it is at all practicable, but it would be highly judicious if. . . some way could be found to see to it that individuals of the undesirable type did not get into Columbia College, no matter what their record in the very important matter of As and Bs" (Wechsler, 1977: 166). His comment also suggests that the Columbia administration had discovered that universalistic selection devices such as the IQ test did not really handicap Jews at all. By 1934, Director of Admissions Frank H. Bowles was able to report that of the entering freshman class 58 percent were Protestants, 25 percent Catholics, and 17 percent Jews. Butler urged that they "continue to build up the Freshman Class in the College along the lines that have recently been followed," which meant pursuing wide geographic distribution and subordinating academic performance to "character" (Wechsler, 1977: 168). This suggests that not only were geographic quotas being used precisely to limit the Jewish population, but that meritocratic standards were being abrogated to do so as well. By such methods was Columbia able to halt its "Jewish invasion."

PENN

Admissions

From 1850 until 1890 the admissions requirements at Penn exhibited no formal changes. All candidates had to present themselves at the university for a battery of examinations in various subjects. By 1890 students could be admitted either by the conventional examination system or by "certificate." Thus, perhaps out of financial necessity, Penn had placed itself in the less than distinguished company of the western state universities by implementing the certificate plan. Entrance exams were also offered in a variety of cities across the country in an effort to attract a larger and more national student body. This plan of admission continued in force through 1901 with only minor revisions.

By 1910 Penn had pulled back somewhat from the method of full certification. Admission was granted by either examination or the submission of a school record which satisfied the Committee on Admission that the requirements had been covered. Rather than being any kind of discriminatory mechanism, it appears that this procedure was designed to recognize the special qualities of different schools. Exams were offered under the auspices of the university or the College Board, of which Penn was a charter member, and the classical languages were no longer required, thus removing a barrier to many lower-status students.

In 1922 the required entrance subjects and their distribution had been standardized into the credit or unit system, popularized by the College Board. There were three methods of admission: examination in required entrance subjects; school record and certificate, for those from accredited schools; and school record and alternative exams, for those from schools without unlimited accreditation. These alternative exams could take the form of either four CEEB comprehensive examinations or two special exams in English usage and mental power. Coinciding with the timing of its implementation at Columbia, this last exam was the first evidence of the use of the IQ test at Penn. The use of these tests may have been animated by a desire to discriminate, but in Penn's case the surest way to do so would have been to abolish the certificate system. More likely the third method of admission was begun to increase the pool of eligibles for the university; that is, its intention was more inclusive than exclusive.

By 1930, however, the SAT was required of all candidates regardless of the admission method chosen. Schools were apparently no longer certificated by the university, but had to be accredited by one of the regional school associations. That there was some effort to modify the unconditional certificate is indicated both by the SAT requirement and the stipulation that only those graduating in the top quarter of their class were eligible. These were modest limitations, but they do indicate an attempt to limit the extreme democracy of the certificate. The entrance requirements for 1940 were substantially the same as those a decade earlier with minor modifications, though a modest retreat from the more stringent standards of 1930 may have been a response to declining applications during the depression.

By 1950 only two methods of admission were possible. Graduates of accredited secondary schools who had taken the required courses and were fully recommended by their principal were required to take the SAT and three scholastic achievement tests in English, a foreign language, and either natural or social science. Thus, content exams were required of all applicants. The only other method of admission was by examination in the senior subjects in a series of aptitude and achievement tests given by the CEEB. This was the only method open to nongraduates of secondary schools or to graduates of unaccredited secondary schools.

In 1960 the entrance requirements were basically unchanged, but only at this time was there any suggestion that admissions were becoming truly selective at Penn. "Applications for admission now greatly exceed the available places in the freshman class. It is apparent that we are now in a truly selective admissions situation" (*U of P Registrar's Notebook*, 1960). What is noteworthy is that "truly selective admissions" came to Penn at such a late date. In his 1965 *Annual Report to the President*, the provost indicated that "thought should be given to the eventual size of the student body." This suggests that Penn had never before considered limiting the size of the student body, a problem which Harvard,

Yale, and Princeton had addressed as early as the 1920s. Columbia first considered such a move before World War I and implemented it in 1919.[16]

The evidence on Penn's admissions policies suggests two important conclusions. First, Penn democratized early, implementing the certificate system in 1890. In its democratic thrust this policy was somewhat analogous to Butler's work at Columbia that modernized the curriculum and standardized exams through the College Board. Yet it goes beyond anything Butler was able to institutionalize in this regard. By the use of the unconditional certificate, responsibility for the admission of students was effectively handed over to the secondary schools. Undoubtedly this procedure had opened up the university to a much more heterogeneous clientele than would otherwise have been the case. Like Columbia, however, Penn appears to have later placed some limitation on certification, though whether these measures had as their object particularistic exclusion is unclear.

Second, it would appear that Penn's admissions requirements remained less rigorous than Columbia's at least until the 1960s. By 1949 Columbia required the achievement tests of all students and assumed high school graduation. It was not until the late 1960s that Penn eliminated the nongraduate provision and developed entrance requirements equivalent to Columbia's of 1950. In short, admissions procedures at Penn invited relative openness, both socially and academically.

Geographic Origins

Like Columbia, Penn has been for most of its history a local school, drawing students primarily from Philadelphia and Pennsylvania (see Table 4.4). In 1850 fully 96 percent of the students came from Pennsylvania, 92 percent from Philadelphia. The Pennsylvania figure remained above 90 percent until 1890 when it began a fairly steady decrease to 55 percent in 1920. The interwar period showed a slight recovery to 61 percent in 1940, but thereafter the Pennsylvania contingent steadily declined to 34 percent in 1970. The proportion from Philadelphia declined in a parallel way.

Although both Penn and Columbia were predominantly home-state schools throughout their histories, Columbia seems to have remained more so than Penn. Recently the home state constituted nearly half of Columbia's student body and only a third at Penn. (On the other hand, the remainder of Penn's student body was divided equally between the Middle Atlantic region and all others, whereas Columbia received only 10 percent of its students from the other Middle Atlantic states and 45 percent from other regions.) Moreover, for a considerable time, New York City students were more apt to make Columbia "their" school than

Philadelphians made Penn "theirs." In 1870 students from each city made up more than 70 percent of the student bodies of their respective schools. From 1880 until 1920 the representation of New Yorkers dropped to between 50 and 60 percent at Columbia; during this same period at Penn the Philadelphia group declined from 78 to 36 percent. This steady decline did not abate until 1930, when the Philadelphia contingent stood at 27 percent.

TABLE 4.4
Geographic Origins of Penn Undergraduates (%)

Region	1850	1860	1870	1880	1890	1901	1910	1920	1930	1940	1960	1970
Pennsylvania	96	91	93	94	89	85	71	55	58	61	45	34
(Philadelphia)	(92)	(74)	(79)	(78)	(76)	(62)	(44)	(36)	(27)	(29)	(25)	(12)
Mid-Atlantic	2	4	5	5	7	6	14	21	26	25	28	34
New England	1				1	2	2	3	5	5	9	11
Midwest			2		1	3	4	7	5	4	6	7
South	1	5		1	1	2	6	10	4	4	6	9
West					1	1	2	4	2	1	4	3
Foreign					1	1	1	1	1	1	2	2
Total	100	100	100	100	101	100	100	101	101	101	100	100

Just how to account for this pattern is unclear. Unlike Columbia's New York City contingent, which precipitously declined in the 1920s, the drop in students from Philadelphia began in 1890. It is extremely unlikely that the changes at Penn can be construed as evidence of some kind of discriminatory quota system, for several reasons. First, the drop in the number of Philadelphians began after 1880, before concerns about Jews and other immigrants would have prompted much action. Second, there were no precipitous drops parallel to New York City's at Columbia between 1920 and 1930; the decline was consistent and gradual. If a quota were in effect, it would have had to have been incrementally applied beginning in the 1880s—an unlikely institutional response.

Finally, as shown above, Penn's admissions procedure, especially the certificate plan, could in no way be construed as an attempt to limit the enrollment of Philadelphians. On the contrary, it could only have had the effect of increasing access for local students, especially graduates of public schools. Perhaps the certificate plan was implemented to stem the flow of Philadelphians away from Penn, since the plan was adopted in 1890, a decade after the decline began. The evidence is that it met with limited success, if that was its intended purpose. On the other hand, Penn built dormitories in the 1890s and began to offer examinations in other cities around the country, thereby recruiting a less local student body. One possible explanation for the decline in the Philadelphia contingent is competition offered by other local colleges. Temple was founded in 1884 and Drexel in 1891; they may have siphoned off local students who would otherwise have gone to Penn.

Secondary School Backgrounds

The secondary school background of the students at Penn and Columbia changed in much the same way (see Table 4.5), though with some noteworthy variations. In 1890 the private school graduates constituted about half of Penn's student body, and public high schools accounted for only a tenth. At the turn of the century the public and private school graduates were nearly equally represented, but by 1910 public schools were contributing more than twice the amount of the private component, 60 percent to 24 percent, and the upward trend of public school students continued until 1920, when it reached 82 percent. During the decade of the depression the public group declined to slightly above 70 percent, where it has remained since.

TABLE 4.5
Secondary School Backgrounds of Penn Undergraduates (%)

Type	1890	1900	1910	1920	1930	1940	1960	1972
Private	47	44	24	16	15	27	28	28
Public	11	42	60	82	83	72	72	72
Transfer	7	14	16	2	1	1		
Tutor	35							
Total	100	100	100	100	99	100	100	100

This pattern clearly shows the influence of the democratic certificate admissions policy implemented in 1890, as well as the rise to prominence of the public school system. At Penn, however, a resurgence of private school graduates occurred by 1940, whereas at Columbia this reversal trend did not happen until around 1970. Penn seems to have reached its peak in the public school representation sooner than Columbia (1920 versus 1940) and "readjusted" sooner. Possibly Columbia's quota policies and the absence of the certificate system accounted for the slower rise of its public population, but the anomaly here is why Penn's public school group dropped off in the 1930s. This may have been an effect of the depression, or it may have been the result of some deliberate policy. The two schools have nevertheless wound up with roughly the same public-private composition.

Religious Backgrounds

According to a study conducted by the *American Jewish Yearbook* in 1918-1919, 14.5 percent of the total student population at Penn was Jewish. This compares with the 21.2 percent figure at Columbia. In 1934-35 a student religious census was undertaken by the Office of the Chaplain, W. Brooke Stabler, with the following results. For the total university, 58 percent were Protestant, 12 percent Catholic, and 22 percent Jewish; in the college, however, 45 percent were Protestant, 15 percent Catholic, and 35 percent Jewish. From the figures for Penn it seems clear that there was no attempt, at least no successful attempt, to limit the number of Jewish students. From 1919 to 1935 the percentage of Jews in the university and the college rose notably, whereas at Columbia during the same period the proportion of Jewish undergraduates declined by more than half (40 percent to 17 percent). This difference seems to reflect Penn's greater commitment to nondiscriminatory admissions procedures.[17]

However, at the same time there were some efforts, initiated by alumni, to change the course that the university was taking. By the eve of World War I Penn had become a multifaceted, democratic university complete with a summer school, evening school, extension courses, college courses for teachers, as well as a large complement of professional and graduate schools and various undergraduate courses. All of these components contributed to a substantial increase in the size of the university. To this was added a great influx of potential students after the war. It was in response to this situation that a large and influential body of alumni began to criticize the university and urge reform.

> The rapid increase in numbers of the University, its growing depen-
> dence on state appropriations, its development, since the beginning of
> the century, into a great many-sided, democratic institution, in which
> the College was only one of many departments, drawing its students
> largely from distant regions yet subject to the influences of its location
> in a large industrial city, were all displeasing to many members of the
> alumni societies. The University, even the College, was drawing into its
> student body the more ambitious boys of the city masses and in its
> other departments ever more and more yielding to the pleas for admis-
> sion of women, however rigorously they were excluded from the Col-
> lege proper. Through the Extension and Evening Schools and Saturday
> classes it was serving and including classes of the community that before
> had no access to its opportunities, and it necessarily came to reflect to
> certain extent these interests. (Cheyney, 1940: 384)

The alumni urged that the mission of the university ought properly to be to train for "leadership." This proposal was not intended to promote meritocratic selection or to reform the content of education but rather to advance a particularistic selection process. Specifically pitted against "mass education," they argued that the university ought to seek to educate a special class of people with superior ability but also with superior social and economic credentials. The aim was to restore the hegemony of the traditional Protestant elite, which perceived itself in a threatened position. The model was the ancient English universities. So seriously was this proposal taken that two professors were dispatched to Oxbridge in 1930 "in search of suggestions that might be of value in reconstructing the educational work of the College" (Cheyney, 1940: 387).

A second proposal made by the alumni was to move the entire university out of the city to Valley Forge, a rural setting conducive to creating the proper atmosphere and making the college inaccessible to city commuters.

> The ideal of a relatively small college, located in the country, well away from the interruptions, confusions, and social admixtures of city life, making possible a closer intercourse among the students and with the faculty, providing more healthy and attractive surroundings and allowing more leisure for reading and conversation, hovered before the eyes of many of the most thoughtful of the alumni as a refined and attractive contrast to the numbers, the mixture, the democratic tone which the University was more and more taking. The smaller colleges of New England, or a detached university, like Princeton, seemed to them a better ideal of college life, and they regretted that their own University was not like these.(Cheyney, 1940: 395)

In 1926 a graduate of the college class of 1896 purchased 178 acres near Valley Forge and offered it to the university. The alumni remained enthusiastic, but the trustees demurred, and the plan eventually languished.

These episodes do not manifestly reflect an attempt at religiously grounded discrimination. Yet the criticism of democracy, the masses, and corrupt city influences were precisely the euphemisms current in the 1920s for referring to immigrant groups, especially Jews. It can hardly be doubted that the intent of such proposals was to limit the number of Jews, just as Butler, Hawkes, and others at Columbia contrived through geographic quotas and other admissions devices to achieve the same end. At Penn, however, such proposals apparently fell on deaf ears in the administration, whether out of adherence to democratic principles, financial necessity, or sheer inertia. Whatever the explanation, that 35 percent of Penn's undergraduates were Jewish in 1935 and that the university today remains in West Philadelphia testify that the exclusionary course was abjured.[18]

HARVARD, YALE, AND PRINCETON[19]

Proceeding from a position of institutional strength, Harvard, Yale, and Princeton followed a substantially different, less democratic course in their selection of students during this critical period. None of the Big Three adopted any kind of certificate procedure, unlike Penn, which used it as early as 1890. Columbia stands with the former in this regard, but it was Columbia that initiated the discussions about standardized examinations which led to the formation of the College Board in 1900 under Butler's auspices. Harvard, Yale, and Princeton were very suspicious of the board, wishing to administer their own exams and maintain their relationships with their traditional feeder schools. Even Harvard's Eliot, who had been urging some kind of standardization as a means of recruiting more students from the further reaches of the country, balked at Low's invitation in 1895 to put his proposals into practice: "A preliminary difficulty seems to me to be the weakness of the proposed group of insitutions. The University of Pennsylvania has but a very small department of arts, being in the main a school of medicine and of law. At Columbia also the undergraduate department has by no means the importance of the professional schools" (Wechsler, 1977: 96). Yale and Princeton were even more conservative. Although both Penn and Columbia were charter members of the College Board, Harvard did not join until 1904, Yale in 1909, and Princeton in 1910. Even then, however, they retained their own examinations alongside those of the new system. Not until 1915 did they fully adopt the exams of the board, and then it was less for democratic reasons than for the desire to tap talent nationally. Also to that end, in 1911 Harvard pioneered in the so-called New Plan of admission, a compromise between the certificate and examination systems whereby a student could enter on the basis of record in an approved high school and his performance on four comprehensive examinations.

Of course, at least part of the explanation of the caution of the Big Three in accepting new methods of admission was quite simply that they could afford to be cautious. None of them suffered any want of students or money. Indeed, by the 1920s all three had adopted a ceiling on enrollment. This permitted selection on nonuniversalistic grounds. According to Synnott (1979), Princeton explored the full range of methods of selective admission—psychological tests, personal interviews, alumni preference, geographical distribution, character references—for precisely that purpose. Harvard and Yale did likewise. As noted above, Columbia, too, began to limit class size by 1920 in an effort to introduce particularism into "selective" admissions, but Penn did not consider the possibility of limiting numbers until the 1950s.

Information on students' geographic origins at the Big Three is scant. Harvard is alleged to have drawn principally from upper New England, the Middle Atlantic states, and the West Coast, Princeton from the South and Middle Atlantic states, and Yale was strong in the Midwest. All three doubtless drew a more national and less local clientele than either Columbia or Penn, whose urban contingents constituted so much of their student bodies for so long. On this basis it would be expected that Harvard, Yale, and Princeton were rather less socially heterogeneous than Columbia and Penn.

This inference is dramatically supported by the secondary school backgrounds of Big Three students. From 1900 to 1940 the percentage of private school graduates at each of these schools never dropped below 40 percent: Harvard varied between 40 and 60 percent, Yale between 50 and 60 percent, and Princeton between 70 and 90 percent. In 1927 Princeton was 75 percent private school graduates, and during the 1930s it was 82 to 86 percent. It was not until after World War II that the number of public school graduates began to exceed the privately educated. This stands in sharp contrast to Penn and Columbia, where the majority of undergraduates were educated publicly as early as 1910. The proximity of the large urban populations of Philadelphia and New York were certainly factors in this development, but so were the less stringent admissions requirements of Penn and Columbia. Whatever the reasons, Penn and Columbia democratized their student bodies almost forty years before the Big Three.

According to Synnott, Harvard, Yale, and Princeton, in addition to having more exclusive entrance requirements by whatever criteria, all developed particularistic quotas in the 1920s, focusing especially on Jews. At Princeton, whose country club image probably discouraged non-WASPs from bothering to apply, Jewish students made up only 2.6 percent of the undergraduates in 1918. This figure rose to around 6 percent in the mid-1920s, when a quota was applied limiting Jews to 3 percent of enrollment. The proportion remained under 10 percent until after World War II, though by 1970 it had risen fractionally to just under 15 percent. At Yale between 1901 and 1927 the percentage of Jewish undergraduates rose from 2 to about 13 percent. In 1927 a quota limiting the Jewish population to no more than 12 percent was invoked, and until World War II the figure never went much above 10 percent. After the war the

Jewish group accounted for 13 percent in 1952 and rose to 33 percent by 1972. Harvard's Jewish students grew from 7 to 21.5 percent of the total from 1900 to 1922. In 1926 quotas were begun to limit the proportion to between 10 and 16 percent, down from a high of over 25 percent in 1925. Again, there is little evidence of change until after World War II, when the percentage rose to 25 percent by 1952, where it has remained at least until 1971.

In short, during the pre-World War II period the percentage of Jews never exceeded a quarter at Harvard, and Yale with 13 percent and Princeton with 6 percent were no more than half that figure. On the other hand, the proportion exceeded 40 percent at Columbia in the 1920s and 35 percent at Penn in the 1930s. The Big Three were obviously less religiously heterogeneous; they all adopted quotas limiting Jewish students to no more than 15 percent. Columbia, too, enforced some kind of quota which more than halved the Jewish contingent, but there is no evidence that Penn ever had a quota. Apparently the administrations of the Big Three were not unmindful of the popular opinion expressed as early as 1911 that "the Jews had ruined Columbia and Pennsylvania" (Slosson, 1910: 105-6).

CONCLUSION

In his masterly study of the American university from 1865 to 1910, Laurence Veysey distinguished three ideal types of academic institutions in terms of their undergraduate atmospheres. The first, the homogeneous eastern college, was marked by its internal cohesion and sharp isolation from the surrounding society. Demands for conformity to particular collegiate traditions, undivided loyalty, and homogeneous student populations characterized these schools, primary examples of which were Princeton, Yale, the early Columbia, and most of the small New England colleges. The second type, the heterogeneous eastern university, was in many respects the social opposite of the first. "It contained a great variety of discordant elements among its student population, and mirrored, if in a top-heavy fashion, the social gamut of the area at large" (Veysey, 1965: 283). Principal examples of this more socially diverse type were Penn and Columbia, though also the latterday Harvard.[20]

Of the five schools considered in this paper, Penn seems to be the most heterogeneous, at least the least exclusionary. "It welcomed commuters, immigrants, and socialites alike; it was said to have the democracy of the street car" (Veysey, 1965: 288). Penn's admissions criteria, including the certificate as early as 1890, were certainly the most demo-

cratic, and none of the evidence on geographic origin, secondary education, or religion indicates that quotas of any kind were used.

Columbia, although obviously falling into the heterogeneous category as well, at least by 1900, shows indications of having attempted to
be slightly more restrictive, probably because it had become "too heterogeneous." Columbia's faculty never acceded to Butler's overtures for
the certificate system, but Butler did succeed in developing the College
Board, standardizing admission requirements, and bringing Columbia
into closer articulation with the New York public school system. Having
succeeded in drawing greater numbers to Columbia, however, the administration reversed its course after World War I when it realized that many
among those numbers were of Jewish or other immigrant background.
To administrators concerned about institutional reputation it was becoming clear at that time that the financial status of a university had to be
balanced with a concern for its social prestige. Numbers alone were no
longer necessarily desirable. Having the "right" people was the required
base for building a general reputation of excellence. The geographic,
admissions, and religious evidence all confirm that various steps were
taken to repel the "alien invasion" and that by the 1930s they had
succeeded to the satisfaction of the administration. Nevertheless, even
with these policies, Columbia was a decidedly heterogeneous university.

This fact is made all the more evident when Columbia and Penn are
contrasted with Harvard, Yale, and Princeton. None of these three
adopted any kind of certificate system, they were all reluctant partici-
pants in the CEEB, and their religious and secondary education statistics indicate that they were distinctly more homogeneous than Penn and
Columbia. For the period under consideration here the social composition of Harvard occupies something of an intermediate position between
Penn and Columbia on the one hand and Yale and Princeton on the
other, though it is distinctly closer to the latter. Of these Princeton was
evidently the most homogeneous, though whether that homogeneity
resulted from exclusion, self-selection, or simply from location is unclear.[21]

In short, Columbia and Penn both democratized their student bodies sooner and much more thoroughly than either Harvard, Yale, or
Princeton. At Penn and Columbia this process was already in motion
before the tremendous influx of students after World War I. By that
time, under Lowell's leadership, Harvard was already beginning to pull
back from Eliot's diversity. Yale and Princeton had never really aban-
doned homogeneity, and it was not until after World War II that the Big
Three would begin to approach the level of diversity exhibited by Columbia and Penn prior to 1915. These findings present almost the mirror
image of patterns of upper-class college attendance (Farnum, Chapter 3).

By World War I Harvard, Yale, and Princeton had become the premier national upper-class colleges, and Columbia and Penn had lost even their own local upper classes to these schools. The inference is irresistable that the democratization of Penn and Columbia played a major role in their declining prestige.[22]

If democratization made a contribution to the diminished prestige of Penn and Columbia, it must be realized that democratization, per se, was not responsible but democratization at a specific historical time. Since World War II the Big Three have all universalized their admissions criteria and democratized their student bodies to the extent that they are probably socially indistinguishable from those at Penn and Columbia. What residual differences may exist are probably the result of self-selection. The point is that since World War II it has become socially acceptable, even desirable, to have a heterogeneous or diverse student body. Before World War I it was apparently neither desirable nor acceptable, at least to the upper classes. It was the timing of this apparently ineluctable trend toward greater universalism and democracy that was crucial.

Ben-David (1972) has pointed out that in order to sustain prestige American universities have had to be sensitive to shifts in its criteria. When the modern university system emerged in the late nineteenth century, the Ivy League universities had an established fund of prestige that was based on wealth, but especially a historical association vith the most cultured and socially elevated parts of the population. Ben-David cites Harvard, Yale, Princeton, Columbia, and Penn, to a lesser extent, as examples. In order to sustain their prestige these schools had to be alert to shifts in the values of their clients. "When scholarly excellence began to replace general cultural atmosphere and social graces, they had to be able to attract outstanding scholars and scientists" (Ben-David, 1972: 39). They also had to be on the lookout for rising new elites. If they acted either too early or too late, their prestige would be devalued. In these terms Penn and Columbia mishandled their prestige funds; for whatever reasons they both acted too early in the matter of democratization, alienating their traditional clientele and very likely new elites along with them. Harvard, Yale, and Princeton, on the other hand, delayed democratization, retaining the support of their upper-class constituencies, and were able build the quality of their academic programs on the solid base of social prestige. They thus have sustained their position as America's most prestigous undergraduate institutions in an era that stresses considerations of academic quality and individual merit.

This paper suggests that institutional prestige depends not just on important contemporary features such as endowment, material facilities, faculty eminence, and student achievement levels but is also importantly related to the history of the institution. In particular, association with an upper class at strategic periods in its development is crucial to the generation and maintenance of institutional prestige. To be sure, as Karabel (1984) suggests, such association provides necessary material support without which prestige could not be sustained. He argues that the Big Three, because they depended so heavily on the upper class for money, did not democratize in the interwar period because they could not afford to alienate this essential constituency. The development of quotas at Columbia could be interpreted in the same way, though apparently the damage had already been done. It might also be argued that Penn could afford to democratize, indeed was forced to do so, precisely because it was poor and the upper class was not giving it adequate support. It thus had nothing material to lose. But what it lost was nevertheless real; with the defection of the Philadelphia upper class to Princeton, Penn lost a substantial component of its prestige.

During the twentieth century the relationship of colleges and universities to the class structure has changed functionally from status-confirmation to status-creation. They have become differentiated in such a way as to allow institutions of higher education to make an independent contribution to the configuration of the stratification system. As Parsons argued, this change is reflected in the shift in orientation from ascription and particularism to achievement and universalism. The rise of democratization and meritocracy is itself predicated on the transition in the grounding of social authority and social prestige from tradition to reason. Traditional authority, an important component of which is class, is being supplanted by rational authority, grades, credentials, achievements, and the like. This paper, however, suggests that the transition is incomplete and perhaps must be. The prestige of higher-educational institutions remains significantly based on traditional elements, in particular a historical association with the upper class. There are many colleges and universities today which are the universalistic equals of the Big Three in many respects. Nevertheless, none of their names resonates so strongly in the popular imagination as do Harvard, Yale, and Princeton.

NOTES

1. This is not to say, of course, that nonscholastic criteria do not figure in the recruitment of students and faculty and the attribution of institutional prestige; it is stipulated only as an ideal type whose truthvalue is entirely compara-

tive. Indeed, it is precisely the burden of this paper to demonstrate how certain particularistic criteria have entered into the above calculations.

2. Until the 1930s the chief executive at Penn was the provost, an anomalous title reflecting a substantive lack of power and responsibility, which were jealously guarded by the trustees, an elite club of upper-class Philadelphians. At the same time the university developed first-rate professional schools at the expense of the liberal arts and the undergraduate college, symbolically evident in its failure to construct dormitories until around the turn of the century. The complete absence of dormitory accommodations ensured a relatively local student body of commuters and prevented the university's reputation from developing nationally.

3. The unwillingness of the trustees to delegate genuine responsibility to a strong president, the enphasis on careerist professional education at the expense of the liberal arts college, the delay in constructing dornitories conducive to a collegiate environment, and the failure of the local upper class to adequately support the university socially and financially are all seen to issue from a secularized Quaker ethic. Baltzell contrasts this situation with that at Harvard, where liberal arts was the center of a collegiate education from the founding, strong presidents were given a relatively free hand, and a self-confident upper class built its university into the pinnacle of the American higher-educational system.

4. In addition to Penn, the Philadelphia upper class was attracted to Haverford.

5. In Baltimore Johns Hopkins was superceded by Princeton in 1905, never to regain its former first rank; in Philadelphia Penn lost out to Princeton around 1915; in New York Columbia dropped below both Harvard and Yale as early as 1890 and by 1910 was surpassed by Princeton as well.

6. Johns Hopkins will not be considered here because it is not a member of the Ivy League.

7. The history of college admissions has witnessed various innovations during its evolution, some of which have been democratic in thrust, and others of which have been restrictive (Wechsler, 1977). By examining the nature of the formal admissions procedure, we can make some inferences about the heterogeneity of the student body.

8. Geographic information can be useful as potential evidence of a direct or indirect admissions quota against immigrant or urban groups, especially Jews (Bloomgarden, 1960).

9. During the late nineteenth and early twentieth centuries, the public high school system was just becoming institutionalized, first in urban areas. Thus, in that period it must be expected that students would be more homogeneously privately educated as well as more upper middle class. With the advent of the public system, more college students would be from families lower in the social

scale and publicly educated. This is expected to be particularly true for Penn and Columbia, located as they are in large East Coast cities.

10. For reasons of either sensitivity or neglect, no systematic religious information was available from official sources at either university. For the period from 1880 to 1910 at Columbia it was possible to obtain some religious data from yearbooks and classbooks. For Penn the only official religious information comes from a religious census made by the university chaplain in 1934-35.

11. At the same time it permitted high school educators to influence the nature of the college curriculum. This was one of the methods whereby college curricula became increasingly open to new subjects.

12. Developed from the Army Alpha test during World War I, it was purported to measure intrinsic mental abilities as opposed to acquired skill or knowledge. This would help the college to identify the students of genuine promise whose records did not otherwise reflect it. It would also help to weed out overachievers, those of inferior talent who made up for it with hard work, most of whom were thought to be Jews. It was then believed that Jews and members of other immigrant groups were of inferior intrinsic intelligence to native Americans; thus, it was supposed that in IQ tests the former would perform less well than the latter (Kamin, n.d.).

13. In 1870 most of the 80,000 students attending secondary school were in private academies. It was in the 1880s that enrollment in public high schools surpassed that in private schools. By 1910, 90 percent of the secondary students were in public high schools.

14. The balance of the students in 1890, 30 percent, were privately tutored. Thus, the above information understates both the total private component (around 80 percent) and the magnitude of the shift to the public component by 1905.

15. The level of both ignorance about and prejudice against Jews is evident in two examples from class publications. On the twenty-fifth anniversary of the class of 1886 the class record reported that the class valedictorian, Oscar Cohen, had become a "Jewish minister." In the yearbook for the class of 1920 were included four caricatures of rival colleges, among which was the following on CCNY.

"A Glimpse of Peasant Life in Roumania"

Now last and quite least to our eye,
Comes Ikey from CCNY.
A radical chap,
Vy should he gif a rap?
"Bolshevisn come kvick" is his cry.

16. As early as 1914 Dean Frederick Keppel had lamented that Columbia would never again be a "fashionable college per se" but nevertheless felt that something could be salvaged. "In view of the present rapid rate of growth, it is very possible that a limitation of numbers in the near future will enable the College to strike a more definite note" (Keppel, 1914: 111). Butler supported this policy in 1917 and implemented it in 1919 (Wechsler, 1977: 154-57). Levine has observed that in 1920 Penn rejected more applicants (750) than any other college except for Dartmouth and Princeton (1986: 139). The grounds for this rejection are unclear, but it apparently was not the effect of a limitation on enrollment, since class size continued to expand.

17. Far from attempting to hide its Jewish students, Penn's provost drew attention to their need for organizational support. "In 1920 Provost Edgar Fahs Smith pointed out that the Jewish community until that time had failed to display real interest in the spiritual welfare of the Jewish students on the campus. Under the leadership of Dr. and Mrs. Cyrus Adler, the Philadelphia Branch of the United Synagogue of America undertook to supply that need, and the present house was dedicated on October 12, 1926" (Dowlin, 1940).

18. One other proposal by the alumni was to secure the services of General Leonard Wood as provost, to succeed E.F. Smith on his retirement in 1920. Wood was one of the "drillmasters of Americanization" in the post-World War I era. He was "one of the leading advocates of preparedness and suggested that universal military service would itself offer the best means of making unassimilated groups understand that they are Americans" (Higham, 1968: 247). Though he was avidly courted for the position and even elected to it, he never served.

19. For the comparative information on Harvard, Yale, and Princeton I rely heavily on and am indebted to the comprehensive work of Marcia Synnott (1974, 1979).

20. The third type, the heterogeneous western university, is irrelevant here.

21. Veysey places Harvard in the heterogeneous category, however. This is because his study dealt with the period 1865-1910, almost exactly coincident with Eliot's tenure as president. It was under Eliot that Harvard implemented the elective system, established professional and graduate schools, and developed an extremely heterogeneous student society. The cost of these policies was a rather naked internal system of stratification among the students as well as the desertion of Harvard for smaller colleges by many upper-class New Englanders after 1900. In 1911 Eliot was succeeded by A.L. Lowell, who attempted to turn Harvard more in the direction of policies pursued at Yale and Princeton. In curricular terms Lowell reasserted the primacy of the college; socially he moderated diversity and its effects by imposing quotas and building the houses. This entire Harvard episode parallels Columbia's efforts at democratization and its subsequent retrenchment, though Harvard was apparently more "successful" in the latter.

22. Why Columbia and Penn democratized at this time is an interesting question, at least a partial answer to which is to be found in Karabel's notion of institutional autonomy. In these cases the schools' poor financial condition may have afforded them greater freedom with respect to the upper classes that supported Harvard, Yale, and Princeton more generously. Beyond that, the animating ethos of these urban institutions may have constituted an attraction for a more diverse clientele. As Veysey shows, Penn and Columbia were characterized by a service or professional orientation toward college education, whereas at Yale and Princeton, and Harvard under Lowell, culture and the liberal arts predominated. Baltzell(1979) has argued that the emphasis on the liberal arts and classical culture as opposed to pragmatic professional training emerged from the earlier religious traditions of the colleges. Where that tradition was weak, there was little resistance to more utilitarian concerns. Similarly, undergraduate collegiate life remained vital where there existed a prior religious emphasis on the socialization of the whole individual, intellectually, morally, and religiously. Penn and Columbia, lacking such a religious background, lacked also a collegiate life and a primary concern with culture. In this sense it might be said that they "secularized" too soon.

REFERENCES

Baltzell, E. Digby. 1979. *Puritan Boston and Quaker Philadelphia: Two Protestant Ethics and the Spirit of Class Authority and Leadership.* New York: The Free Press.

Ben-David, Joseph. 1972. *Trends in American Higher Education.* Chicago: University of Chicago Press.

Bloomgarden, Lawrence. 1960. "Our Changing Elite Colleges." *Commentary,* February, 150-54.

Bressler, Marvin. 1973. *Princeton University: Report of the Commission on the Future of the College.* Princeton, N.J.: Princeton University Press.

Broome, E.C. 1903. *Historical and Critical Discussion of College Admission Requirements.* New York: The Macmillan Company.

Broun, Haywood, and George Britt. 1931. *Christians Only: A Study in Prejudice.* New York: The Vanguard Press.

Burt, Nathaniel. 1963. *The Perennial Philadelphians.* Boston: Little-Brown.

Cheyney, Edward P. 1940. *History of the University of Pennsylvania, 1740-1940.* Philadelphia: University of Pennsylvania Press.

Columbia College.
Annual Register: 1880, 1890.
Catalogue of Officers and Students: 1870.
Class Book: 1903, 1905.
The Columbian: 1891, 1900, 1920, 1930, 1940, 1950, 1960.
Directory: 1962, 1972.
A History of the Class of 1911.
Record of the Class of 1886.

Columbia University.
Annual Report of the President: 1920, 1930, 1940, 1948.
Report of the President: 1969, 1977.

Columbia University Quarterly, Vol. III (1900-01) and Vol. XII (1909-10).

Coon, Horace. 1947. *Columbia, Colossus on the Hudson.* New York: Dutton.

Davis, Allen F., and Mark Haller, eds. 1973. *The Peoples of Philadelphia: A History of Ethnic Groups and Lower Class Life, 1790-1940.* Philadelphia: Temple University Press.

Dowlin, Cornell M., ed. 1940. *The University of Pennsylvania Today.* Philadelphia: University of Pennsylvania Press.

Elliott, Edward C., ed. 1937. *The Rise of a University, Vol. 2, The University in Action, From the Annual Reports, 1902-1935, of Nicholas Murray Butler.* New York: Columbia University Press.

Farnum, Richard. "Patterns of Upper Class Higher Education in Four American Cities: 1870-1970." Chapter 3, this volume.

Fiske, Edward B. 1982. *Selective Guide to Colleges, 1982-83.* New York: Times Books.

Goddard, David R., and Linda C. Koons. 1973. "A Profile of the University of Pennsylvania." Pp. 225-248 in *Academic Transformation: Seventeen Institutions Under Pressure,* edited by David Riesman and Verne Stadtman. New York: McGraw-Hill.

Higham, John. 1978. *Strangers in the Land: Patterns of American Nativism, 1860-1925.* New York: Atheneum.

Hires, William L. 1972. "Josiah Harmar Penniman, Educator: 1868-1941." Unpublished Ph.D. dissertation, Graduate School of Education, University of Pennsylvania.

Kamin, Leon J. n.d. "Heredity, Intelligence, Politics and Psychology." Unpublished manuscript.

Karabel, Jerome. 1984. "Status-Group Struggle, Organizational Interests, and the Limits of Institutional Autonomy: The Transformation of Harvard, Yale, and Princeton, 1918-1940." *Theory and Society* 13: 1-40.

Karen, David. 1985. "Who Gets Into Harvard? Selection and Exclusion at an Elite College." Unpublished Ph.D. dissertation, Department of Sociology, Harvard University.

Keppel, Frederick P. 1914. *Columbia.* New York: Oxford University Press.

Levine, David O. 1986. *The American College and the Culture of Aspiration, 1915-1940.* Ithaca, N.Y.: Cornell University Press.

Lipset, Seymour Martin, and David Riesman. 1975. *Education and Politics at Harvard.* New York: McGraw-Hill.

Mathews, Brander, ed. 1904. *A History of Columbia University.* New York: Columbia University Press.

Meyerson, Martin, and Dilys Pegler Winegrad. 1978. *Gladly Learn and Gladly Teach: Franklin and His Heirs at the University of Pennsylvania, 1740-1976.* Philadelphia: University of Pennsylvania Press.

Morison, Samuel Eliot. 1936. *Three Centuries of Harvard, 1636-1936.* Cambridge: Harvard University Press.

Oren, Dan A. 1985. *Joining the Club. A History of Jews and Yale.* New Haven, CT: Yale University Press.

Pierson, George. 1969. *The Education of American Leaders.* New York: Praeger.

Robbins, Michael David. 1955 "Princeton, 1920-1929: An Historical Study of a Problem in Reputation." Unpublished senior thesis, Department of History, Princeton University.

Russell, Willian F., ed. 1937. *The Rise of a University, Vol. 1, The Latter Days of Old Columbia College from the Annual Reports Of Frederick A.P. Barnard, President of Columbia College, 1864-1889.* New York: Columbia University Press.

Schudson, Michael J. 1972. "Organizing the Meritocracy: A History of the College Entrance Examination Board." *Harvard Educational Review 42: 34-69.*

Shryock, Richard Harrison. 1959. *The University of Pennsylvania Faculty. A Study in American Higher Education.* Philadelphia: University of Pennsylvania Press.

Slosson, Edwin. 1910. *Great American Universities.* New York: The Macmillan Company.

Steinberg, Stephen. 1971. "How Jewish Quotas Began." *Commentary* 52: 67-76.

———. 1974. *The Academic Melting Pot: Catholics and Jews in American Higher Education.* New York: McGraw-Hill.

Stone, Lawrence. 1974. "The Size and Composition of the Oxford Student Body, 1580-1910." Pp. 3-110 in *The University in Society*, edited by Lawrence Stone. Princeton, NJ: Princeton University Press.

Synnott, Marcia Graham. 1974. "A Social History of Admissions Policies at Harvard, Yale, and Princeton, 1900-1930." Unpublished Ph.D. dissertation, Department of History, University of Massachusetts.

_____. 1979. *The Half-Opened Door: Discrimination and Admissions at Harvard, Yale, and Princeton, 1900-1970.* Westport, CT: Greenwood Press.

The New York Times. 1977. "The University of Pennsylvania Is Suffering From an Identity Crisis." October 22.

Tomberlin, George E., Jr. 1971. "Trends in Princeton Admissions." Unpublished senior thesis, Department of Sociology, Princeton Unversity.

University of Pennsylvania.
  Catalogues: 1850, 1860, 1870, 1880, 1890, 1901, 1910, 1920, 1930, 1940.
  Freshmen Directories: 1960, 1972.
  History of the Class of 1890.
  Record, The Senior Class Yearbook: 1900, 1910, 1920, 1930,1940, 1950, 1960, 1970.
  Registrar's Notebooks, Enrollment Information: 1950, 1960, 1970.

Veysey, Laurence R. 1965. *The Emergence of the American University.* Chicago: University of Chicago Press.

Wechsler, Harold S. 1977. *The Qualified Student: A History of Selective College Admission in America.* New York: John Wiley and Sons.

PAUL WILLIAM KINGSTON
LIONEL S. LEWIS

Chapter Five

Undergraduates at Elite Institutions: The Best, the Brightest, and the Richest

The avalanche of applications to the nation's most prestigious private colleges and universities attests to the widespread belief that where one goes to college matters—academically and, later, to one's career. Those who make it through the highly competitive admissions process are seen as the best and the brightest, those qualified—perhaps even destined—to have the most prized careers. What is often overlooked, however, is that the student bodies of these colleges and universities are drawn heavily from affluent families. The chances of the less economically privileged attending an elite private institution are quite limited. Not enough attention has been given to the fact that admissions policies that stress high school grades and standardized test scores systematically create not only student bodies of high academic achievement, but also highly affluent student bodies.

In earlier eras the connection between economic status and the prestige of the college or university a student attended was direct, unquestioned, and clear: for the most part, only the children of the rich had any real chance of attending an elite private institution of higher learning. If an offspring of a middle- or working-class family did go on to higher education, as a rule, he or she went to a local institution with little prestige. Indeed, the elite stature of institutions like those in the Ivy League largely reflected their connection to those with money, not the intellectual capacities of their students. As wags at the turn of the century mocked: "College is a rich man's bread—a four year loaf."

Not until well into this century were admissions to the elite private institutions academically competitive in any meaningful way. Even then, with course requirements most readily met by affluent students who were often educated at private schools, only limited financial aid available for needy students, and with favored treatment of alumni children, these institutions were still quite socially exclusive. Research has shown that between 1900 and 1940 at least 40 percent of the students at Harvard, Yale, and Princeton Universities were private secondary school graduates.

The postwar years have been the much heralded time of the democratization of American higher education. The most dramatic symbol of this thrust has been the huge growth of the relatively low-cost public sector. College and university enrollments were about eight times larger in 1985 than they were in 1940.

Keeping in step with the increasing opportunities in public higher education, officials at elite private institutions since at least the 1960s have repeatedly stated a commitment both to more diverse student bodies and to meritocratic admission policies. Their efforts to admit less privileged students are said to be unflagging and successful. Although there is evidence which indicates that particularistic criteria have not been expunged from admissions decisions, that students are not sorted in the academic hierarchy by intellectual talent alone, the current practice of looking carefully at the academic merit of applicants is undeniable. Even while ratcheting up admissions standards, there is still a question, however, of how closely the elite private institutions remain linked to an upper-status constituency *within* this putative meritocratic order: that is, how socioeconomically diverse are undergraduate students at the most prestigious American institutions of higher learning?

This question of how far elite private institutions of higher learning have moved to reflect the diversity of American society has drawn increasing attention as the costs of attending such a college or university, or indeed any private institution, have soared. Middle-class parents vociferously complain about being "squeezed out," of having their children denied full educational opportunities (which they believe involve a number of things, from small classes and individual attention to consistency in the application of academic standards) because private education is simply far too expensive. Working-class families seldom complain, at least in part because they do not see an education at an elite private college or university for their children as a realistic possibility.

Some educators lament the reemergence of a "two-tier" system in higher education—one for the rich, one for all others. There is good reason to take these concerns seriously. According to an estimate by the College Board, the national admissions association, by 1987-88 the average charges (tuition and fees, books and supplies, room and board, transportation, and miscellaneous costs) for resident students in all private institutions had reached $11,982, up 7.3 percent from the previous year. Comparable costs for residential students at public institutions were $5,189. As is clear from Figure 5.1, tuition and fees at private colleges and universities more than doubled in the decade 1978 to 1987, and every year between 1981 and 1987 increases in costs exceeded the rate of inflation. In four consecutive years, tuition and fees increased by 10 percent or more. (Although sizable, the overall increase in tuition and fees at public four-year institutions was not as great.)

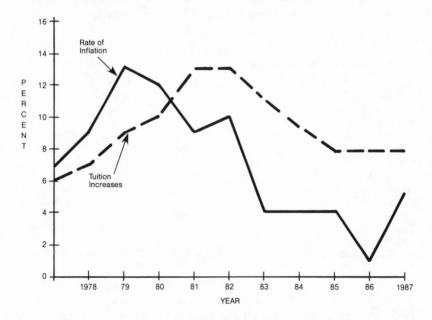

FIGURE 5.1
U.S. Rate of Inflation and Tuition Increases at Private Institutions, 1978-87.

In 1981, the inflation rate as measured by the Consumer Price Index was 8.9 percent, while tuition and fees for a student entering a four-year private institution had increased by 13 percent over the previous year. In 1986, when inflation was 1.1 percent, tuition at the average private institution was up 8 percent. Costs at private colleges and universities have risen by not less than 8 percent annually for each of the six years following 1981, although for four of these years inflation was only 4 percent or less.

Even more staggering are the costs of an education at an elite private institution. As Table 5.1 makes evident, the most expensive colleges and universities in the United States are for the most part elite private institutions. Moreover, when compared with the costs at most other elite private institutions, the figures in Table 5.1 do not seem to be particularly large. In 1987-88, total costs at Princeton University were $16,918, at Stanford University they were $16,835, and at Williams College they were $15,666. With the addition of other expenses, the final cost of going to an elite private institution for one year can actually total over $20,000. Expenses at elite private institutions continue to spiral. Oberlin College increased its tuition for the 1988-89 academic year by 9.5 percent. Dartmouth College increased its tuition by 6.4 percent.

TABLE 5.1
Ten Most Expensive Colleges and Universities, 1987-88 School Year

	Tuition and Fees	Room and Board	Total Costs
Bennington College	$14,850	$3,140	$17,990
Sarah Lawrence College	12,375	5,065	17,440
Barnard College	12,104	5,192	17,296
University of Chicago	12,460	4,730	17,190
Columbia University, Columbia College	12,170	4,950	17,120
Harvard/Radcliffe Colleges	12,890	4,210	17,100
Dartmouth College	12,474	4,600	17,074
Brown University	12,960	4,075	17,035
Tufts University	12,088	4,940	17,028
Yale University	12,120	4,900	17,020

To be sure, elite private institutions admit very qualified students. As can be seen in Table 5.2, of the 41 colleges and universities whose 1987 freshman class had Scholastic Aptitude Test scores averaging 1,200 or more, only 3—the College of William and Mary, the University of North Carolina at Chapel Hill, and the University of Virginia—were public. Few, if any, of the remaining 38 institutions would be omitted from a consensus listing of elite private institutions,and not a large number of colleges and universities not found in Table 5.2 would be added.

It is also clear from Table 5.2 that elite private colleges and universities are very well endowed. Six of the 7 private institutions with an endowment of over $1 billion in 1987 are listed in Table 5.2. (There were a total of 10 with an endowment of over $1 billion; the 3 that were public were the University of Texas System, the Texas A & M University System, and the University of California.) Fully two-thirds of the 55 colleges and universities which in 1987 had endowments of $200 million or more are found in Table 5.2. (This percentage is not larger because some of the institutions found in the table are quite small. Carlton College and Mount Holyoke College, for example, each have total enrollments of fewer than 2,000 students but substantial endowments of approximately $150 million.) Along a number of dimensions these colleges and universities are at the top.

TABLE 5.2
Colleges and Universities Whose 1987 Freshmen Class
Had Average SAT Scores of 1,200 or More and Their 1987 Endowments

Amherst College ($248,354,000)	Princeton University ($2,291,110,000)
Brown University ($347,520,000)	Reed College ($67,942,000)
Bryn Mawr College ($109,922,000)	Rice University ($857,155,000)
California Institute of Technology	Smith College ($299,625,000)
($408,946,000)	St. John's College (Maryland) ($21,984,000)
Carelton College ($144,190,000)	Stanford University ($1,676,950,000)
Claremont McKenna College ($83,743,000)	Swarthmore College ($276,019,000)
College of William and Mary ($56,157,000)	Trinity University (Texas) N/A
Columbia University ($1,387,060,000)	University of Chicago ($913,600,000)
Cornell University ($725,096,000)	University of North Carolina at Chapel Hill
Dartmouth College ($537,272,000)	($127,282,000)
Davidson College ($66,931,000)	University of Pennsylvania ($648,528,000)
Duke University ($363,706,000)	University of Virginia ($396,329,000)
Emory University ($798,549,000)	Vassar College ($224,351,000)
Grinnell College ($226,783,000)	Washington and Lee University
Harvard University ($4,018,270,000)	($93,400,000)
Haverford College ($73,792,000)	Wellesley College ($298,000,000)
Johns Hopkins University ($534,809,000)	Wesleyan University (Connecticut)
Massachusetts Institute of Technology	($258,130,000)
($1,169,740,000)	Williams College ($262,588,000)
Mount Holyoke College ($151,916,000)	Worcester Polytechnic Institute
Northwestern University ($802,670,000)	($78,320,000)
Oberlin College ($203,673,000)	Yale University ($2,098,400,000)
Pomona College ($232,675,000)	

The implications of these numbers have been much discussed, though largely in anecdotal fashion. We now examine recent enrollment patterns at elite institutions by students' family income from two complementary perspectives. The first is institutional: what are the family income characteristics of the student bodies at elite private institutions? The second considers attendance rates: how is the probability of attending an elite private institution related to family income?

DATA AND MEASURES

We base this analysis on data presented in *The American Freshman: National Norms for Fall,* 1980-86, a large annual survey of first-time, full-time freshmen enrolled at a highly stratified sample of institutions. In 1986, the published norms were based on 204,491 respondents from a total of 372 institutions; these data provide a relatively accurate picture of the students' family income at institutions of similar standing in the collegiate hierarchy.

We examine two categories of elite private institutions, those labelled by a standard selectivity index for colleges and universities as *four-year private nonsectarian colleges-very high selectivity* (46 institutions) as and *private universities-high selectivity* (28 institutions). The average combined Scholastic Aptitude Test score for incoming freshman at these institutions was at least 1,175 in the mid-1970s, when the index was constructed. The "eliteness" of these institutions, then, is in large part defined in terms of their selectivity in admissions. (Parenthetically, it is of some interest that only 47 of the 157 colleges and universities rated as the "best and most innovative" in one of nine categories by college presidents in 1987 selected fewer than 50 percent of those who applied for admission, and that only 7 of the 47 were public institutions. The tuition and fees at 30 of the 47 were $10,000 or more.)

Although all of the 76 institutions included in this study enroll unusually competent students, their general prestige varies significantly. The top category of universities includes Ivy League institutions as well as Rensselaer Polytechnic Institute, Tulane University, Vanderbilt University, and Yeshiva University. The top category of colleges includes the Little Three (e.g., Amherst College) and some of the Seven Sisters (Smith College, Wellesley College, etc.), as well as Franklin and Marshall College and Hobart and William Smith College. Clearly not all of these institutions enjoy equally high standards and stature. This list of institutions is more inclusive than we wished it to be; with the data available, it is not possible to study family income and enrollments at the very most elite private institutions.

THE IMPORTANCE OF FAMILY INCOME

As Table 5.3 details, the freshmen at the private highly selective colleges and universities are decidedly affluent, much more so than the population of college students as a whole. Just less than a quarter of the freshmen of the private highly selective colleges and universities reported 1986 parental incomes exceeding $100,000, a figure that places them in the top few percent of all families in the general population. Little more than 7 percent of all freshmen come from such affluent families.

TABLE 5.3
Family Income of 1986 Freshmen (in percent)

Family Income	All Institutions	4-Year Colleges	Universities	Private Very Highly Selective Colleges	Private Highly Selective Universities
Less than $10,000	7.6	7.0	4.2	2.7	2.8
$10,000-19,999	12.9	12.0	8.2	5.3	5.1
$20,000-29,999	16.1	15.4	12.2	8.8	8.3
$30,000-39,999	20.1	20.1	18.1	13.5	12.5
$40,000-49,999	12.4	12.7	12.7	10.2	10.7
$50,000-59,999	10.2	10.5	12.6	11.2	11.8
$60,000-74,999	8.3	9.0	11.8	12.0	13.3
$75,000-99,999	5.3	5.6	8.2	11.3	11.8
$100,000-149,999	3.6	3.8	6.1	11.9	10.9
$150,000+	3.6	3.9	5.9	13.0	12.8
Total*	100.0	100.0	100.0	100.0	100.0
Enrollment	1,607,586	630,485	393,976	21,299	29,790

*Totals do not add exactly to 100% because of rounding.

Furthermore, a majority (more than 60 percent) of the freshmen at the private highly selective colleges and universities reported having family incomes exceeding $50,000. Although a family income in excess of $50,000 is hardly rare among the total population of freshmen (31 percent), the proportion is almost double at the private highly selective institutions. Since less than one-fifth of all American families reach this income level, it is clear that these institutions are primarily attended by upper-middle-class students.

Correspondingly, these private highly selective institutions have few middle- or low-income students. One in twelve of the students come from families with incomes below $20,000, and the proportion from poor families is minuscule. (To place these figures in perspective, the 1985 median family income was about $28,000.)

In sum, although the family income distributions at the private highly selective institutions indicate that they are not solely upper class preserves, their student bodies are very disproportionately skewed to the top end of the stratification system.

ANY CHANGE?

From a long-term perspective, the social and economic diversity of the most elite private colleges and universities has clearly increased. As a matter of course, prep school graduates no longer fill the rolls at these institutions. The greater availability of financial aid in the last few decades has brought them within reach of a more socially and economically diverse cohort of college-bound teenagers. At the same time, in the face of the rapidly escalating costs of these institutions and cuts in assistance available to moderate-income families, the question remains whether their exclusive economic character has actually increased in the 1980s.

To address this issue, in Figure 5.2 we present the percentage of students at private highly selective institutions with family incomes above $100,000 for 1980-86. It is obvious from Figure 5.2 that there was a huge increase in the proportion of such affluent students in this short-time period. The proportion more than doubled—from just over a tenth to almost a quarter.

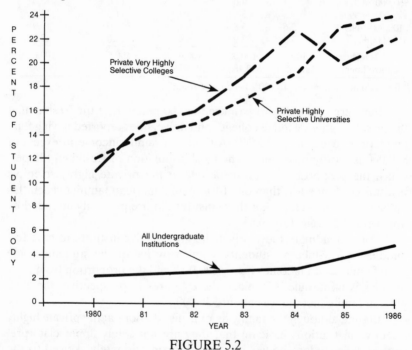

FIGURE 5.2
Enrollments of Freshmen with Family Incomes Exceeding $100,000, 1980-86

Although the economic meaning of a $100,000 income was not constant over these six years, the dramatic change which we see in Figure 5.2 undoubtedly still points to some increase in economic exclusiveness. In spite of the fact that the real value (purchasing power) of a $100,000 income did decline, inflation was relatively modest in these years. As the result of inflation and some real growth in family income in parts of the country, the *relative* standing of families at this income level declined. Not surprisingly, then, the proportion of students from these affluent families grew at all institutions (see the bottom line in Figure 5.2), not just at private highly selective institutions. If, however, the private highly selective institutions merely retained the same relative number of economically privileged freshmen, the trend lines in Figure 5.2 would be parallel. Yet clearly they are not: the trend lines for the private highly selective institutions are much steeper than the one for all undergraduate institutions.

From 1980 to 1986 the proportion of all students with $100,000+ family incomes increased from just over 2 percent to just over 7 percent. The comparable increases were much greater at private highly selective institutions: by 12.8 percent at the most selective colleges and by 13.9 percent at most selective universities. Quite simply, from 1980 to 1986, students from affluent families became more commonplace at private highly selective institutions. The reasons for this change are not apparent from these data, but the outcome is unmistakable: the most selective private institutions have become notably more economically exclusive in recent years.

INDIVIDUAL PROSPECTS OF ATTENDANCE

Up to this point we have considered the income characteristics of the students at private highly selective colleges and universities—an institutional perspective. Now, in a complementary light, we analyze how students' *chances* of attending an elite institution are related to family income level.

At the outset of this analysis it is important to note that the data relate only to college or university entrants, not the total age cohort. Since college or university attendance is positively related to family income level, the analysis understates the full advantage of the children from middle-class and upper-class families.

To make the presentation of data more manageable, we only examine the chances of students in three income categories (see Table 5.4):

1. Students from families with income greater than $100,000.
2. Students from families with income in the $35,000-49,999 range. (In relation to the general population, these families are considerably above the middle. In 1985, a $35,000 income would place a family in the top 37 percent of the income distribution.) In 1986, these students

represented about the middle third of all college students, and the economic burdens of their attending an institution of higher learning and their fates have been the subject of popular worries and official attention. Since the family incomes of these students generally place them just above the eligibility cutoffs for many government aid programs, they are the "middle class" that presumably is being squeezed out of the more costly institutions.

3. Students from families with incomes below $20,000. Although only some of these students come from the very bottom of the economic ladder (34 percent of American families in 1985 had incomes below $20,000), they are generally eligible for the full range of assistance plans.

TABLE 5.4
Probability of Enrolling at a Selective Private Institution,
by Family Income Categories, 1980, 1982, 1984, 1986

| Family Income | Percent Enrolling | | | |
	1980	1982	1984	1986
$100,000+	13.1	13.9	15.9	10.7
$35,000 - 49,999	4.5	3.3	2.9	2.5
Less than $20,000	1.2	1.1	1.1	1.2
All Freshmen	2.9	2.9	3.1	3.2
Number of Freshmen with $100,000+				
Family Income	37,656	60,934	57,232	115,746

The most obvious point to be made about Table 5.4 is that going to a private highly selective institution is quite unusual, at all income levels. The important implication of this fact is that these institutions cannot be a major mechanism by which affluent families in American society reproduce themselves. Only a small minority of their children will be able to earn and benefit from a prestigious undergraduate degree.

At the same time, the fact remains that the chances of enrolling at a private highly selective institution increase greatly with income level. Very few of the low-income students go to one of these institutions, and the chances are only slightly greater for middle-income students. Only students from families with incomes of more than $100,000 have any notable prospects—for example, about 11 percent in 1986 and nearly 16 percent in 1984. To place the favorable prospects of rich students in perspective, note that 3.1 percent of all freshmen in 1984 went to one of these institutions; thus rich students were overrepresented by a factor of more than five.

Have the chances of students from various levels of the economic hierarchy changed in recent years? For the reasons noted in the preceding section, it is problematic to use static income categories, unadjusted for inflation, to assess change. The data, however, are adequate to suggest some rough conclusions.

For students from all income levels, there has been, as would be expected, no major transformation in the prospects of going to a private highly selective institution in the 1980s. It has never been likely that low-income students would enroll at one of these colleges or universities —only about one in a hundred throughout this time. At the same time there is not much to indicate that a great number of middle-income students have been squeezed out because of rising tuition costs or a decrease in aid. In 1980, 4.5 percent enrolled in one of these selective private institutions; 2.5 percent did so in 1986. To be sure, the proportional decline is large, but only because the initial figure is so small. And, in part, the decline reflects the fact that a $35,000-$49,000 income in 1986 represents a lesser real income than it did in 1980.

The pattern among rich students is somewhat odd. From 1980 to 1984, their attendance rates rose slightly: from 13.1 percent to 15.9 percent. In 1986, however, the proportion dropped to 10.7 percent. Some of this decline undoubtedly reflects the great overall increase in the number of freshmen from families with $100,000+ incomes. (See Figure 5.2.) In absolute numbers, more students from such affluent families attended a private highly selective institution in 1986 than in 1984.

In sum, throughout the 1980s only a small minority of rich college students were enrolled at a private highly selective institution, but, as Figure 5.2 shows, they account for an increasing proportion of the students at these colleges and universities. At the same time, since total enrollments at these institutions are so small, they have not become significantly more likely to attend.

STRATIFICATION AND POLICY

All of these figures on family income clearly establish that the offspring of rich families continue to be the prime beneficiaries of an elite undergraduate education—with the concomitant credentials. Affluent and upper-middle-class students predominate at these schools. Even in an era believed to be guided by intellectually meritocratic principles that is said to have supplanted an era committed to the more direct advancement of class concerns through higher education, their monied tone is still very much in evidence, despite some sincere efforts to increase diversity.

Undoubtedly the predominance of a racially and religiously exclusive, self-conscious WASP upper class has waned at these institutions, even if the student bodies are still drawn so heavily from the top of the income hierarchy. (As both the established snob and the arriviste recognize, "money isn't everything.") The upper class and their institutions have long incorporated some ethnic and other types of social diversity. By and large, students at the most selective institutions of higher learning are rich or at least materially comfortable; they are not upper class in the sense of having direct control of substantial private property or an encompassing common cultural identity.

The goodly concentration of rich students at these institutions certainly constricts the socialization experiences that the schools might provide. To be sure, students can readily find comfort and reinforcement from many like themselves, and nonaffluent students have no shortage of models who have enjoyed the comforts of life at the top. (It is hardly surprising that admissions officers complaining about a small applicant pool report that a smaller proportion of academically meritorious students from poor families than from rich families seek to enroll at elite private institutions.) Rather than learning the ways of a traditional property-based upper-class culture, undergraduates at elite private institutions are immersed in a milieu that seems fertile ground for developing a sense that being the best and the brightest is linked to the possession of the right credentials, and upper-middle-class membership.

In greater measure than heretofore, students at elite private institutions are the offspring of families that attained affluence through the possession of educational attainment and certificates. Their inheritance is "educational property"; it is their cultural capital that places them in the running for high-level positions in the credential-dominated realm of professional and managerial work. Prestige diplomas—widely believed to be the most valued coin of the realm—are appropriated and claimed by those privileged by birth. This process contributes to the reproduction of a stratification system in which the role of education looms large. As it turns out, the prestigious credential route to occupational success is available to only a very small proportion of students from below the top reaches of the income distribution.

At the same time, the limited impact of elite private institutions in this overall process of marketing undergraduate degrees must also be recognized. The data make clear that only a fairly small proportion of rich college students go to elite private institutions. To the extent that affluent parents pass on privilege, they must often do so by other means.

Whatever their actual impact on the stratification system, the prominence of these elite private institutions in our collective thinking about education, equity, and opportunity has made them a focus of public concern. From both outside and inside academe, these elite private institutions have been under pressure to "open up"—to make admissions a reflection of academic merit, not financial status—particularly to increase minority representation, even if this might mean some modification of admissions criteria. Governmental and private financial aid programs have been directed to this end.

Elite private institutions have been much heralded as concrete symbols of America's commitment to equality of opportunity. It would appear, however, that the increased educational opportunities for middle- and working-class students that have been so evident in recent years are almost totally the result of the growth of public education, the creation of vast state university, state college, and community college systems in every state in the nation, not the result of changes in the admissions policies or programs of elite private institutions. It is difficult to assess whether admissions policies are genuinely "money blind" (as administrators at many elite private institutions profess them to be), but the aggregate impact of all aid programs has not significantly increased the chances that students from families of limited means will attend these institutions.

It has been shown that, all things being equal (which they never are), parental income has a modest effect on where students go to college. By comparison, academic ability, as conventionally measured, has a larger impact on what types of colleges students attend. Some greater availability of financial support for academically capable low- and middle-income students would further increase the economic diversity of undergraduates at elite private institutions. Yet, if elite private institutions remain committed to the conventional measures of "merit" in their admissions decisions—high scores on standardized tests, the ability to fit in socially, being well balanced in terms of interests, having a special skill—any increase in aid is likely to have only a slight impact on the social background of their students. Most students who are meritorious in the broad sense are raised in high-income families where they have enjoyed special opportunities. Generally speaking, children from the lower social classes compared with those from the higher social classes acquire fewer linguistic and cultural skills and so have a decided disadvantage in their schoolwork. The "all-round man" is an upper-class value. And the dominance of this value in the admissions process has made it possible for elite private institutions of higher learning to tighten their academic requirements for admission and still cater to the privileged.

The link between elite private institutions and the stratification system may, nonetheless, be marginally shaped by the vicissitudes of public policy. Expressed in 1982 dollars, the total amount of financial aid (including loans) from all sources declined from $18,958,000,000 in 1980 to $18,482,000,000 in 1985—a drop of 2.5 percent. Moreover, even though the total aid available in many key programs actually increased in real terms in these years, a greater number of students receiving aid generally meant no increase in benefits to individual recipients. This occurred at a time when tuition costs were escalating sharply at elite private institutions.

Quite simply, even with the much touted financial aid that is supposed to eliminate class barriers to attending, costs at elite private colleges and universities are now beyond the means of a large percentage of undergraduates. For example, 65 percent of the freshmen who received financial aid—grants, employment in a work program, loans—at Middlebury College in 1984 came from families in which the total parental income was $30,000 or more. In 1984, the comprehensive fee billed by Middlebury College was $12,600, and it was estimated that additional expenses, which included books and supplies, would be another $1,000. The average amount of financial aid from all sources for a freshman whose parents had an income between $15,000 and $30,000 was $8,800, so the student and his or her family were expected to contribute at least $4,800 from savings or other assets. Thus, only 15 percent of the students who received grants at Middlebury College in 1984 were from families where the parental income was $15,000 or less, and 25 percent were from families where the parental income was $45,000 or more.

In sum, a small decrease in recent years in the ability of low- and middle-income students to pay for an elite private education is associated with some increase in the economic exclusiveness of these institutions. Many elite private institutions partially offset the declining ability of lower- and middle-income students to meet total costs by increasing institutional assistance. (Indeed, some institutions have tried to justify their tuition increases by citing these new financial burdens.) Nonetheless, these additional expenditures have not halted the increasing affluence of their student bodies.

Although there is not yet solid evidence that middle-income students have "traded down" because of a new inability to pay for an expensive selective college or university, it is clear that public encouragement for increasing opportunities for the less economically privileged at elite private institutions has waned. Hardly anyone today asks their admissions officers to justify why they continue to set aside a number of places in their freshman class for those they decide to admit in order to get the correct mix of hockey players, Californians, trumpet players, Texans, and aspiring lawyers, regardless of credentials, or why the children of their undergraduate alumni are given an advantage in the admissions process.

Since the children of privilege do better on standardized achievement tests and in their schoolwork than their less affluent counterparts, there are more than enough of them to fill the freshman classes at elite private institutions. The public is told that there are too few students from lower- or working-class families with the academic credentials for and interest in attending a private elite institution. It is hard to believe that of the approximately one million such students who begin college every year there not are enough who meet the standards set by elite private institutions; and without evidence to support it, this contention need not be taken seriously.

Apparently, administrators at elite private institutions take it for granted that their students will come from affluent families. In responding to concerns about increases in tuition and fees, the financial vice-president for Radcliffe College writes that it is not realistic to make comparisons with changes in the Consumer Price Index: "Unlike higher education, many of the consumer items are highly 'price sensitive'—that is, they are subject to a good deal of product substitution when their cost gets out of line. A more relevant comparison would be, for example, the 7.5 percent increase in college tuition with the 9 percent rise in cost of living revealed in a 1987 national survey of families with income of $75,000 or more" (Morrell 1985: 12). Although certainly reality directly influences how people think about a problem, this quotation suggests that administrators at elite private institutions will have to think hard about their attitudes if they want to institute changes that will affect the composition of their student bodies.

When it suits their purpose, the elite private colleges and universities can admit students on the basis of so-called academic merit; when it does not, even the most elite private institutions contend that they must look at other criteria in order to have well-rounded individuals and a good balance in their student bodies. A look at the great variability in standardized test scores of any freshman class shows that elite private institutions fall short of being academic meritocracies.

In any case, without fundamental changes in the definition of academic merit, the educational mission of elite institutions, and the stratifying aspects of early education, elite private colleges and universities are likely disproportionately to enroll children from financially and academically privileged families. There is little to suggest that these institutions seek an active role in developing social policy that will foster change.

We can thus expect that the bachelor's degree from an elite institution will continue to be given and received as a ticket for continued privilege.

REFERENCES

The American Freshman: National Norms for Fall, 1980-1986. Los Angeles: Cooperative Institutional Research Program, University of California at Los Angeles.

Morrell, Louis R. 1988. "The Tuition Policies of Higher Education Are Not Divorced From Economic Reality." *Chronicles of Higher Education.* July 27, 1988: 1B.

Chapter Six

Pathways to Attendance at the Elite Colleges*

Educational leaders, scholars, and the general public share a rough consensus regarding the prestige hierarchy among U.S. colleges and universities (Ben-David, 1974; Clark, 1983). Although the American higher-education system may not be dominated by a discrete institutional elite on the order of England's Oxford and Cambridge, a relatively small group of well-known colleges has produced since colonial times a disproportionate share of the national leadership in industry, politics, education, and the professions (Mills, 1959; Pierson, 1969).

There is some dispute, however, over the extent to which those institutions themselves, as institutions, have shaped the contours of U.S. social stratification. Early analyses of this question often assumed that the colleges themselves were most responsible for their graduates' extraordinary successes. If Harvard produced more U.S. Presidents than the University of Massachusetts, then a Harvard education was assumed critical. Recent scholarship has questioned this conclusion, however, suggesting that the successes of the graduates of elite institutions may have less to do with the nature of those colleges themselves than with the nature of their student clientele. When students' academic and socioeconomic characteristics as entering freshmen are statistically controlled in regression models of occupational and income attainment, the distinctive positive effects of prestigious institutions decline (Alwin, 1974; Trusheim and Crouse, 1981), although college prestige does still seem to confer some economic benefit (Kingston and Smart, Chapter 7 in this volume).

Whatever the extent of the advantages conferred by a degree from a prestigious school, it is the entering characteristics of the schools' students that are most striking. Importantly, the elite schools disproportionately enroll affluent students. For example, about one-fourth of the 1986 freshmen at the most selective private colleges and universities had family incomes exceeding $100,000, as opposed to only about 7 percent at all U.S. colleges and universities (Astin, et al., 1986). Many of the potential beneficiaries of elite degrees are therefore already advantaged by family background at the time of college entry. (For further detail, see Chapter 5 in this volume.)

Nevertheless, economic privilege does not appear to "buy" admission to elite institutions. In multivariate models, students' socioeconomic status (SES), gender, and racial and ethnic characteristics have been found to be of only secondary direct significance in entry into those institutions. National studies of college attenders by Karabel and Astin (1975), Alexander and Eckland (1977), and Hearn (1984) have suggested that students' entry into the more selective institutions is rooted more in their notable academic talents (individual ability and achievement) than in their ascriptive characteristics. Although ascriptive factors exert undeniably important indirect influences on entry into such institutions, via their early effects on the formation of academic characteristics (Sewell, 1971), the most immediate influences are clearly academic. The higher a student's ability and achievements, the more likely it is that he or she will attend a selective institution.

Of the ascriptive characteristics, socioeconomic status shows the most direct influence, but that influence is minor compared to that of academic factors. Gender and race have been found to have minor effects in varying directions. These national results are supplemented by intriguing findings from Klitgaard's analysis (1985) of admissions decisions in a sample of elite colleges: elite colleges vary substantially in the ways they evaluate students' credentials in admissions decisions, but generally seem either to disregard ascriptive factors or to show some limited favoritism to minority applicants.

The existing empirical evidence on the pathways to entering the more selective colleges may therefore be summarized as follows: (a) the dominant direct influences on entry into such colleges are students' academic characteristics; (b) economic characteristics have significant, but clearly secondary, direct influences; (c) the influences of gender and racial and ethnic characteristics are mixed; and (d) elite institutions exhibit no overt ascriptive biases in evaluating their applicants, and may slightly favor minorities. In other words, although there are significant nonmeritocratic tendencies in the matching of students and the most selective colleges, the evidence gives no indication of strong ascriptive biases or channeling in entry into the elite colleges.

Nevertheless, although class influences appear minor, it is intriguing to examine further the conjunction of findings (b) and (d). All else equal, lower-SES college attenders are less likely to attend selective schools, but there is no available evidence that such schools overtly discriminate on the basis of SES. The tendency of SES to be positively associated with the selectivity of college entered, in spite of an absence of evidence of discrimination, may be interpreted in two general ways. First, the data on admissions may be somewhat misleading. Admissions bias may exist, but may be efficiently hidden behind an unmeasured correlation between SES and certain aspects of "cultural capital" (Bourdieu, 1977) which are evaluated by counselors or admissions officers. Alternatively, the national enrollment data may incorrectly suggest that some SES effects exist because of problems in the way academic talent is measured. Such measurements may be so imperfect (or so rooted in class considerations) that variance which is in reality based on talent emerges in regression results as based on class.

A second way of interpreting the conjunction of (b) and (d) is to consider how high-school-level decisions affect where one will apply. College admissions officers cannot exhibit direct bias against students who never apply to their schools. Lower-SES parents may steer their children away from applying to elite schools, perhaps for reasons of perceived costs (Olson and Rosenfeld, 1984 a,b). High school counselors and teachers may also do so in their dealings with college-bound lower-SES students, but studies at the high school level do not show the especially strong class-based organizational biases and stuent channelling suggested by elite-oriented theories (Hurn, 1978; Heyns, 1974).

Such results have led John Meyer, in a perceptive essay, to question dominant modes of explanation in the sociology of education (1986). Two of Meyer's major "evidentiary embarrassments" for the field seem particularly applicable to the issue of entry into selective colleges. First, once intellectual ability is controlled, ascriptive group differences in academic achievement and access to elite education are minor and are sometimes in unexpected directions. Second, evidence of distinctive organizational influences (such as effects of systematic counselor bias in track placement and college advising, or effects of wealthy secondary schools) is weak. Clearly, those who believe there are distinctive and important class biases active in the U.S. educational system find little support in most analyses of college entry.

Meyer may well be right in his skepticism, but further exploration of the possibility of nonmeritocratic influences in students' pathways to elite colleges seems advisable. Perhaps earlier analyses have failed to find important systematic influences because of their research designs rather than because of any flawed theoretical underpinnings. Much of the existing research on college entry may be criticized for relying on research designs with universe samples and the assumption of linear effects. In such designs, slightly brighter students are hypothesized to attend slightly more prestigious (i.e., selective) schools, which, in turn, are hypothesized to have slightly more positive attainment effects throughout the empirically observed range of ability, prestige, and attainment values. This kind of reasoning lies at the heart of linear multiple regression studies in which the characteristics of nationally representative samples of college attenders are statistically related to the selectivity of the colleges they attend, out of the diverse national pool of colleges. Similarly, this kind of reasoning lies behind studies in which college selectivity, across its entire range, is related to attainment outcomes, across their entire range. Such designs may allow too much "noise" to creep into the analysis, obscuring any distinctive pathways to, or effects of, elite colleges.

To develop this argument further, assume that (a) an elite corps of prestigious and highly selective colleges does indeed uniquely improve graduates' socioeconomic outcomes, and (b) these colleges' freshmen average 100 Scholastic Aptitude Test (SAT) points (or 5 American College Testing Program Assessment (ACT) points) higher than freshmen in the "effect-less" schools in the next lower rung of the hierarchy. With the traditional research design, the special attainment effects of the elite schools in our assumed world might well be dwarfed by an absence of comparable differential effects between institutions in America's vast nonselective institutional pool. For example, students from two essentially nonselective four-year state colleges with respective average freshmen SATs of 850 and 950 might have very similar levels of career success. In regression analyses, this "no-differences" pattern would blur the differential effects of a school in our elite corps (average SATs = 1,250) and a school in the next lower rung in the hierarchy (average SATs = 1,150). It follows from this example that the wide variation in admissions test scores among all American institutions may be largely irrelevant to an analysis of the distinctive characteristics of the elite sector of American higher education. The great majority of U.S postsecondary institutions are not truly selective, and as many as one-third are "virtually open-door" (*New York Times,* November 2, 1986; Clark, 1983). For this reason, the difference between any two institutions in average SAT or ACT scores may more often be a trivial artifact than a substantive indication of differences in quality or "eliteness."

It would not be hard to construct a parallel example of research design limitations for studies of entry into elite colleges: perhaps powerful ascriptive effects on entry occur only among the academically talented and only for the choice between applying to the most elite institutions and those on the next lower rung in the prestige hierarchy. If true, a significant pattern of status transmission via the elite college sector would go largely unnoticed by standard analytic approaches. To find distinctive paths to elite colleges, then, research designs must concentrate more cleanly upon the students and institutions most likely to be involved. What is more, these designs must allow for tests of hypotheses about thresholds in multivariate models, that is, points on variable ranges at which effects and other statistical relationships are increased.[1]

The focus here is on one aspect of this large issue: the characteristics and behaviors of those academically talented students who enter the most highly selective colleges. The central question is: do these students significantly differ from equally talented students entering other schools, even from those entering schools in the next lower rung in the prestige ladder? In a methodological sense, can we assume that attendance chances at such schools rise linearly with students' academic and socioeconomic credentials, or are there discontinuities and nonlinearities in this relationship? In other words, do the linear gradations in the prestige hierarchy roughly correspond to the linear gradations in students' characteristics?

THE ISSSUE IN HISTORICAL FOCUS

One might argue that twentieth century education in the United States has been notable for its elevation of the universal and linear and its derogation of the categorical as norms for the matching of high school graduates and collegiate institutions. In the years before 1900, there existed a small, identifiable class of elite institutions, most of them private in control, located in the Northeast, and chartered in the years before the Revolutionary War. Entry into these colleges seems to have been as dependent upon family circumstances and attendance at an elite secondary school as upon academic ability (Veysey, 1965). As the nineteenth century drew to a close, however, two developments began to blur the picture. First, the expansion of higher education into the former "frontier" states of the Midwest and West grew in vigor, breaking the association of eastern institutions with the nation's views of quality in higher education. Wisconsin and Chicago were particularly prominent among the new, legitimate claimants to elite status. In the case of Wisconsin and its emerging sister state universities, the very notion of quality was being revised to a more inclusive vision in tune with the progressive education movement (Brubacher and Rudy, 1976). Second, a growing meritocratic impulse led many prestigious institutions to place greater emphasis on the academic characteristics of prospective students. In fact, according to Brubacher and Rudy (1976), the founding of the College Entrance Examination Board in 1900 was in part due to the desire of several eastern institutions to reduce their reliance on secondary school origins and familiar educational networks in admission criteria.

As the boundaries of the elite institutional class became blurred, and as attention to family and school origins fell into disfavor in collegiate admissions processes, the appearance of unfairness and class-based elitism began to erode in the nation's higher education system. Problems of equity in access and attainment may remain, however. For one matter, the meritocracy may function perfectly in both theory and reality, but be blunted in its effectiveness by the nonrandom, class-based distribution of talent in the society. If institutions are ranked in a meritocratically- based prestige hierarchy that affects graduates' occupational placements, and if students' measured academic ability is strongly associated with their social origins, then educational meritocracy may serve indirectly, and paradoxically, to maintain certain families' socioeconomic advantages over generations, under a legitimated "cover" of equitable allocations (see Karabel, 1972; Bowles and Gintis, 1976; Bourdieu, 1977). A perhaps more fundamental problem is the possibility that the meritocracy itself may work imperfectly. Meritocratic norms may not have been as fully realized as the "covering" arguments sometimes presuppose. Institutional origins, individual status characteristics, and arbitrary cutoff scores may be used as proxy markers in place of more detailed efforts to rank individuals' ability to succeed and advance in various settings. Such reliance on the categorical would represent a breakdown in meritocratic standards. These possible weaknesses in meritocratic norms, structures, and procedures inform the rationale for this chapter.

THE RESEARCH APPROACH

Two aspects of the pathways followed by students to attendance at the elite colleges in the United States are critical in this analysis: the influences of ascriptive factors on students' entrance into elite colleges, and the connections between these influences and academic (meritocratic) influences. To explore these issues, the research approach is grounded in two fundamental decisions. First, it uses a categorical definition of an "elite" institution. Much earlier research assumed that institutions may be arrayed along a continuum of selectivity (as evidenced by average freshman entrance examination scores) that roughly reflects quality. Instead, the chapter's analysis specifies a high cutoff level in average SAT/ACT scores of entering freshmen in order to explore the nature of a circumscribed group of elite institutions. The institutions identified in this way correspond closely to those named by most scholars and the general public as "elite." Students attending these distinctive institutions are then contrasted to students entering other institutions. Second, the study focusses mainly on those especially able students most likely to consider, and be considered by, the elite institutions.

Data

This analysis employs some of the latest and most comprehensive data available: information for a sample of college attenders, drawn from the national High School and Beyond (HSB) survey of the high school graduates of 1980 (see National Opinion Research Center [NORC], 1983). This data base has the advantage of both recent origin and extraordinary breadth and depth of coverage of critical relevant variables.

For the present analysis, these survey data for graduating seniors were merged with two-year follow-up data for the same sample to ascertain the graduates' college attendance behaviors. Data for the white college attenders among the larger sample were then merged with institution-level selectivity data from the Higher Education Research Institute (HERI) (1984).[2] The sample thus consists of 1879 whites in the HSB data base who entered, within one year of their 1980 high school graduation, a postsecondary institution in the HERI data set (see Peng, 1983, for details of the college attendance patterns of students in the HSB senior sample). The analysis pays special attention to the 964 of these 1,879 attenders who scored in the top quartile of American high school graduates on the HSB cognitive tests. For all analyses, sample weights suggested by the U.S. Department of Education were used to allow inferences about all white college attenders from the high school class of 1980.

The basic selectivity indicator used for the "elite-status" cutoff score in this chapter is a combined verbal and mathematics SAT score average of at least 1,176 for all freshmen at the institution in 1978, the closest year to 1980 available on the HERI data set. (When the institution tended to rely more upon scores from the ACT assessment, a conversion was made to SAT scaling, using a procedure agreed upon by the producers of the two instruments.) The cutoff score is rather arbitrary, and perhaps a bit liberal. Freshmen at the institutions most frequently termed "elite" (Harvard, Yale, Stanford) tend to average over 100 points above this minimal level. Nevertheless, it was only at this level that sufficient student cases could be drawn from the HSB sample for the analysis proposed. In the HERI sample of 2,537 institutions, only 23 schools averaged above 1,250. Seventy-four averaged above 1,175, however. These schools appear to coincide roughly with those termed "highly selective" by the recent Carnegie Report on undergraduate education in America, as well as to those most often mentioned in lists of "elite colleges" (*U.S. News and World Report*, 1985; Pierson, 1969; Useem and Karabel, 1986).

Of the 74 schools, 68 are privately controlled. Of these, 29 are universities, 36 are nonsectarian four-year colleges, and 3 are four-year colleges controlled by Protestant denominations. Of the 6 public institutions represented in the sample, 1 is a university and 5 are four-year colleges.[3] Not surprisingly, all Ivy League institutions (Brown, Columbia, Cornell, Dartmouth, Harvard, Pennsylvania, Princeton, and Yale) easily met this minimum level, as did other similarly well-known research universities around the country (e.g., Stanford, Chicago, MIT, Johns Hopkins, Duke, Northwestern, Rice, California Institute of Technology, Virginia, and Carnegie-Mellon). Among the distinguished private colleges easily making the cutoff were Williams, Barnard, Bryn Mawr, Amherst, Smith, Mt. Holyoke, Carleton, Haverford, Swarthmore, Reed, Harvey Mudd, Colgate, Wesleyan, and Bowdoin. The lower reaches of the acceptable SAT range, however, included more of a mix. Some less recognizably elite institutions were mixed with some good-quality regional and national institutions. Among the schools just making the cutoff score were Notre Dame, Colorado College, Davidson College, Brandeis, Tufts, Kalamazoo College, Washington University, Bucknell, Franklin and Marshall, Lehigh, and Rochester. Interestingly, each of the four U.S. service academies (for the army, navy, air force, and coast guard) were over the 1,175 SAT level, although none would have made a cutoff score of 1,250.

Independent Variables and Their Indicators

The dependent variable indicator for the study, institutional selectivity, is described above. The independent variables hypothesized to relate to the selectivity of the institution attended are described below. College attenders' gender is in dummy form (0 = male, 1 = female).

Four independent variables relate to college attenders' socioeconomic characteristics. Father's education and mothers education are each indicated by an ordinal measure with nine values ranging from attainment of less than a high school degree (coded 2) through attainment of a Ph.D., M. D., or other advanced professional degree (coded 10). Family size is also used as an SES indicator because each sibling represents a potential drain on family financial resources. The family size indicator is a composite of several HSB items. It is coded from 0 (=no siblings) through 5 (=five or more siblings). The fourth and final SES variable indicator is for 1980 family income. This indicator was coded in seven categories, with the lowest (a code of 1) being under \$7,000 and the highest (a code of 7) being \$38,000 or more. The income indicator is based on student reports made when they were seniors in high school, and is therefore imperfect. Nevertheless, these student-reported estimates have been shown to be quite close to verified (parent-reported) data on annual income in the HSB sample (see NORC, 1983).

There are eight indicators in the model relating to the academic characteristics of the college attenders. The indicator for cognitive competence is the HSB Base-Year Test Composite score, an equally weighted composite of scores on tests assessing competence in vocabulary, reading, and mathematics. For all seniors (college attending and non-attenders), the weighted mean of the composite test item is 50 and the quartile break between the top and second quartiles falls at 56.44. The HSB tests are termed "cognitive" by their designers and analysts, and are aimed at assessing a broad range of student characteristics, including basic intellectual skills, achievement, developed ability, and scholastic aptitude (e.g. , see NORC, 1983; ETS, 1985). As such, the tests are somewhat more broadly framed than the basic SAT or ACT tests, which are less concerned with student achievement. Nevertheless, for brevity, the indicator is hereafter termed "tested ability" in this chapter.

The indicator of high school grades is based on a self-report; there are eight categories (1= "mostly below D" through 8= "mostly As"). The indicator for high school curriculum track is a dummy, where 1 = an academic (college preparatory) curricular track, and 0 = a vocational or general curricular track.[4] The next four indicators of students' academic characteristics relate to their participation in high school student government, a departmental or preprofessional club, journalism (the student newspaper or yearbook), and drama or debate. Each of these four indicators is in dummy form (0 = no, 1 = yes). The final indicator of students' academic characteristics relates to the students' educational expectations as high school seniors. This indicator is coded

on a nine-point scale, ranging from 1 = "less than high school graduation" through 9 = a "Ph.D. , M.D., or other advanced professional
degree."

FINDINGS

Table 6.1 reveals that both family income and academic talent
are related to placement in the collegiate hierarchy. The top category
of family income, at least $38,000 per year, contained approximately
14 percent of the nation's 1980 high school seniors, whereas the lowest
category, income under $7,000, contained approximately 6 percent.
For the table, students were classified as having "exceptional ability"
if their scores were over one standard deviation above the test score
mean for the top ability quartile of all high school seniors, including
those not going to college. Students were classified as having "high
ability" if their scores placed them in the top quartile of all high
school seniors, and were classified as having "moderate ability" if their
scores placed them in the second quartile of all seniors (because of
the relationship between college attendance and senior year test scores,
about half of all college attenders are in the top ability quartile of
all seniors).

Lower-ability students were excluded from the Table 6.1 analysis,
since they do not usually attend elite colleges. Even among the included
students of moderate ability, very few entered the most selective institutions. This relationship between students' talent and their colleges' selectivity class is, of course, not surprising. What is more interesting is the
systematic relationship *within ability groupings* between income and
selectivity class. Among high-ability students, 28 percent of the highest-
income students attended moderately selective institutions and 16 percent attended the most selective institutions, for a total of 44 percent
enrolled in the two kinds of institutions. Within the same ability group,
however , only 35 percent of the lowest-income students attended such
institutions. The relationship of income and attendance patterns is even
stronger among the exceptional-ability students. In this special group,
more than one-third (35 percent) of the highest-income families sent
their offspring to the most selective schools, whereas only about a tenth
of the families with incomes below $16,000 sent their children to such
schools. Overall, the results of Table 6.1 strongly suggest that analyses
of attendance at the most selective institutions must focus only upon
talented students, and must consider the nature of SES influences in
some detail.

TABLE 6.1
Selectivity of College Attended, by Student Ability and Family Income Range

	Selectivity of College Attended		
	Non-Selective Colleges: Mean SAT ≤ 1000	Moderately Selective Colleges: Mean SAT 1001 to 1175	Highly Selective Colleges: Mean SAT ≥ 1176
Student Ability Level and Family Income Range	*(percent)*		
Exceptional-Ability Students			
$38,000 or more	33	32	35
$25,000 to $37,999	50	37	13
$20,000 to $24,999	50	35	15
$16,000 to $19,999	60	29	11
$12,000 to $15,999	42	50	8
$7,000 to $11,999	54	36	11
Under $7,000	*	*	*
High-Ability Students			
$38,000 or more	56	28	16
$25,000 to $37,999	63	32	6
$20,000 to $24,999	71	25	5
$16,000 to $19,999	77	20	3
$12,000 to $15,999	74	24	2
$7,000 to $11,999	76	21	3
Under $7,000	64	33	2
Moderate-Ability Students			
$38,000 or more	79	21	0
$25,000 to $37,999	91	8	1
$20,000 to $24,999	88	12	0
$16,000 to $19,999	90	10	0
$12,000 to $15,999	94	4	1
$7,000 to $11,999	90	10	0
Under $7,000	86	14	0

Note: Table 6.1 data are for white college attenders only, within the various ability group-ings and income ranges. Each cell contains the percentage of a row attending a college in the selectivity class noted. For example, the uppermost cell on the right side indicates that 35 percent of the "exceptional ability," highest-income students attended the most selec-tive institutions. Seniors in the HSB sample were placed in ability quartiles on the basis of the scores of all 1980 U.S. high school seniors, including those who did not attend college. No data are presented here for nonattenders or for college attenders scoring below the median test score for high school seniors (i.e., falling into the third or fourth ability quar-tile). "Exceptional-ability" students are those having an HSB cognitive test score above 65 (approximately one standard deviation above the test score mean for top quartile seniors). "High-ability" students are those who had scored in the top quartile, and "moderate-ability" students are those who had scores in the second quartile. College selec-tivity is indexed by average SAT scores of entering freshmen. Percentages are rounded. Cells marked '*' are in a row category which contains too few cases (N = 7) for interpre-tation. All other rows contain at least 25 cases. See text for details.

To assess this matter further, linear multiple regressions were run with selectivity as the dependent variable, both for all students and for high-ability students alone (as before, high ability was indicated by a student's having test scores in the top quartile of all high school seniors). Table 6.2 presents these results. The differences between the two regressions are not great, but do suggest that the process of college matching is somewhat distinctive among the especially able. High school grades and family income appear to have somewhat greater impact among the high-ability students than among the larger group of all college attenders.[5] For each of these factors, both the metric and standardized coefficients were greater among the high-ability students.

TABLE 6.2
Influences on Selectivity of College Attended: Linear Regressions

Independent Variable	Coefficients for All Attenders (N = 1,879)		Coefficients for High-Ability Attenders (N = 964)	
	Metric	Standard	Metric	Standard
Female	-7.41	-.03	-4.20	-.02
Father's Education	2.44	.06*	3.58	.07*
Mother's Education	3.21	.06**	3.71	.07*
Family Income	5.67	.07***	9.44	.11**
Family Size	.51	.01	2.18	.02
Tested Ability	3.86	.23***	9.12	.24***
H.S. Grades	7.69	.08***	14.05	.12***
H.S. Academic Track	26.79	.11***	36.32	.11***
H.S. Student Government	16.92	.06**	20.49	.07*
H.S. Departmental or Preprofessional Club	-7.16	-.03	-15.26	-.05
H.S. Journalism	4.57	.02	4.05	.01
H.S. Drama or Debate	-2.23	-.01	-8.19	-.03
Educational Expectations	11.28	.15***	18.16	.17***
Intercept	499.82	—	40.62	—
R-square	.27***		.27***	

Note: Data are for white college attenders only. Students were classified as "high ability" when their HSB test scores placed them in the top ability quartile relative to the nation's other high school seniors of 1980. Metric and standardized regression coefficients are reported. *** = $p \leq .001$, ** = $p \leq .01$, * = $p \leq .05$.

As discussed earlier, however, much of the institutional selectivity range is irrelevant to an analysis of elite college entry. Because only a small minority of even the most able enter the nation's most selective institutions, a categorization based on a selectivity *cutoff*, rather than the entire selectivity continuum, seems appropriate. In support of this approach, Table 6.3 suggests that those attending the most selective institutions are distinctive from other youth in certain ways not likely to be captured in linear regressions. For example, the table suggests that students attending institutions with selectivity levels over 1,175 are appreciably more advantaged financially than other students. There is also a lesser break in parental education levels at the same point. Academic factors appear linearly related to the selectivity of institution attended, but the high school activities data show at least one break of the kind noted above: notably higher numbers of students in the most selective institutions participated in high school student government.

TABLE 6.3
Characteristics of High-Ability Students in Various College Types

| | Selectivity of College Attended | | |
	Non-Selective Colleges: Mean SAT ≤ 1,000 (n 618)	Moderately Selective Colleges: Mean SAT 1,001 to 1,175 (n 277)	Highly Selective Colleges: Mean SAT > 1,175 (n 69)
Percent Female	51	40	45
Father's Education	5.66	6.67	7.63
Mother's Education	4.92	5.73	6.24
Family Income	5.05	5.34	6.06
Family Size	2.48	2.32	2.29
Tested Ability	60.96	62.68	64.71
H.S. Grades	6.80	7.14	7.60
Percent in H.S. Academic Track	74	90	91
Percent in H.S. Student Govt.	20	31	50
Percent in H.S. Departmental or Preprofessional Club	32	30	27
Percent in H.S. Journalism	26	35	42
Percent in H.S. Drama or Debate	23	26	30
Educational Expectations	7.25	7.82	8.40

Note: Data are indicator means unless otherwise indicated. Data are for white students in the top ability quartile relative to the nation's other high school seniors of 1980 (N = 964).

The breaks in the data of Table 6.3 are not dramatic, but they seem important enough to encourage the strategy of categorizing selectivity outcomes for multivariate regression analysis (see Table 6.4). Logistic regression was employed for this final analysis because the dichotomous, highly skewed nature of the dependent variable of concern (attendance at an elite college versus attendance at another college) precluded following the more traditional multiple linear regression approach. The partial derivative values reported in the second column for each model in Table 6.4 may be interpreted as indicating the change in the probability of attendance at an elite college that is associated with a unit change in the independent variable in question (evaluated at the mean attendance probability, i.e., 7 percent).[6]

TABLE 6.4
Influences on Attendance at Highly Selective Colleges:
Logistic Regression for High-Ability Attenders

Independent Variable	Background Model Logistic Coefficient	$\overline{dP}/dX$	Full Model Logistic Coefficient	$\overline{dP}/dX$
Female	-.07	-.00	-.11	-.01
Father's Education	.15*	.01	.08	.01
Mother's Education	.05	.00	.02	.00
Family Income	.41**	.03	.44***	.03
Family Size	-.06	-.00	.03	.00
Tested Ability	—	—	.19***	.01
H.S. Grades	—	—	.55**	.04
H.S. Academic Track	—	—	.06	.00
H.S. Student Government	—	—	.81**	.05
H.S. Departmental or Preprofessional Club	—	—	-.67*	-.04
H.S. Journalism	—	—	.23	.01
H.S. Drama or Debate	—	—	-.17	-.01
Educational Expectations	—	—	.79***	.05
Intercept	-6.07	—	-28.20	—
R-square	.08***		.25***	
% Concordant Predictions	75%		87%	

Note: A "highly selective" college is defined as a college with average freshman SAT scores greater than 1,175. Data are for white students in the top ability quartile relative to the nation's other high school seniors of 1980 (N=964). Logistic coefficients and the partial derivative at the mean elite college attendance rate of 0.07 are reported here (see text for details). *** = $p \le .001$, ** = $p \le .01$, * = $p \le .05$.

Table 6.4 presents the results of two logistic regressions. The sample for both is composed of high-ability students only. Both regressions discriminate between attenders at highly selective institutions (i.e., attenders at any institution with average freshman SAT scores above 1,175) and all other students. One regression (the full model) assesses direct effects of all factors in the model, including background and academic factors. The second regression (the background model) uses the causal logic of path analysis, transformed for logistic regression format (see Marini, 1984; Hanushek and Jackson, 1977): the total (direct and indirect) effects of background characteristics on college destinations are estimated by an equation containing only those characteristics. By contrasting the results from the background model and the full model, it is possible to discern the total influence of ascriptive factors.

The full model regression for attendance at a highly selective college indicates that only one ascriptive (nonmeritocratic) characteristic is directly significant, beyond the effects of the various academic factors: family income played an especially positive role in attendance at such schools. The derived coefficient of 0.03 suggests that, all else being equal, students from the top income category (income over $38,000) were more than 20 percent more likely to attend an elite school than otherwise similar students from the bottom income category. A similar difference is apparent in the purely descriptive data of Table 6.1, suggesting that the addition of academic factors as controls does not appreciably dampen the effects of income in this special sample.

Test scores and grades were also influential, especially the former.[7] For every gain of one point on the HSB test battery (mean for all high school seniors = 50, top quartile break = 56.44), a student's odds of attendance at an elite school, increased 1 percent. Among the activity factors, as suggested by Table 6.3, student government participation alone was positively associated with entry into selective schools. Having had such participation increased attendance chances by 5 percent at the mean. On the other hand, participation in departmental or preprofessional clubs decreased attendance chances by 4 percent. Educational expectations apparently played a major role in college placement, perhaps suggesting a human capital interpretation: students with high expectations may choose to attend those schools most likely to certify their talents in the competition for graduate and professional school placement.

Overall, the full model explained 25 percent of the variance in elite college entry. (The proportion of concordant predictions, a useful index of model precision in logistic regression, was 87 percent.) In this model, the direct role of ascriptive factors, with the notable exception of income, was minimal. To what extent is the process indirectly influenced by the ascriptive background factors, however? In other words, how do background ascriptive factors affect academic factors, which in turn affect elite college entry? The results for the background model suggest that the total effects of background factors are substantial, though they do not dominate the process of institutional placement. The explained variance for this model was 8 percent, under half of that totaled by the full model with academic factors included, but 75 percent of the model's predictions were concordant with observed outcomes. Once again, it was income that dominated the results, at a level similar to its effects in the full model. Thus, income's effects seem to be almost entirely direct, rather than indirect via influences on the accumulation of secondary school academic credentials. The one sign of indirect effects in the results came from fathers education, which was of minor significance in the background model but not directly influential in the full model.

These findings support the charge that entry into elite institutions is more than a purely meritocratic matter of having greater talent or achievements than other students. Independent of academic factors, upper-income youth, for whatever reasons, were especially likely in 1980-81 enter into America's elite colleges. The findings also suggest, as hypothesized earlier, that there are nonlinearities in the determination of institutional entry. The factors that separate students attending institutions with different selectivity levels, *across all institutions and all college-attending students*, are somewhat different from the factors that separate students attending institutions with average SAT scores over 1,175 from other students. In other words, the relative importance of the various student characteristics changes somewhat as one begins to focus more clearly upon higher-ability students and upon decisions to attend schools at the higher levels of selectivity.

IMPLICATIONS

As educational attainments continue to rise in the society, the significance of stratification among postsecondary institutions continues to rise in concert (Karabel, 1972). In its attention to the recruitment and channelling of students into the collegiate elite, this chapter provides new information on how the odds of benefitting from a prestigious institution are distributed.

As is usual, some limitations of the analysis should be noted. The HSB information on private secondary school attendance was insufficient for this analysis, and racial minorities were excluded because of sample limitations. Furthermore, the sample contained only 69 students attending the most elite colleges, institutional selectivity had to be used as a proxy for elite status, and the definition of elite status was fairly inclusive. What is more, the process of college choice among the brightest students is clearly far from being strictly a matter of student merit and background socioeconomic status. Other factors are involved. These unidentified factors no doubt reflect matters of chance, geography, misinformation, programmatic offerings, personality, and culture (for intriguing reviews of this literature, see Hossler, 1984; Litten et al., 1983;

Rosenfeld, 1980; and Olson and Rosenfeld, 1984a,b). Even so, the findings sharpen our understanding of the undergraduate hierarchy and student placement within it.

As argued in the introductory section, if the elite sector of higher education has some of the characteristics of a distinctive "sector," like the private sector of secondary education, one might expect its students to follow distinctive paths to entry. Nonetheless, although limited by relying on selectivity cutoffs to indicate elite status, the findings here suggest that the boundaries of the sector and its student populace are far from clear. One can make certain statistical distinctions among high-ability students in schools with selectivity at an average SAT level of 1,000 or less, between 1,000 and 1,175, and more than 1,175, but a dramatic series of important distinctions in student characteristics does not appear at a certain level of selectivity. The differences among the three groups are generally more linear than categorical in nature: that is, the students in the most selective sector are somewhat brighter, more accomplished, more ambitious, and higher in SES than those in the moderately selective institutions, who in turn are somewhat brighter, more accomplished, more ambitious, and higher in SES than those in the nonselective institutions. Although there are certainly other ways to identify a distinctive elite sector, the approach adopted here seems to offer only limited promise.

Moreover, even though the affluent have relatively greater odds of attending elite schools, it should be recognized that rather small numbers of the nation's most able youth enter the most prestigious colleges. Only 7 percent of the highly able youth in the sample attended the most prestigious institutions. Thus, it seems that only a handful of these talented youth will be in a position to trade on a prestigious degree. Even among exceptionally able students from the highest-income families, only about one-third attended the most selective institutions. In light of these numbers, it is evident that the elite colleges can only be facilitators of life chances, not major reproducers of the class structure of the society.

Despite the small numbers involved, the analysis specifies how social background is related to collegiate selectivity and, more particularly, elite college entry. Parental education levels played no direct role, and only a modest indirect role, in entry into a highly selective college among high-ability students. Parental income did play a significant role, however, especially for entry into the top institutions by the most able students. Among higher-ability youth, the lower-income students tended to avoid the most elite colleges in favor of relatively nonselective institutions. By contrast, among all students, including those of moderate ability, the effects of income on selectivity of college entered were less important. Since the most selective schools are usually somewhat more costly than others in the U.S. system (Hearn, 1988), and since the income effects found here were largely direct, there is a strong suggestion that the barriers to elite college entry are more material than social. Family income seems to channel some highly able youth into higher-cost schools and other highly able youth into schools in the lower-cost sectors. In the absence of other SES effects, especially effects of parental education, the advantages of higher family income do not appear to represent a subtle, deep-rooted socialization effect but instead a rather more immediate matter of material resources, and perhaps of information concerning student financial aid offerings. Overall, therefore, the factors predominantly influencing high-ability students' behaviors regarding elite college entry are not the deeply rooted ascriptive factors some might expect. Indeed, the social structures influencing entry into elite colleges appear to be largely meritocratic in nature, supplemented by some notable advantages extended toward the offspring of families having greater material resources.

Of course, the possibility of more covert inequalities exists. For example, the positive effects of student government participation might be interpreted in the cultural capital terms of Bourdieu (1977). More fundamentally, the direct advantages associated with high test scores, grades, and academic expectations can be viewed as a result of powerful class-based socialization and channelling (Bowles and Gintis, 1976), even among the high-ability college attenders. Although the total effects of background factors were relatively modest in the analysis, they are worth further attention. A number of possible hypotheses flow from such an interpretation of the results, even if testing some of these ideas may be impossible using the currently available data sets and the recursive analytic techniques employed here. From such a perspective, the toughest challenge of further research in college destinations may be untangling, through qualitative, quantitative, or eclectic methodological approaches, a web of causation cloaked under an outwardly efficient meritocratic system and extending far back in time. In the end, the process of postsecondary student choice and institutional selection is just one part of a long stream of attainment-related decisions and events in young people's lives. Analyzing it independently of the earlier twists and turns of that stream inevitably leads back to questions of first causes.

NOTES

*The research reported in the chapter was partially supported by a research grant to the author from the Spencer Foundation. Support was also provided by the University of Minnesota, in the form of a single-quarter research leave and separate grants for computing and faculty research. The author wishes to thank Jeff Owings of the U.S. Department of Education for his help with the High School and Beyond data base; Susan Urahn and Mary Peterson for their help with the data analysis; and Melissa Anderson, Bob Fenske, Greg Jackson, Paul Kingston, Sam Peng, and Richard Richardson for their insightful suggestions and criticisms.

1. This point is not new. In perceptive articles on elite college effects on attainment, Tinto (1980) and Useem and Karabel (1986; Chapter 8 in this volume) have described their findings of nonlinear effects of college quality on career entry and progression.

2. Asians, Hispanics, and blacks were dropped from the analysis because of data limitations for the college attenders in the sample. Weighted, the HSB sample for whites is reasonably representative of the nation's white college attenders from the high school class of 1980. By focussing only upon whites, the study gained a clearer picture of attendance causation for those students traditionally associated with elite higher education. The unfortunate trade-off was an absence of useful findings on a population whose attendance at such institutions seems threatened in the 1980s (see Evans, 1987).

3. It is worth noting that, of the six public institutions meeting the SAT score cutoff, only two are state supported (the other four are federally-supported service academies). Even more interesting is the fact that both of the state-supported schools are located in Virginia: the University of Virginia and the College of William and Mary.

4. Ideally, we would be able in this analysis to consider information on whether or not the student attended an "elite" secondary institution, such as Groton. Unfortunately, as noted by Falsey and Heyns (1984) and many others, the HSB data set does not contain enough students attending such institutions to support analyses of the effects of elite secondary schools on college attendance patterns.

5. Separate analyses were run for minorities, bearing in mind the previously mentioned caveat about the HSB minority sample. The findings of these analyses hint that Asian ancestry may generally have a positive influence on the selectivity of the institution attended.

6. As Hanushek and Jackson (1977) and others have noted, there are potentially serious problems of bias and inconsistency in linear regression results for dichotomous dependent variable indicators. A probabilistic maximum likelihood estimation (MLE) approach is often superior in such circumstances. However, a logistic regression coefficient has limited interpretability, and cannot be com-

pared directly to a linear regression coefficient. In the logic of logistic regression, the effects of an independent variable are dependent upon where in the continuum of outcome values it is evaluated. For example, among lower-income students relatively unlikely to attend elite schools, a difference of 10 in test scores may more powerfully affect the probability of attending such a school than a similar difference among higher-income students. To be able to make inferences about the effects of an independent variable in logistic regression, one must take the partial derivative of the dependent variable (p) at a particular value with respect to the independent variable (X) of interest. The following formula from Hanushek and Jackson (1977) can be employed:

$$dP/dX = B(X) \, (P) \, (1 - P)$$
where B(X) is the logistic coefficient for X

In practice, analysts have generally summarized the various effects of an independent variable by concentrating on the effects of the independent variable at the mean likelihood outcome, that is, the mean sample value of P (e.g., see Marini, 1984). This approach was taken here. The weighted mean value of the focal outcome variable (attendance at a highly selective institution) is 0.07: that is, only 7 percent of the top-ability students in the sample attended such a college. When P is set to 0.07 in the above formula, the partial derivative is equal to 0.065 (i. e., 0.07 x 0.93) of the logistic regression coefficient B for each independent variable.

7. Perhaps the reason that test scores proved in this analysis to be powerful explanatory factors for selective college attendance, contrary to the claims of some admissions officers, may lie in the special nature of the HSB test battery. As noted before, the SAT and ACT assessment instruments focus more clearly on issues of basic aptitude, whereas the HSB battery focussed an a blend of aptitude and achievement concerns in its design.

REFERENCES

Alexander K., and B. Eckland. High school context and college selectivity: Institutional constraints in educational stratification. *Social Forces,* 1977, 56:166-188.

Alwin, D.F. College effects on educational and occupational attainments. *American Sociological Review,* 1974, 39: 210-23.

Anderson, C.A., M.J. Bowman, and V. Tinto. *Where Colleges Are and Who Attends.* New York: McGraw-Hill, 1972.

Astin, A.W., K.C. Green, W.S. Korn, and M. Schalit. *The American Freshman: National Norms for Fall, 1986.* Los Angeles: Higher Education Research Institute, 1986.

Astin, A.W., and L.C. Solmon. Measuring academic quality: An interim report. *Change,* September, 1979, 48-51.

Ben-David, J. *Trends in American Higher Education.* Chicago: University of Chicago Press, 1974.

Bourdieu, P. Cultural reproduction and social reproduction. In J. Karabel and A.H. Halsey (eds.), *Power and Ideology in Education,* 487-511. Oxford: New York, 1977.

Bowles, S., and H. Gintis. *Schooling in Capitalist America.* New York: Basic Books, 1976.

Brubacher, J.S., and W. Rudy. *Higher Education in Transition.* New York: Harper and Row, 1976.

Carnegie Council on Policy Studies in Higher Education. *Three Thousand Futures: The Next Twenty Years for Higher Education.* San Francisco: Jossey-Bass, 1980.

Clark, Burton R. *The Higher Education System.* Berkeley: University of California Press, 1983.

Coleman, J.S., with E.Q. Campbell, C.J. Hobson, J. McPartland, A.M. Mood, F. Weinfield, and R.L. York. *Equality of Educational Opportunity.* Washington, D.C.: U.S. Government Printing Office, 1966.

Coleman, J.S., T. Hoffer, and S. Kilgore. *High School Achievement: Public, Catholic and Private Schools Compared.* New York: Basic Books, 1982.

Cookson, P.W., and C. H. Persell. *Preparing for Power: America's Elite Boarding Schools.* New York: Basic Books, 1985.

Educational Testing Service (ETS). *Contractor Report Factors Associated with Decline of Test Scores of High School Seniors, 1972 to 1980 - A Study of Excellence in High School Education: Educational Policies, School Quality, and Student Outcomes.* Washington, D.C.: U.S. Government Printing Office, 1985.

El-Khawas, E. *Better Information for Student Choice.* Boulder, Colorado: Education Commission of the States, 1977.

Evans, David L. Self-help at its best. *Newsweek,* March 16, 1987, page 8.

Falsey, B., and B. Heyns. The college channel: Public and private schools revisited. *Sociology of Education,* 1984, 57: 111-122.

Fife, J.D. *Applying the Goals of Student Financial Aid.* AAHE/ERIC Higher Education Research Report No. 10, 1975. Washington, D.C.: American Association for Higher Education, 1975.

Hammack, Floyd M. Private school graduates and college attendance: Patterns of transition. Paper presented at the annual meeting of the Association for the Study of Higher Education. , Washington, D.C., March 1981.

Hanushek, E.A., and J.A. Jackson. *Statistical Methods for Social Scientists.* Orlando: Academic Press, 1977.

Hearn, J. C. The relative roles of academic, ascribed, and socioeconomic characteristics in college destinations. *Sociology of Education,* 1984, 57: 22-30.

―――. Attendance at higher-cost colleges: Ascribed, socioeconomic, and academic influences on student enrollment patterns. *Economics of Education Review,* 1988, 7: 65-76.

Hearn, J.C., and S. Urahn. Alternative approaches to understanding postsecondary attendance patterns in the 1980's. Paper presented at the joint meeting of the Association for the Study of Higher Education and Division J of the American Educational Research Association, San Francisco, October, 1984.

Heyns, B. Social selection and stratification within schools. *American Journal of Sociology,* 1974, 79: 1434-1451.

Higher Education Research Institute (HERI). *Tape File Documentation: HERI SAT File with Additional Institutional Data.* Los Angeles: Higher Education Research Institute, 1984.

Hossler, Don. *Enrollment Management: An Integrated Approach.* New York: College Board, 1984.

Hurn, C. *The Limits and Possibilities of Schooling.* Boston: Allyn and Bacon, 1978.

Karabel, Jerome. Community colleges and social stratification: Submerged class conflict in American higher education. *Harvard Educational Review,* 1972, 42: 521-562.

Karabel, J., and A.W. Astin. Social class, academic ability, and college "quality." *Social Forces,* 1975, 53: 381-398.

Kingston, Paul W., and J.C. Smart. Chapter 8 in this volume.

Klitgaard, R. *Choosing Elites: Selecting the "Best and Brightest" at Top Universities and Elsewhere.* New York: Basic Books, 1985.

Kohn, M.G., C.F. Manski, and D.S. Mundel. *An Empirical Investigation of Factors Which Influence College-Going Behavior.* Rand Report R-1470-NSF. Santa Monica, California: Rand Corporation, 1974.

Litten, L.H., D. Sullivan, and D.L. Brodigan. *Applying Market Research in College Admissions.* New York: College Board, 1983.

Marini, M.M. The order of events in the transition to adulthood. *Sociology of Education,* 1984, 57: 63-84.

Meyer, John. The effects of education as an institution. *American Journal of Sociology,* 1977, 83: 55-77.

_____. Types of explanation in the sociology of education. In John Richardson (ed.), *Handbook of Theory and Research for the Sociology of Education,* 341-359. New York: Greenwood, 1986.

Mills, C. Wright. *The Power Elite.* New York: Oxford, 1959.

National Center for Education Statistics (NCES). *Data Base Documentation for Institutional Characteristics of Colleges and Universities, 1980-81 (IC Survey HEGIS XV).* Washington, D.C.: U.S. Government Printing Office, 1983.

_____. College attendance after high school. *Statistical Highlight.* Washington, D.C.: U.S. Government Printing Office, 1984a.

_____. *The Condition of Education.* Washington, D.C.: U.S. Government Printing Office, 1984b.

_____. Trends in college enrollment. *Statistical Highlight.* Washington, D.C.: U.S. Government Printing Office, 1984c.

National Opinion Research Center (NORC). *Contractor Report, High School and Beyond, 1980 Senior Cohort First Follow-up (1982), Data File User's Manual.* Washington, D.C.: U.S. Government Printing Office, 1983.

New York Times. Colleges in U.S. need overhaul, study contends. November 2, 1986.

Olson, L., and R. Rosenfeld. Parents and the process of gaining access to student financial aid for higher education. *Journal of Higher Education,* 1984a, 55:455-480.

_____. Parents, students, and knowledge of college costs. Paper presented at the annual meeting of the American Sociological Association, San Antonio, Texas, September 1984b.

Peng , S.S. Changes in postsecondary education: 1972-1980. Paper presented at the annual meeting of the American Educational Research Association, Montreal, March 1983.

Peng, S.S., J.P. Bailey, Jr., and B.K. Eckland. Access to higher education: Results from the National Longitudinal Study of the High School Class of 1972. *Educational Researcher,* 1977, 6: 3-7.

Pierson, George W. *The Education of America's Leaders.* New York: Praeger, 1969.

Rosenfeld, R. *Postsecondary Education Plans and Choices: Review of the Literature and Design for Analysis of the Parents' Data.* Report for the High School and Beyond study to the National Center for Education Statistics (NCES) and the NCES Office of Evaluation and Dissemination, under NCES Contract No. 300-78-0208. Chicago: National Opinion Research Center, 1980.

Rosenfeld, R., and J.C. Hearn. Sex differences in the significance of economic resources for choosing and attending a college. In P. Perun (ed.), *The Undergraduate Woman: Issues in Educational Equity,* 127-157. Lexington, Massachusetts: Lexington (Heath) , 1982.

Rubinson, R. Class formation, politics, and institutions: Schooling in the United States. *American Journal of Sociology,* 1986, 92: 519-48.

Sewell, W.H. Inequality of opportunity for higher education. *American Sociological Review,* 1971, 36: 793-809.

Smart, John C. College effects on occupational status attainment. *Research in Higher Education,* 1986, 24: 73-95.

Solmon, L. The definition of college quality and its impact on earnings. *Explorations in Economic Research,* 1975, 2: 537-87.

Thomas, G.E., K.L. Alexander, and B.K. Eckland. Access to higher education: The importance of race, sex, social class, and academic credentials. *School Review,* 1979, 87: 133-56.

Tinto, V. College origins and patterns of status attainment. *Sociology of Work and Occupations,* 1980, 7: 457-86.

Trusheim, Dale, and James Crouse. Effects of college prestige on men's occupational status and income. *Research in Higher Education,* 1981, 14: 283-304.

Useem, Michael, and Jerome Karabel. Pathways to top corporate management. *American Sociological Review,* 1986, 51: 184-200.

U.S. News and World Report. America's best colleges. November 25, 1985, 46-51.

Veysey, L. *The Emergence of the American University.* Chicago: University of Chicago Press, 1965.

Weisbrod, B., and P. Karpoff. Monetary returns to college education, student ability, and college quality. *Review of Economics and Statistics,* 1968, 5: 491-97.

PAUL WILLIAM KINGSTON
JOHN C. SMART

Chapter Seven

The Economic Pay-Off
of Prestigious Colleges

Even as annual costs approach $20,000, record numbers of high school students apply to the nation's elite undergraduate institutions—vivid testimony to the firmly held popular conviction that graduation from these schools makes a difference to life chances. To the parents and students who are willing to bear such costs and anxiously await admissions decisions, the appeal of these schools is not simply the intellectual quality of their educational programs. Economic fates are seen linked to acceptance letters. It is believed that where one goes has financial consequences: elite education is translated into privileged economic status. Whether because the elite institutions provide better access to desirable positions and a certification of being the right sort, or actually better training for lucrative careers and postgraduate education, the economic benefits are perceived as substantial.

Students are paying much more for this education than ever before. For all the concern about the middle class being priced out of higher education, costs at *public* institutions have remained fairly flat in real terms, yet the costs at the elite schools have risen sharply, far in excess of the inflation rate or purchasing power. Presumably, families believe that the extra investment promises a desirable return.

The continuing appeal of the elite institutions is particularly remarkable in light of recent developments in American higher education. Nationwide, students have deserted liberal arts programs for business and other job-oriented studies in the belief that employers want such practical training. Yet, for the most part, the elite schools remain firmly committed to liberal arts. As careerist as students at elite colleges may be, their curricula have been little affected by these impulses, and students have "bought" this traditional commitment. One does not go to Princeton to study business.

One apprised of the social science research on this matter, however, might counsel against this investment—at least if the aim is a *monetary* return. In summarizing the literature (much of it quite technically sophisticated), this investment counselor would indicate that institutional differences have little or no effect on income or other measures of career attainment. In saying this, the counselor would mean that graduation from a higher-quality institution is not substantially rewarded. Although graduates of higher-quality institutions do have demonstrably more successful careers, their greater success largely reflects greater intellectual and personal endowments and advantaged family backgrounds. The advice to a bright affluent high school student would be: go to college and graduate, but don't worry about where you go because you are likely to do as well in any case.

Our intention is to evaluate the evidentiary base for this advice. We will examine the analytical shortcomings of previous research and present some findings suggesting that the common wisdom, not sociological analysis, has considerable merit: where one goes does matter. As we will make clear, our own analyses have their own shortcomings, but the accumulated evidence points to a credentialling process in which certain prestigious degrees are distinctly rewarded. These findings raise theoretical issues that are addressed in the final section.

PREVIOUS RESEARCH

Early studies indicated through bivariate analysis that the graduates of prestigious colleges had greater career success than other graduates (Havemann and West, 1952), but such analyses do not establish that an elite credential in itself provided economic advantages. The brightest, most affluent, and perhaps most motivated students were disproportionately likely to graduate from the top institutions, and thus the economic advantage of the elite college graduates might be attributed to either the schools or the individual characteristics of the graduate from these schools (Foster and Rodgers, 1979).

Using a variety of data sets, subsequent analyses therefore attempted to specify the net effect of college quality on earnings and occupational status. This generally meant running multiple regression models that included independent variables measuring family background and other sociodemographic characteristics, intellectual ability and academic performance, and personality traits, along with various indicators of institutional quality. Though the impact varied somewhat across data sets, the quality measures uniquely accounted for a few percent or so of the explained variance in the models of attainment. This finding generally seems to prompt a dismissal of the significance of institutional distinctions on life chances.[1]

Many of these analyses suffer a confusion as to what they are about: the fact that measures of college quality (generally measured as some continuous variable—e.g., expenditures per student or mean SAT of the student body) explain rather little variance across the full range of income does *not* mean that *all* distinctions among schools are inconsequential. Within the logic of the linear assumptions of multiple regression, most of the research has established that measures of college quality, across their entire range, are quite modestly related to measures of career attainment, across their entire range. (See Hearn, Chapter 6 in this volume, for a similar point.) Although informative, such analyses do not directly address whether going to Princeton (and the few similar institutions) instead of Podunk makes a difference. Any distinctive impacts of small sets of schools (e.g., the Ivy League) are inevitably obscured in the coefficients for quality—in effect, the *average* impact of quality differences throughout the academic hierarchy. It is entirely conceivable that differences throughout most of the academic hierarchy are inconsequential for life chances—thus a small overall effect for "quality"—but that going to an elite school does make a difference. In other words, going to Central State College instead of Northeast State University may not matter, but going to Princeton may—"holding constant" the personal characteristics of the students at these schools.

By including categorical measures of institutional quality or prestige, some analyses avoid the technical limitations just noted. However, in several frequently cited studies using this approach, the samples do not adequately represent the graduates of elite private universities and colleges, the institutions that are commonly thought to make a difference in life chances. For example, using a subsample of the Panel Study of Income Dynamics, Trusheim and Crouse (1981) analyze the effects of eight prestige categories (entered as dummy variables in multiple regression models), but their top category, high prestige private, includes only ten cases, and this category incorporates the three highest categories in the prestige scale on which their analysis is based. Not only is the eliteness of this category questionable, but the predicted (net) income of respondents in this category is lower than that of respondents in a less prestigious category. Although the coefficients for all prestige categories, including the top category, are statistically insignificant, this finding flies in the face of other research and calls into question the representativeness of those ten cases.

Alwin's (1974) detailed analysis is also based on an inadequate survey—a sample of the Wisconsin high school class of 1957—to assess the impact of elite institutions. Virtually all of the respondents in this survey went to a college in Wisconsin; graduates of the elite eastern institutions appear unrepresented. Alwin does show some modest net differences in career attainments of the graduates of different types of institutions, but any distinctive role of the national elite institutions is not considered.

This review suggests, then, that we need (1) categorical measures of institutional differences with especially fine distinctions at the top of the hierarchy because a relatively few prestigious institutions are widely perceived to have distinctly consequential effects; (2) samples with adequate representation of respondents from the most prestigious institutions; and (3) appropriate statistical control for factors affecting career attainment in order to show any net effects of degree prestige.

To somewhat varying degrees, the three analyses that follow meet these requirements. The designations of elite status are perhaps not as fine-grained as desirable, and inferences of prestige effects rest on the always questionable assumption that all other relevant factors have been held constant. However, by looking at the experiences of three separate cohorts, we can make a good case that going to Princeton instead of Podunk has made a financial difference throughout the postwar years.

We first look at the experiences of a recent cohort of college graduates to show the current impact of degree prestige. We then back up historically and consider the fates through mid-career of a cohort educated just after World War II and the early career experiences of the college class of 1961.

RECENT GRADUATES: THE EARLY CAREER

To summarize our findings at the outset, in recent years graduation from an elite institution does count, even in the early stages of a career. Elite institutions not only disproportionately channel graduates into lucrative careers but also confer direct benefits on graduates independent of their other personal characteristics.

Data for this analysis were obtained from respondents to the 1971 and 1980 Cooperative Institutional Research Program (CIRP). All respondents— 10,326 students from 487 different colleges and universities— completed the survey on entering college in fall 1971. This survey obtained information on students' family backgrounds, high school experiences, occupational aspirations at the time, and other personal characteristics. In 1980 respondents were resurveyed to collect data on their collegiate experiences and their subsequent educational and occupational achievements. (See Astin, 1982, and Smart, 1986, for details of the sampling scheme and design.)

With this design, we can control for the effects of personal factors that existed prior to attendance at college (e.g., early aspirations) without having to rely on reconstructions that may be distorted by the passing of time. The limited span between the survey dates means, however, that the respondents with a bachelor's degree could have had at most five years of posteducation work experience. Thus, this analysis is necessarily restricted to analyzing the early career of college graduates. This restriction may lead us to underestimate the long-term benefits of an elite degree: economists in the human capital tradition argue that the full value of a job includes the "pay" of on-the-job training, and to the extent that the prestigiously credentialled get jobs with valuable training (or access to lucrative career ladders), analysis of early-career salaries may understate the financial benefit of elite credentials. On the other hand, it is conceivable that the effects of degree prestige are relatively pronounced in the early career as employers use credentials to sort job entrants, but these effects may become muted later on as employees become rewarded for their individual performance.

In this analysis we focus on the 2,213 respondents who attended a single undergraduate institution, had completed no more than a bachelor's degree, were employed full-time in 1980, and had complete data on all variables included in the regression models.[2]

Measuring Quality

As argued in the introductory chapter of this volume, there is no sharply demarcated hierarchy of quality in American higher education— or, indeed, even conceptual agreement about the meaning of quality. Our point here is not to resolve conceptual ambiguities, much less set out some definitive ranking scheme. Instead, reflecting the stratification procedures in the CIRP sample design, we created a seven-category schema based on control (public versus private) and selectivity: in effect, the average standardized test scores at a school.[3] In a rough sense this schema seems to correspond to rankings based on other criteria, but the cutting points are largely determined by the structure of the data set, not by conceptual rationale. Even so, we have distinguished a fairly small group at the top; most of the institutions, though not all, can reasonably lay claim to some genuine elite status. Our main intent is to see whether graduation from these top-ranked schools affects careers. The quality categories are the following.

Elite. These are the private universities and private nonsectarian colleges with combined SAT scores of 1,175 or more. Some 74 institutions met these criteria in 1968, and 42 of these participated in the 1971 survey. Included are four Ivy League institutions (Dartmouth, Pennsylvania, Princeton, and Yale), the Little Three colleges (Amherst, Wesleyan, and Williams), prominent technical schools (Cal Tech, Carnegie-Mellon, and RPI), three of the Seven Sisters (Vassar, Mount Holyoke, and Wellesley), private universities such as Northwestern, Johns Hopkins, Rice, and Tulane, and numerous small liberal arts colleges, such as Carleton, Colby, Davidson, and Dickinson.

This top category does not isolate the most elite segment of the higher-educational system: some Ivy League schools are mixed in with a fair number of institutions whose national reputations are far less prominent, whatever the quality of the educations they provide. Nonetheless, we are able to focus on a small and select group of graduates, a few percent at most of the college graduates in this cohort.

Private Highly Selective. These are the four-year and university private institutions with average SATs of about 1,025 to 1,175. Some 185 institutions met these criteria. A few examples are Lewis and Clark College, Hamline University, Manhattan College, Randolph Macon College, and Drake University.

Public Highly Selective. These are the public universities with average SATs of 1,100 or more and public colleges with SATs above 1,025—65 institutions. Included are such nationally prominent institutions as the University of North Carolina, the University of California -Berkeley, and the University of Michigan, as well as others like the University of Colorado, Framingham State College, and SUNY at Geneseo.

Private Medium Selectivity. These are the private institutions with average test scores approximately in the 950-1,025 range. Examples are Webster College, Upsala College, and the University of Dayton.

Public Medium Selectivity. Public institutions with test scores in the 950-1,099 range. Examples are Western Illinois University, the University of Delaware, and the University of North Dakota.

Private Low Selectivity and Public Low Selectivity. These two lowest categories include all other four-year institutions. Average board scores are below 1,000 (as are the average individual scores on these tests). CIRP data indicate that more than 800 institutions are included in these two categories; they account for almost half of total full-time, first-time freshmen enrollments at four-year institutions.

In our regression models each of these categories is entered as a dummy variable; the category *Public Low Selectivity* is the reference (excluded) category. With this technique (similar to Trusheim and Crouse, 1981) we can look for nonlinear relationships between degree prestige and career success.

Other Factors

At issue is whether degree prestige has any net effect on early career success. In the subsequent regression models we therefore entered a substantial set of variables that are related to both degree prestige and income:

Sociodemographic factors: race (white or other), sex, parental income in 1971 (i.e., on entrance to college), paternal and maternal education.

Precollegiate academic and personal characteristics: high school academic achievement (a three-item measure based on high school grade point average, class rank, and membership in a scholastic honor society), high school type (private-nonparochial or other), occupational aspirations on enrollment (a single item with 44 occupational codes converted to occupational status), and self-estimates of academic intellectual ability and drive to achieve or lead. (Whatever the accuracy of these assessments, they provide an indirect measure of self-image.)

College experiences: College grade point average and science major (yes/no).

Have we controlled for all possibly relevant factors? The question is unanswerable, but it is worth emphasizing that this set includes a standard set of ascribed characteristics related to socioeconomic status, measures of high school and college academic performance, as well as crude indicators of personality characteristics (prior to college) that would seemingly provide an advantage in the labor market. These equations, then, largely follow the specification suggested by the status attainment tradition (Jencks et al., 1979). Clearly, it would be desirable to include test scores (presumably a standardized measure of academic ability or aptitude), but they should be quite strongly correlated with school grades, a more direct indicator of actual knowledge and willingness to apply natural intellectual endowments. Moreover, grades are relatively visible indicators of ability: employees may look at grade point averages but are not inclined to ask for SATs.

It should also be recognized that we may have in a sense overcontrolled for relevant factors. The measure for occupational ambition and the indicators of personality were obtained prior to any substantial collegiate experience, therefore negating the possibility of any direct socialization effects of different kinds of institutions. However, students entering prestigious schools may know that such institutions are chartered to channel their students to the top, thus indirectly creating heightened aspirations and self-images among the entrants (Meyer, 1977). Some of the effects of college prestige on career success may be rooted in such anticipatory socialization mechanisms: students act and think in accord with the allocative roles of their institutions.

Our main indicator of career success is 1980 income. If money does not convey the full meaning of career success, it is a compelling and readily measurable dimension. Unfortunately, the CIRP income measure is precoded in twelve categories of varying increments. In our regression models we handled the difficulties posed by this limitation in two ways: (1) We created a dichotomous dependent variable indicating whether the respondent earned more than $20,000 in 1980.[4] This measure allows us to assess whether degree prestige affects the probability of being at the front of the race for high income. Those earning more than $20,000 were in the top fifth of our sample of full-time employed college graduates without an advanced degree. (2) We scored each respondent's income to the midpoint of the designated category. Since many of the categories represented $5,000 increments, this procedure is crude. Mean income for this cohort was $15,252 with a standard deviation of 6,062.

The Effects of Quality

The results presented in Table 7.1 indicate that going to an elite institution is rewarded in the early career.[5] The coefficient for elite institution in Equation 1 may be interpreted in this way: graduates of elite institutions have nearly a 15 percent greater chance of earning at least $20,000 than graduates of low selectivity public institutions after accounting for differences in family background, academic performance, and personality traits. And apparently the only institutional prestige distinction that makes any difference in reaching this income level is graduation from an elite institution. In itself, graduation from a school of any lesser prestige level does not improve prospects of earning at least $20,000.

In analyzing 1980 income as a continuous variable (Equations 2 and 3), we also see a distinctive pay-off to an elite degree. On average, the elite graduates earned almost $3,500 more than their counterparts from low selectivity institutions, an advantage that only partly reflected differences in their personal characteristics.

TABLE 7.1
The Effects of Undergraduate Type on Early Career Income

| | $20,000+ Income in 1980 | 1980 Income[c] | |
Institutional Type	Equation 1[a]	Equation 2[b]	Equation 3[a]
Elite	.145*	3462.8*	2102.6*
	(.10)	(.17)	(.10)
Private High Selectivity	.04	1572.7*	937.6*
	(.04)	(.10)	(.06)
Public High Selectivity	.06	2411.4*	1130*
	(.04)	(.12)	(.06)
Private Medium Selectivity	.03	908.6	897.5*
	(.03)	(.05)	(.05)
Public Medium Selectivity	.04	1055.5*	886.9
	(.03)	(.06)	(.05)
Private Low Selectivity	.01	-78.7	178.4
	(.01)	(.00)	(.01)
R²	.15	.033	.19
N	2,213	2,213	2,213

a. Equation 1 and 3 include all the independent variables listed in the text; "public low selectivity" is the excluded category.
b. Equation 2 includes only the measures of undergraduate type.
c. As noted in text (p. 154), this 1980 income measure represents the mid-point of one of twelve income categories.
*p < .05.

Note: Unstandardized regression coefficients ("b") are reported; standardized "b" in parentheses.

Compared with graduates of low-selectivity public institutions of otherwise similar attributes, the elite institution graduates averaged about $2,100 more. There was also a pay-off—roughly about equal size—to graduating from public and private highly selective and private medium selective institutions instead of a low-selectivity public institution, but this pay-off is only about half or less than the advantage enjoyed by the elite graduates. In short, graduating from a school of some middle-level prestige provided a modest boost to income, but graduating from a school at the very top of the prestige hierarchy provided a decidedly large advantage. The effects of prestige in this analysis, then, are not directly linear; income levels do not rise with each step on the prestige ladder.

Nor do the advantages of a prestigious degree equally benefit women and men. (We separately ran the equations in Table 7.1 for each sex.) The net advantage of graduating from an elite school was $1,556 for men and $2,959 for women. Furthermore, chances of earning at least $20,000 were 18 percent higher for women and 12 percent higher for men than their counterparts from low selectivity public institutions.

The fact of this discrepancy makes sense in light of the changing role of women, especially college-educated women, in the occupational structure. We suspect that in previous generations the prestige of a woman's degree would have made relatively little difference because so many women were concentrated in low-paying "female" professions, no matter what their alma mater: that is, both the Mount Holyoke and State Teachers College graduate earned pittances as teachers; neither had any real prospect of entering lucrative "male" careers. By comparison, however, the women of the class of 1975 were inclined to enter traditionally male occupational preserves. (Only because so many women entered the male occupational world did the variance in women's earnings become notable.) These women were strange and even threatening newcomers to the male gatekeepers, who may have been particularly anxious to reassure themselves that the women were the right sort. In the absence of other recognizable cues, these gatekeepers may have placed a particular emphasis on degree prestige for female applicants, an extra validation that was not as necessary for their male competitors. Although this interpretation emphasizes the credentialling function of degrees, we cannot discount the possibility that the socialization effects of going to an elite institution were different for men and women. Something about the actual education at an elite school may have enhanced women's productive capacities more than men's.

Besides analyzing differences in the prestige effect between the sexes, we also briefly looked at whether graduation from particular schools was especially rewarded in certain sectors of the labor market. We ran the equations in Table 7.1 for all respondents with a job in a private business organization on the presumption that private-sector gatekeepers had relatively great leeway in their recruitment and promotion procedures and would be relatively attracted to the social and intellectual cachet associated with a prestigious degree. However, there was no support for this line of reasoning: the pay-off to an elite degree was not notably greater in the private sector. Yet, on the basis of this analysis, it may be premature to say that the pay-off to an elite degree holds equally across all sectors of the economy. Indeed, the disproportionate concentration of elite college graduates at the top of the corporate ladders in certain industries (e.g., banking) suggests the value of a fine-grained analysis of narrowly defined labor markets.

Further Credentials

Of course many of the high-income aspirants in this recent cohort did not merely attempt to trade in on their undergraduate credentials. They came of age at a time when certain high-pay-off professional degrees, especially the M.D. , J.D., and M.B.A., had become a secure and common route to great material comfort (Kingston, 1980b). Applications to such professional programs soared accordingly, and competition for entrance remains fierce, though the number of medical school applications has recently declined.

We should expect that graduates of prestigious undergraduate institutions are disproportionately successful in being admitted to these professional schools. After all, they are generally academically able, and admissions criteria emphasize academic achievement. Thus, elite undergraduates would seem tracked to the top of the income hierarchy through professional degrees, even if undergraduate prestige itself does not provide any advantage in gaining admittance to these professional schools. The issue remains whether an elite undergraduate education provides some edge in getting on this track, thus conferring indirect benefits on later career prospects.

With the limited time span of the CIRP data, we cannot assess whether undergraduate prestige has indirect effects on financial success through professional school attendance, but we can assess how attainment of high-pay-off degrees varies by undergraduate quality. We regressed attainment of a high-pay-off degree (yes/no) on (a) the prestige categories alone (Equation 1, Table 7.2), and (b) on prestige categories and the set of personal attributes discussed above (Equation 2, Table 7.2).[6] To reiterate, precollege occupational aspirations as well as college grades are included in this second equation. This analysis includes all respondents with at least a bachelor's degree.

In comparison to low-selectivity public graduates, only the graduates of elite institutions are significantly more likely to have earned a M.D., J.D., or M.B.A. degree—a 20 percent greater chance. Graduates of institutions in all prestige categories below the very top did not take this high-income professional route more often than their counterparts at the lowest-level public institutions. Of course, some of the elite graduates' substantial advantage reflects their personal characteristics. Controlling for all relevant factors that we have measures for, however, the elite graduates still have an 11 percent advantage (see Equation 2). Only initial occupational aspiration (beta $= .27$) has a larger net effect than the elite institution variable; the latter and undergraduate grades have a similar impact (beta $= .15$).

TABLE 7.2
The Effects of Undergraduate Type on
Attainment of M.D., J.D., or M.B.A.

Institutional Type	High-Pay-off Professional Degree	
	Equation 1[a]	Equation 2[b]
Elite	.20*	.11*
	(.27)	(.15)
Private High Selectivity	.03	.00
	(.04)	
Public High Selectivity	.03	.00
	(.03)	
Private Medium Selectivity	.02	.00
	(.02)	
Public Medium Selectivity	-.00	-.01
Private Low Selectivity	.01	-.00
	(.01)	
R^2	.07	.19
N	3,402	3,402

a. Equation 1 includes only the measures of undergraduate type; "public low selectivity" is the excluded category.
b. Equation 2 includes all the independent variables listed in the text.
* $p < .05$.

Note: Unstandardized regression coefficients ("b") are reported; standardized "b" in parentheses.

Let us emphasize that this analysis does not establish that elite graduates are favored in professional school admissions decisions because of their undergraduate credentials. Rather, it simply shows that they were more successful in getting these professional credentials—more so than their counterparts at less prestigious schools with equal precollege aspirations, family resources, self-image, and college grades. Their greater success probably reflects some combination of greater institutional and informal encouragement to apply to these professional schools (a socialization effect related to institutional differences), favorable treatment in the admissions process because of their undergraduate degree (a credential effect), and some greater academic merit not reflected by overall grade point average (especially scores on standardized test scores). Although we cannot assess the relative weight of these potential factors, there is clearly *something* about going to an elite undergraduate school that boosts chances of getting on the high-pay-off professional track.

Elite Schools: A Large Advantage?

The prestige effects we note here all reach conventional levels of statistical significance, but the more crucial question is whether these coefficients point to substantively important differences. Against the usual standard of contribution to explained variance, degree prestige does not go far in explaining early career income for college graduates. Indeed, our most complete model of 1980 income—Equation 3, Table 7.1—explains only about a fifth of the variance. However, the fact that, net of many crucial factors, elite graduates have a 15 percent greater probability of earning at least $20,000 and have an average income advantage of $2,100 suggests a benefit that is far from trivial. This latter advantage should be viewed in the context that the mean income of the respondents in the sample was a little more than $15,000; $2,100 represents a substantial proportional difference. Similarly, the 11 percent edge in earning a high-pay-off professional degree cannot be readily dismissed. Advantages of this magnitude are ones that few would turn down and most would covet.

That the elite institutions have a current impact on careers is perhaps our most noteworthy finding. After all, in an era in which admissions decisions are primarily meritocratic (though see Chapters 2, 6, and 9 in this volume) and hiring processes are also presumed to be ever more governed by considerations of individual merit, the existence of prestige effects appears somewhat anomalous. They suggest the possibility of particularistic processes that are more readily expected in previous decades. We lack data for systematically assessing whether the pay-off accruing to prestigious degrees has changed, but we can document that elite institutions made a difference throughout the postwar years, America's era of increasingly explicit claim to a meritocratic order.

AFTER THE WAR: GREY FLANNEL MEN

Even though now dated, perhaps the best data source for analyzing college prestige effects on high-income prospects in the postwar era is the NBER-Thorndike Hagen longitudinal survey of World War II aviation volunteers (all white males).[7] *Before* most of them completed college, these men were given a general intelligence test, and they were resurveyed in 1968 about their careers. By this year, having worked for about twenty years (median age was forty-six), they were at or near the peak of their careers. For the most part, those who were going to succeed in their careers had already done so by this time.

Rather than attempting to explain variance, we focus here on the relationship between college prestige and chances of getting to the top of the income hierarchy—hence, the cross-tabular analyses and an informal odds ratio approach. Operationally, we define being rich as a 1968 income of at least $25,000, an income level that was in approximately the highest 2 percent in the general population. Our measure of prestige is based on institutional selectivity. The four-category classification is based on Cass and Birnbaum's (1968) widely used guidebook.[8]The category of primary concern is *high prestige*—all 28 institutions are private and are the most selective in the country. In the mid-sixties SAT scores for these institutions were in the middle 600s or higher, though admissions were not as rigorously determined by academic qualifications in the immediate postwar years when most of these men went to college. This category consists of the Ivy League, other private universities such as the Massachusetts Institute of Technology, the California Institute of Technology, Stanford, and Johns Hopkins, and some nationally esteemed liberal arts colleges. The other categories are *good*—49 institutions, primarily private, many with notable regional reputations; *select*—125 institutions, mostly private but also a number of large state universities; and *low prestige*—the less prominent state universities, state colleges, and the least selective private schools.

In analyzing the economic careers of this cohort, one fact is dramatically evident: chances of being rich were strongly associated with undergraduate degree prestige. Among the college graduates, success rates were linear: Ivy League—52 percent, other high prestige—41 percent, good—34 percent, select—33 percent, and low prestige—22 percent. To a slight extent, this "prestige advantage" reflects the greater professional school graduation rates of the elite collegians, but the pattern is largely similar among those with only a bachelor's degree.

In a society that prides itself on meritocratic principles, such a skew of life chances is not disturbing if an elite college credential represents productive abilities that are rewarded in the marketplace. Again, the issue is: does an elite degree itself count, or do elite collegians have greater endowments of personal characteristics that are rewarded?

To approach this matter, consider the analysis presented in Table 7.3. For each prestige level, the respondents are divided into quintiles based on their performance on an intelligence test administered before they completed their higher education. Since above-average intelligence

TABLE 7.3

Probability of Being Rich in 1968 by College
Prestige Level of College Graduates, Controlling
for IQ Quintile: The NBER-TH Cohort

Income Level	College Prestige of Graduates																								
	High Prestige					Good					Select					Low Prestige					Total
IQ Quintile*	1	2	3	4	5	1	2	3	4	5	1	2	3	4	5	1	2	3	4	5	
Percent more than $25,000 (N)	53	60	44	15	29	35	36	29	39	20	36	30	30	31	39	27	24	22	22	16	27
	(39)	(15)	(8)	(2)	(2)	(34)	(16)	(12)	(12)	(4)	(53)	(33)	(33)	(26)	(17)	(89)	(68)	(66)	(68)	(40)	(637)
Percent less than $25,000 (N)	47	40	56	85	71	65	64	71	61	80	64	70	70	69	61	73	76	78	78	84	73
	(35)	(10)	(10)	(11)	(5)	(62)	(28)	(29)	(19)	(16)	(93)	(78)	(76)	(59)	(27)	(244)	(216)	(233)	(238)	(208)	(1,697)
Total (N)	100	100	100	100	100	100	100	100	100	100	100	100	100	100	100	100	100	100	100	100	100
	(74)	(25)	(18)	(13)	(7)	(96)	(44)	(41)	(31)	(20)	(146)	(111)	(109)	(85)	(44)	(333)	(284)	(299)	(306)	(248)	(2,334)

* 1 = highest fifth; 5 = lowest fifth. As explained in text (p. 162), these quintile rankings in the sample roughly correspond to the five top decile rankings in the general population.

was a prerequisite for consideration in the aviation program from which the sample was drawn, these quintile rankings roughly correspond to deciles in the general population. Thus, those included in IQ Quintile 1 in the table were probably in the upper tenth or so of the IQ distribution. We might parenthetically note that the prestige hierarchy was hardly a strict hierarchy of intellectual capacity. A large proportion of the graduates of relatively prestigious schools had modest intellectual ability—or at least modest ability to perform well on this test.

A revealing pattern emerges:

- The least able graduates of select colleges had a higher chance of becoming rich than the most able graduates of low-prestige colleges.
- The good and select graduates did about equally well, but there was no consistent increase in income prospects by IQ within each of these levels.
- Among those in the top three IQ fifths, high-prestige graduates did much better than those with equal measured intelligence at less prestigious institutions. For example, in the top intelligence fifth, 53 percent of the high-prestige graduates got rich—1.5 times the rate of those who went to good and select institutions, and two times the rate among the graduates of low-prestige schools.
- Among the high-prestige graduates, measured intelligence was not directly associated with success rates. (With the very small number of cases in the lower IQ categories, we cannot generalize from these numbers.)

As we will discuss in our concluding section, these substantial prestige effects, net of intelligence, are difficult to reconcile with a human capital interpretation. Recall that the human capital school within economics assumes that people are paid in proportion to their marginal productivity; and since education supposedly enhances productivity, and the well educated are in short supply, they end up earning the most. Now, measured intelligence is surely not a direct indicator of productivity, but human capital theory can begin to explain these different success rates by college prestige only if the elite college graduates had greater endowments of truly productive skills than equally intelligent men who went to less prestigious colleges. It is worth noting, though, that human capital theorists often try to make their own case by using some measure of intelligence as a proxy indicator of productivity.

If not because of intelligence, then, did the elite collegians do better simply because of advantaged family background? If so, the results would undermine human capital theory as well as the implications of credentialism suggested in Table 7.3. The results in Table 7.4 indicate, however, that degree prestige in itself affects life chances. Obviously some cells are too small for analysis and all interactions cannot be tested, but several crucial comparisons are possible.

To minimize the problems caused by small cell counts, the intelligence measure is dichotomized (top and lower halves in the sample) and family status is measured simply as working class (blue-collar fathers) versus middle class (white-collar fathers). Since distinctions within white-collar occupations were not systematically related to high-income prospects, this status division is sensible.

Consider the income prospects of those with middle-class backgrounds and high intelligence (top quarter of the general population) — the largest group within each prestige category and presumably those with the best prospects. Much like the bivariate rates, chances of becoming rich still increased strongly with institutional prestige: low prestige — 27 percent, select and good — 40 percent, and high prestige — 59 percent. Prestige also paid off for bright working-class graduates, though to a lesser extent; but these bright working-class graduates did somewhat less well than their middle-class counterparts at each prestige level except the lowest: that is, there appears to be a class divide of sorts in the benefits of a prestigious degree.

In short, putting this all together, where one went to college certainly appears to have counted in these years, though the extent of the pay-off was mediated by family status and, to a much lesser extent, measured intelligence. Graduation from a high-prestige institution was particularly an advantage to relatively bright middle-class graduates. Of course, this analysis cannot show conclusively that degree prestige, per se, is rewarded because the elite school graduates may have had greater career-enhancing capacities besides the advantages of brains and family status. Nonetheless, the very size of these net effects and the absence of other important factors related to life chances but unrelated to status and intelligence create a strong case for considering the merits of credentialling theory.

THE COLLEGE CLASS OF 1961

Having considered the experiences of a cohort that mostly entered the labor force after the war, we now summarize the results of a study of a group that is about a decade younger, the college class of 1961.[9] We use here the same categorization of institutional prestige as in the analysis of the NBER-TH survey. The continuing class-stratified nature of Ameri-

TABLE 7.4
Probability of Being Rich in 1968, by College Prestige of College Graduates, Controlling for Family Status and IQ: The NBER-TH Cohort

Income Level IQ Half[a]	College Prestige of College Graduates																Total
	High Prestige				Good				Select				Low Prestige				
	Top ½		Lower ½		Top ½		Lower ½		Top ½		Lower ½		Top ½		Lower ½		
Family Status[b]	White Collar	Blue Collar	White Collar	Blue Collar	White Collar	Blue Collar	White Collar	Blue Collar	White Collar	Blue Collar	White Collar	Blue Collar	White Collar	Blue Collar	White Collar	Blue Collar	
Percent more than $25,000 (N)	59 (43)	36 (9)	31 (4)	36 (4)	40 (32)	31 (18)	38 (15)	23 (5)	40 (56)	26 (34)	40 (31)	19 (13)	27 (86)	25 (71)	26 (73)	14 (40)	28 (534)
Percent less than $25,000 (N)	41 (30)	64 (16)	69 (9)	64 (7)	60 (49)	69 (40)	62 (24)	77 (17)	60 (85)	74 (98)	60 (45)	81 (56)	73 (229)	75 (216)	74 (203)	86 (241)	72 (1,365)
Total (N)	100 (73)	100 (25)	100 (13)	100 (11)	100 (81)	100 (58)	100 (39)	100 (22)	100 (141)	100 (132)	100 (76)	100 (69)	100 (315)	100 (287)	100 (276)	100 (281)	100 (1,899)

a. Respondents are divided into two intelligence groups: The "top ½" corresponds to the highest quarter in the general population; the "lower ½" corresponds to the second quarter (50-75%).

b. The status categorization is collapsed here to white-collar fathers and blue-collar fathers.

can higher education and some consequences for career attainment are readily evident.

As for previous cohorts, those graduates in a position to reap the benefits of a prestigious degree were already advantaged in their family backgrounds. Though these graduates were not rigorously sorted in the prestige hierarchy by socioeconomic background, the sons of affluent parents (in the top 5 percent of the income distribution) were clearly favored. About a third of the graduates from these high-income families went to a high-prestige institution, whereas only a few percent of college graduates from the lower two quintiles in the income distribution did so. Given these distributions, the elite schools had a distinctly monied tone: about half of the high-prestige graduates were raised in families in the top 5 percent of the income distribution.

Moreover, many with an elite undergraduate education had enjoyed the advantages of an elite secondary education. At this time prep schools were quite effective conduits to elite colleges: almost two-thirds of the college graduates who had been educated in these exclusive secondary schools earned their degree at a high-prestige college. For public and parochial school graduates a high-prestige degree was a rare attainment. The institutional connection between prep schools and the top echelon of higher education was so strong that about a fifth of the elite college graduates had first attended private schools. Further, the largely affluent prep school graduates were much more likely to have earned an elite degree than equally rich graduates of other high schools—69 percent versus 28 percent for those in the top 5 percent of the income distribution.

High-Pay-off Degrees

Once out of college, graduates of the elite institutions distinguished themselves, though only modestly so, in graduation rates from high-pay-off professional schools and, to a lesser extent, in the race for high income. Graduation rates from these professional schools were as follows: Ivy League—33 percent, other high prestige—25 percent, good—21 percent, select—16 percent, and low prestige—7 percent. For the elite college graduates, then, a high-pay-off degree was a fairly typical next step in the educational and occupational career ladder, but the much greater number of low-prestige grads had few classmates who took this route. Professionals in this cohort with affluent origins were especially likely to have turned elite undergraduate credentials to their advantage in pursuing a high-pay-off degree.[10] Such facts point to an important feature of the American higher-educational system: institutions at various levels in the prestige hierarchy have different roles in the linkage of education and the world of work, and these different roles are associated with class distinctions.

Not only were elite colleges effective conduits to professional schools, but a prestigious undergraduate credential in itself provided an extra advantage. Graduates with prestigious college backgrounds had higher professional school attendance rates than the less prestigiously credentialled of roughly equal college performance.[11] (See Table 7.5.) Within the ranks of high college performers, the high-prestige graduates had by far the greatest graduation rates from one of these professional schools: 3.3 times greater graduation rates than students from low-prestige colleges. Within the ranks of medium college performers, the advantage of high-prestige grads over good and select graduates was somewhat less pronounced, but again the low-prestige grads trailed those of presumably equal achievement.

It is also worth noting that performance effects within each prestige category were generally slight: that is, although the best students in each prestige category (except the good colleges) had unsurpassed professional school attendance rates, the lower-performing students were only somewhat less likely to continue their education at these high-pay-off schools. This finding casts doubt on the scope of Davis's (1966) famous argument (based on the same survey) in "The Campus as a Frog Pond: An Application of the Theory of Relative Deprivation to Career Decisions of College Men." Presumably the lesser frogs at the competitive ponds (the elite schools) should have become discouraged by their relatively poor academic performance and therefore lowered their career aims. Yet, plainly, a relatively large number of run-of-the-pond frogs in the most competitive swimming holes had sufficient determination, knowledge of how the system works, resources, or self-image to pursue these professional careers. That the top frogs in the most competitive ponds were the most apt to take this route is not surprising, but the lesser frogs in competitive ponds did not seem greatly deterred by their comparatively mediocre performance.

Law and Business School Prestige

Furthermore, the elite college grads who took the professional school route were also the most likely to have gone to the very best professional schools. Of the lawyers in this class (about 4 percent of all graduates), the percentage from each undergraduate prestige level graduating from a National 15 law school was as follows: high prestige—57 percent, good—24 percent, select—48 percent, and low prestige—9 percent. Of the M.B.A.s (about 5 percent of all graduates) the corresponding

TABLE 7.5
Probability of Earning a High-Pay-Off Professional
Degree, by College Prestige, Controlling for
Academic Performance Index: Men in
the College Class of 1961

	Academic Performance											
	High				Medium				Low			
College Prestige:	High Prestige	Good	Select	Low Prestige	High Prestige	Good	Select	Low Prestige	High Prestige	Good	Select	Low Prestige
Percent Earning a High-Pay-off	33	15	21	10	25	25	17	10	30	21	14	5
Degree (N)	(91)	(17)	(43)	(30)	(40)	(42)	(74)	(78)	(6)	(27)	(65)	(78)

chances of having attained a Top Dozen degree were as follows: high prestige—74 percent, good—22 percent, select—12 percent, and low prestige—1 percent.[12] Thus, for those elite college grads with plans for business or law careers, a majority continued their education at the most elite professional schools. In fact, the overrepresentation of elite college graduates at elite professional schools was so pronounced that almost half of the National 15 law school graduates went to an Ivy-high-prestige college, as did almost two-thirds of the Top Dozen MBA graduates.

The very pronounced tracking of elite college graduates with law or business aspirations to the most prestigious professional schools raises the question of whether an elite undergraduate credential was itself a boost to careers in law and business. Using the same data set (augmented by LSAT scores), Joseph Zelan (in Warkov, 1965) establishes that where aspiring lawyers went to college strongly affected where they went to law school. Among the lawyers with high test scores (600+ on the LSAT), all who went to elite colleges were much more likely to have attended an elite law school than all less prestigiously credentialled, no matter what their family origins. For elite college graduates with high scores going to an elite law school was almost routine—more than three-fourths did so. Moreover, elite collegians with below 600 LSAT scores were as likely to have gone to an elite law school as less prestigiously credentialled collegians of equal family status but *higher* LSAT scores.

A similar institutionalized connection between elite undergraduate institutions and elite business schools was also evident at this time. The Top Dozen business schools were the overwhelming choice of high-prestige grads throughout the range of academic performance; and however well they performed in college, all M.B.A.s with less prestigious undergraduate backgrounds predominantly enrolled in less prestigious business schools.

In the Job World

For this cohort, however, a prestigious undergraduate degree did not mean a distinctly high income in the early career. Indeed, one year after graduation, where the graduates with full-time jobs placed in the income hierarchy was virtually unaffected by collegiate prestige, family background, or academic performance. Furthermore, the edge of elite college graduates in getting to the front of the income race was still modest in 1968. Among those with a B.A. as their highest degree at this time, the proportion who earned more than $15,000 (the top 15 percent of this group) was as follows: high prestige—22 percent, good—25 percent, select—12 percent, and low prestige,—11 percent. By no means, then, were the B.A.s distinctly sorted into the income hierarchy by prestige level, and the disproportionate success of the collegians with relatively prestigious degrees largely reflected their greater family affluence and higher academic performance. Even so, the graduates with an affluent background and a high-prestige credential were the most likely (44 percent) to be in the highest-income category ($15,000+).

CONCLUSION

Among those persuaded by the common wisdom on the value of various colleges, our findings of prestige effects should occasion little surprise, but they hardly sit easily with some views prominent in the sociological literature. Before speculating about the theoretical implications of these findings, however, we should highlight what is distinctive about our empirical analysis and how this analysis itself is limited.

Let us be clear about our key finding: graduation from a relatively small set of institutions at the top of the academic hierarchy has been distinctly rewarded, whereas other prestige distinctions have been relatively inconsequential for life chances. The distinctive pay-off of elite schools is particularly evident for the most recent cohort analyzed. Although other research has dismissed the significance of institutional differentiation because continuous prestige (or quality) measures are weakly related to career outcomes, it has overlooked the distinctive role of the elite institutions in the stratification process. By taking a categorical approach to institutional prestige, we highlight this effect. To state these findings in terms of financial advice, we are inclined to say: go to an elite college (and don't worry about your grades unless you want to go to a professional school), but if you can't get into one of these schools, don't worry too much about where else to go because the name of your alma mater won't be important.

We should caution that this advice is subject to some questioning. Inferences of prestige effects rest on the presumption that all personal characteristics that affect career success other than degree prestige have been accounted for in the analysis. This presumption is impossible to justify unequivocally, but we do control for key factors, and thus the likelihood of reporting spurious relationships does not seem great.

On the other hand, we may underestimate the benefits of graduating from the very most prestigious institutions. Especially for the most recent cohort, our elite category is rather inclusive, necessarily so because of data limitations. If we had been able to isolate the institutions that are generally accorded the highest esteem (the Ivy League and a few others), we might have found an even stronger effect at the top end of the hierarchy. Our analysis also uses a rather broad brush in analyzing the extent of financial pay-off to prestigious degrees. By analyzing all graduates together, we report an average effect across all segments of the labor market. To a limited extent we attempted to see if there were differential effects within broadly defined economic sectors, but these analyses do not really bear on the impact of particular credentials in specific niches of the labor market—for example, hiring practices at investment and large commercial banks, where the prominence of the elite-credentialled seems so pronounced.

Although there are questions to be asked about the precise extent of prestige effects, the finding that the prestigiously credentialled do better than their equally bright and economically advantaged counterparts raises a theoretical issue—*why* is education rewarded? Outlined in the Introduction to this volume, the main competing explanations for the existence of prestige effects would emphasize socialization (elite schools provide distinctly productive training) or allocation processes (elite schools provide distinctive access to favored positions because their graduates, as a group, are presumed to have desirable traits, cognitive or cultural).

In themselves, our findings do not allow us to choose definitively between these views. It is conceivable that prestigious schools had some socialization effects that actually enhanced productivity or inculcated some other desirable traits—such as a sophisticated cultural style—that was economically rewarded. However, the so-called college effects literature (Astin, 1977) indicates that different kinds of colleges do not have varying socializing influences: essentially what goes into a particular type of school is what goes out. In other words, there is little reason to conclude that elite college graduates did better because their college experiences *made* them better. Moreover, to argue for the impact of socialization effects, especially related to productive capacities, one must believe that the elite-credentialled acquired distinctly greater supplies of these capacities than their equally intelligent counterparts (see the results for the NBER-TH cohort) or those with similar levels of academic performance (see the results for the NORC and CIRP cohorts).

Although the case for substantial socialization effects seems weak, the pattern of results here indirectly points to allocation processes involving the use of degrees as almost defining markers of desirability. As revealed in Table 7.3, success rates increased with prestige level, and *within* each prestige level did not vary by IQ level (perhaps a proxy for productivity): that is, once a student received a degree from a school of certain prestige, his intelligence had little effect on his chances of becoming rich. The great success of the prestigiously credentialled throughout the intellectual range, then, possibly reflects the tendency of many employers to have assumed that graduation from an elite school in itself ensured at least an acceptable level of intelligence (and other desirable traits) and that further intellectual distinctions had little meaning.

If so, it is the social reactions to particular types of degree holders, not their individual characteristics, that account for prestige effects. Given the prominence of those with elite credentials in gatekeeping positions, and the general tendency of people to favor those like themselves, the role of credential cronyism seems likely.[13] Yet without evidence bearing directly on hiring processes, it is impossible to say to what extent the market signal of a particular degree entails productivity-related capacities or particular sociocultural dispositions. We can only speculate that the appeal of the elite collegians is that they are both bright and the socially "right" sort.

Whatever the basis for employers' attraction to elite college graduates, arguments for the unidimensionality of the educational system (e.g., Treiman and Terrell, 1975) seem misguided. And whatever the precise size of independent direct effects of prestigious credentials on career success, the elite schools are effective institutionalized conduits to elite economic status, benefitting a group that is at once academically able and already economically privileged.

NOTES

1. Indeed, Meyer (1977: 60), in a widely cited essay, argues that the lack of institutional effects at each educational level is "the most puzzling general research paradox in the sociology of American education." Jencks and his collaborators (1979), in perhaps the most noted empirical work on the stratification process, also dismiss the impact of institutional differences on careers.

2. The restriction of attending a single undergraduate institution was necessary to eliminate ambiguity in measures of the college experience (e.g., major) because the 1980 CIRP survey referred only to the last undergraduate institution attended. The restriction of including only the full-time employed was necessary to eliminate those still in degree programs (a time commitment that reduces income) or unemployed for other unknown reasons. By restricting the subsample to those without advanced degrees, we in effect partially standardize the work experience of the respondents, a matter which we cannot directly measure.

3. The CIRP data are categorized into 37 stratification cells reflecting differences in type (college, university, two-year), support (public and private), religious affiliation, predominant race, and selectivity. We have collapsed these cells into seven categories.

4. Although the use of a dichotomous measure as a dependent variable in OLS regression is problematical, estimates of effects do not tend to be severely biased, though their significance levels are questionable. For this reason, we report the findings for an alternative measure of income.

5. For ease of presentation we do not present the coefficients for the independent variables; they are not of substantive interest in this analysis, though we do report the overall coefficient of determination.

6. Our caution about the use of dichotomous dependent variables in OLS regression should be repeated here.

7. See Taubman and Wales (1974) for the best description of the sample and the analysis of response biases. Most of the respondents were at college age in the war years. In addition to having the personal disposition for dangerous duty, the respondents were not representative of the male population of similar age because they had to pass a screening test. The passing mark was roughly equivalent to the mean IQ score in the general population. This lack of representativeness in relation to the general population does not constitute a serious problem for analyzing the impact of college prestige because the overwhelming number of graduates can be expected to be at least moderately intelligent.

8. This guidebook, similar to Barron's guidebook, ranks institutions on the basis of selectivity: presumably the "better" students will want to go to "better" schools and hence their greater selectivity. It is questionable to categorize postwar graduates with mid-sixties ratings, but appropriate ratings on a large number of schools are not available. However, a study based on a 1947 survey (Havemann and West, 1952) identifies virtually the same schools as high prestige, and since the categories are rather large, the slight improvement or drop in quality of a few schools should not upset the basic validity of the classification.

9. The official title of the five-wave NORC survey is "The Career Plans and Experiences of June 1961 College Graduates." See Davis (1964) for details of the sample and data collection. The data reported here represent the responses of the male, fifth-wave (1968) respondents, a subsample of those who had responded to all of the first four waves (Spaeth, 1970).

10. Forty-three percent of these professionals with families in the $15,000+ bracket (then, the top 5 percent of the income distribution) had first gone to a high-prestige college. By contrast, 17 percent of these professionals with families in the less than $7,500 bracket graduated from one of these elite undergraduate institutions.

11. This survey lacks any standardized measure of intelligence or academic ability. NORC researchers devised an Academic Performance Index, a measure based on self-reported grades adjusted for school quality. Three large groups were formed: high (approximately the top fifth), medium (the next 36 percent of the students), and low (all the rest, somewhat less than the bottom

half). See Davis, 1965, for details about construction of the index and analysis of its validity.

12. The *National 15,* our term, are the highest-ranked fifteen law schools as indicated by a survey of "knowledgeable scholars" in various subspecialties of law. The *Top Dozen,* again our term, are the highest eleven schools (plus the Tuck School at Dartmouth) in "The Cartter Report on Leading Schools of Education, Law, and Business," *Change,* February 1977: 44-48.

13. *Credential cronyism,* Judah Matras's (1975) term, refers to the ascriptive process whereby individuals with the right degrees are granted distinctive access to desired positions. People with similar right degrees are drawn to and favor each other. See Useem and Karabel, Chapter 8 in this volume, for evidence on the overrepresentation of elite collegians in top positions in the corporate world.

REFERENCES

Alwin, Duane. 1974. "College Effects on Educational and Occupational Attainments." *American Sociological Review* 39: 210-221.

Astin, Alexander. 1977. *Four Critical Years.* San Francisco: Jossey- Bass.

_____. 1982. *Minorities in American Higher Education.* San Francisco: Jossey-Bass.

Cass, James, and M. Birnbaum. 1968. *Comparative Guide to American Colleges.* 3rd edition. New York: Harper and Row.

Davis, James. 1964. *Great Aspirations.* Chicago: Aldine.

_____. 1965. *Undergraduate Career Decisions.* Chicago: Aldine.

_____. 1966. "The Campus as a Frog Pond: An Application of the Theory of Relative Deprivation to Career Decisions of College Men." *American Journal of Sociology* 77: 1151-1164.

Foster, Edward, and J. Rodgers. 1979. "Quality of Education and Student Earnings." *Higher Education* 8: 21-37.

Havemann, Ernest, and P.S. West. 1952. *They Went to College.* New York: McGraw-Hill.

Jencks, Christopher, et al., 1979. *Who Gets Ahead?* New York: Basic Books.

Kingston, Paul. 1980a. "The High Income Track: The Impact of Academic Credentials and Family Status on Chances of Becoming Rich." Ph.D. dissertation, Columbia University.

_____.1980b. "The Credential Elite and the Credential Route to Success. *Teachers College Record* 82: 589-600.

Matras, Judah. 1975. *Social Inequality, Stratification, and Mobility.* Englewood Cliffs, NJ: Prentice-Hall.

Meyer, John. 1977. "Education as an Institution." *American Journal of Sociology* 83: 55-77.

Smart, John. 1986. "College Effects on Occupational Status Attainment." *Research in Higher Education* 24: 75-95.

Solomon, Lewis. 1973. "The Definition and Impact of College Quality." Pp. 77-102 in *Does College Matter?*, edited by L. Solomon and P. Taubman. New York: Academic Press.

Spaeth, Joe. 1970. "Occupational Attainment among Male College Graduates." *American Journal of Sociology* 75: 632-644.

Taubman, Paul, and T. Wales. 1974. *Higher Education and Earnings.* New York: McGraw-Hill.

Treiman, Donald and K. Terrell. 1975. "The Process of Status Attainment in the United States and Great Britain." *American Journal of Sociology* 81: 563-583.

Trusheim, Dale, and J. Crouse. 1981. "Effects of College Prestige on Men's Occupational Status and Income." *Research in Higher Education* 14: 283-303.

Warkov, Seymour, with J. Zelan. 1965. *Lawyers in the Making.* Chicago: Aldine.

MICHAEL USEEM
JEROME KARABEL

Chapter Eight

Pathways to Top Corporate Management*

Presiding over America's large business corporations and thus occupying the summit of its class structure, is a relatively small cadre of senior managers, primarily the chief executives and ranking vice-presidents. More than any other single set of people, their decisions have decisive bearing on the contemporary contours of the nation's career hierarchies, wage distributions, and plant locations. To understand which individuals finally occupy these positions, of the tens of thousands who strive for them, is to understand better the internal organization of the corporations that selected them for positions of leadership.

Beginning with the landmark study of Taussig and Joslyn (1932), an extensive literature has developed on pathways to top corporate management (Miller, 1952; Newcomer, 1955; Warner and Abegglen, 1955; Mills, 1956; Lipset and Bendix, 1959; Keller, 1963; *Scientific Ameican*, 1965; Pierson, 1969; Diamond, 1970; Taubman and Wales, 1974; Burck, 1976; Swinyard and Bond, 1980; Bonfield, 1980). These studies have consistently demonstrated that the social and educational backgrounds of top senior managers are far higher than those not only of the average citizen, but also of other senior managers as well. The role of higher education in recruitment to the corporate elite has, however, changed dramatically in the course of the past half-century: whereas a solid majority (55 percent) of the managers in Taussig and Joslyn's study had never attended college, a number of more recent studies (Burck, 1976; Bonfield, 1980) suggest that the figure is now well under 15 percent. At the same time, the proportion possessing postgraduate degrees has increased considerably.

These studies have done much to increase our knowledge of pathways to senior corporate management, but they leave a number of critical questions unanswered. Foremost among these is the issue of stratification *among* senior managers. Especially in an era in which managerial hierarchies within firms are becoming ever more elaborate and networks between firms increasingly important (Useem, 1979, 1982), the issue of vertical divisions in the ranks of top managers commands our attention.

Just as many studies view the senior corporate management as homogeneous, so, too, do they portray their college backgrounds as relatively undifferentiated. This is not, to be sure, true of all of the studies: Newcomer (1955), Warner and Abegglen (1955), and Pierson (1969), for example, all distinguished between elite and non-elite colleges and show a vast over-representation of alumni of the former in top management. Yet, none of these studies, to the best of our knowledge, looks simultaneously at the effects of educational credentials *and* class background. They, thus, leave open the possibility that the apparent effects of institutional status on corporate access are artifacts of differences in class origin—or vice versa. Or, to put the matter another way, the oft-found overrepresentation in top corporate management of graduates of elite private colleges may be a consequence not of their prestigious educational credentials, but rather of their upper-class backgrounds.

In contrast to other studies, then, the emphasis of our investigation is on stratification *within* the ranks of senior corporate management as it may be affected by both educational and family background. A key hypothesis is that prestigious educational credentials— defined in this study by a bachelor's degree from a top private college, an MBA from a top program, or a law degree from a leading institution—increase the likelihood that an individual who has made it into the ranks of senior management will advance to become a chief executive officer, a member of the board of directors of another firm, or a participant in the leadership of a major business association. Similarly, we hypothesize that an upper-class background will confer an important advantage, independent of educational credentials, in climbing the corporate ladder. We also anticipate that the value of family background is lowest when educational credentials are highest.

Our theoretical framework is influenced by Max Weber's recognition of the growing importance of refined distinctions among educational credentials in the allocation of rewards in advanced industrial societies, and by the emphasis of such neo-Weberians as Collins (1971, 1979) and Parkin (1979) on the special impact of refined educational distinctions on the careers of elites. We have been influenced as well by the formulations of Bourdieu and his collaboraters (Bourdieu, 1973;

Bourdieu and Passeron, 1977; Bourdieu and Boltanski, 1978; Bourdieu, 1984) who see individuals and groups as possessing varying forms and amounts of "capital" which they then attempt to "convert" into rewards on the labor market.

Within this framework, scholastic capital—a term which refers to educational attainment in its qualitative as well as quantitative dimensions—is a key determinant of access to high-paying and high-status jobs. It is not the only such determinant, however, for there are other forms of capital which are highly relevant to labor market success. Prominent among these are social capital (the class-linked personal contacts or network ties that can be crucial to organizational and professional advancement) and cultural capital (the class-based capacity to decode valued symbolic meanings and objects). Individuals and groups may differ in both the volume and the structure of the forms of capital they possess.

The framework that we propose has affinities with that of the cumulative advantage perspective (see Merton, 1968 and Zuckerman, 1977), with those who possess the greatest initial resources best situated to acquire and convert educational credentials. To state the study's most central hypothesis: those individuals who possess the greatest amount of the relevant forms of capital—in particular, scholastic *and* social capital—will be the most likely to gain access to the core of the American business elite. We predict, in particular, that having an upper-class background will have the greatest independent impact, as is suggested by Domhoff (1970, 1979) and Collins (1971, 1979), in moving beyond the firm into the formal and informal inter-corporate networks that play such a central role in American business.

RESEARCH PROCEDURES

The Sample

To examine these hypotheses, we draw on systematic information compiled on 3,105 senior managers and directors of 208 large American companies. The annual *Fortune* magazine listing of America's largest corporations for 1977 was used to identify the firms (*Fortune,* 1978). This list is generally regarded as the most comprehensive ranked list of publicly held companies, and it includes virtually all large corporations in the U.S. The 208 corporations were selected to represent middle-size and large firms, and companies in both the financial and manufacturing sectors. The sampled companies included manufacturing firms, ranked 1 to 60 and 451 to 500 according to their sales volume; commercial banks ranked 1 to 25 and 41 to 50; insurance companies ranked from 1 to 15, and nine of those ranked 41 to 50 by assets (the tenth company was not included because a complete list of its officers was unavailable); thirteen of the diversified financial firms numbered 1 to 15 and nine of those ranked 41 to 50 by assets (again, the three missing companies were not included because of the unavailability of the identities of the top executives); utilities numbered 1 to 5 by assets; retail firms ranked 1 to 6 by sales; and transportation companies numbered from 1 to 5 by operating revenues.

The managers studied all hold ranks of vice-president or higher, and a significant proportion serve on boards of directors of other major companies and participate in the affairs of the Business Roundtable and other major business associations. Six to eight of the senior-most officers and ten of the outside directors (directors who were not employed by the company) for each company were selected for detailed study, yielding a total of 3,105 managers and directors, or about 15 per company.[2] The eight most senior officers were selected when eight were named by a corporation; fewer were selected when fewer were identified as officers, though in no case were there fewer than six. When a board of directors included more than ten members, ten were chosen for study through random selection. Of those serving as outside directors of one of the sampled firms, three-quarters (74.5 percent) were, themselves, managers of other corporations.

Several dozen sources were used to gather information on the careers, corporate board service, and business association activity of the managers. In addition to the usual biographical references, our sources included annual company reports, alumni directories of preparatory schools and universities, and business association membership rosters.[3]

Of the 3,105 managers in the original sample, no biographical information was available in any of the directories on 376. These managers are excluded from our analysis. If we see these individuals as akin to survey non-respondents (as in survey procedures, most biographical directory information is obtained through solicited disclosure by the entrant), our response rate can be viewed as 87.9 percent.[4]

Variables

In light of our emphasis on stratification among both senior corporate managers and institutions of higher education, the discussion that follows addresses, first, the level of reponsibility within the employing firm, involvement in the governance of other firms as board members, and participation in the major business associations that represent large corporations to the government. We then proceed to define the study's principal independent variable, type of university credential, and, finally, family background.

Seniormost Management. There are large differences among senior managers in their level of responsibility and power. Though an imperfect measure, titles typically connote the differences, beginning with the position of vice-president and followed, in turn, by senior vice-president and executive vice-president, and capped by the president or chief executive officer. The level of ascent within senior management is measured here by whether the manager has reached the highest administrative position in a major company, that of chief executive officer (CEO). Though there is no uniform title associated with this position, most who occupy it carry the titles of company president, chairman of the board, or both. A major firm is defined in this analysis as a company that is among the nation's largest 1,300 corporations in 1978. Two in five of the senior managers (38.9 percent) were serving as chief executive of a major corporation in 1978.

Corporate Governance. Companies are governed by boards of directors of ten to fifteen members, with about one-third of the positions filled by senior managers of the governed company.[5] Approximately three-quarters of the remaining outside directors are senior managers of other companies. As a first sign of managerial accomplishment outside of the strictly internal career ladder of the company, invitation to join the boards of directors of other major companies is considered a singular achievement. Involvement in the governance of other corporations is measured by the number of major corporate directorships held by a senior manager, and we distinguish between those who serve on one board, termed *single directors,* from those who serve on two or more corporate boards, termed *multiple directors.* Approximately one in four of the senior managers in our sample (25.9 percent) were serving as multiple directors.

Business Representative. Corporations actively lobby on behalf of their political interests, and hundreds of trade associations do the same on behalf of firms in the same industry. A few exclusive associations draw membership from the largest companies in all industries, however, and they have the task of articulating the opinion of most large corporations to government agencies, legislative bodies, and the public. The most influential of these associations are the Committee of Economic Development, Business Council, Council on Foreign Relations, and above all, the Business Roundtable.[6] Focusing on these four key associations, we distinguished those who participate in none from the political activists who participate in one or more. Fewer than one in five of the senior managers (18.4 percent) were members of this group—the most exclusive of our three measures of corporate success—at the time of the study.

*University Credential.*The distinguishing university credentials for top company managers are the prestige of the undergraduate university attended and whether their bachelor's degree was followed by professional training in management or law. University quality is identified for a period as closely as possible to when most of the managers were enrolled in college. For undergraduate institutions, Richard Coleman has provided a painstaking evaluation of the status of the nation's colleges and universities in 1940 using a variety of sources (Coleman, 1973).[7] Eleven institutions are at the top of the ranking:[8]

Columbia University
Cornell University
Dartmouth College
Harvard University
John Hopkins University
Massachusetts Institute of Technology
University of Pennsylvania
Princeton University
Stanford University
Williams College
Yale University

In the analysis that follows, a senior manager is considered to hold a superior *college* credential if the manager earned a bachelor's degree from any of these eleven institutions.

The most common form of professional management training is completion of a master's degree in business administration (MBA). Here, too, we focus on completion of a high-ranking MBA program. Various rankings of the nation's MBA programs are available, most placing the same schools at the top of the list. We draw upon one of these for identification of the top eleven programs.[9] They are:

Columbia University
Dartmouth College
Harvard University
Massachusetts Institute of Technology
Northwestern University

Stanford University
University of California, Berkeley
University of California, Los Angeles
University of Chicago
University of Michigan
University of Pennsylvania

A manager is considered to hold a superior *management* credential if he or she received an MBA degree from any of these eleven programs. Another possible educational pathway to top corporate management is to attend one of the nation's leading law schools. Though attending law school as a route to top corporate management has received far less attention in the literature than attendance at a business school, we wished to leave open the possibility that, especially in an era of growing government regulations of corporations and increasingly complex (and, at times, antagonistic) intercorporate relations, a legal education might be an effective pathway to the corporate elite. Based on a survey by Blau and Margulies (1974-1975), we have identified nine law programs as especially prominent:

Columbia University
Harvard University
New York University
Stanford University
University of California, Berkeley
University of Chicago
University of Michigan
University of Pennsylvania
Yale University

A manager is considered to hold a top-ranking *law* degree if he or she received an LL.B. from any of these nine programs.

The distributions of the senior managers among the several types of university credentials is displayed in Table 8.1. We distinguish here among nine groups of managers divided according to the level and quality of their highest degree: those who (1) attended no college; (2) attended college but did not complete a bachelor's degree; (3) completed a college degree at a lesser institution (not one of the top eleven) and received no post-graduate degree; (4) completed a bachelor's degree at one of the top eleven schools and received no postgraduate degree; (5) completed an MBA degree from a lesser institution (not one of the top eleven); (6) earned an MBA degree from one of the top eleven universities; (7) completed a law degree (LL.B.) from a lesser institution (not one of the top nine); (8) earned an LL.B. from one of the top nine law schools; and (9) earned a postgraduate degree other than an MBA or an LL.B. These groups are generally mutually exclusive. In those several instances when both business and law degrees had been earned, the manager was classified as holding the latter.

TABLE 8.1
University Background, Company Position, Board Membership, Business Association Involvement, and Social Origins of Large Company Senior Managers

	Number	Percent
University Background		
No college	291	10.7%
College drop-out	161	5.9
BA only, unranked college	753	27.6
BA only, top college	306	11.2
MBA, unranked program	81	3.0
MBA, top program	385	14.1
Law, unranked program	274	10.1
Law, top program	203	7.4
Other post-graduate degree	275	10.0
Total	2,729	100.0%
Seniormost Management		
Does not hold CEO position	1,667	61.1%
Chief executive officer	1,062	38.9
Corporate Governance		
Serves on one board or none	2,023	74.1%
Serves on two corporate boards or more	706	25.9
Business Representative		
Active in no business association	2,227	81.6%
Active in one or more	502	18.4
Social Origin		
Non-upper social origin	2,287	83.8%
Upper social origin	442	16.2

Upper-Class Origin. If a manager is a descendant of a socially prominent family, he or she is more likely to have the kind of dense network of high-status friends and acquaintances or "social capital" that facilitates advancement within the ranks of top management. The joint impact of an upper-class background and education on managerial career may lead to a partially spurious correlation, however, especially since high-status families are far more likely to send their children to elite colleges and universities (Collins, 1971; Karabel, 1972; Karabel and Astin, 1975; Useem and Miller, 1975; Moore and Alba, 1982). To test this possibility, we have included a measure of upper-class background in our analyses.

A number of studies have documented the over-representation of individuals of patrician origin at the top of corporate management, but they have not identified the extent to which their presence is a direct product of class advantage rather than an outcome mediated through educational advantage. Following our framework of cumulative advantage, in which additional increments of different forms of capital should lead progressively to increased career success, we anticipate that originating in an upper-class family will independently increase the likelihood of rising to the top of the corporate elite.

Whether a manager is of upper-class origin is gauged through the joint use of two sources of background information. One is the manager's inclusion in the *Social Register*, the nationally accepted bluebook of America's first families. The other is whether the manager attended one of the nation's leading preparatory schools, institutions whose entry has traditionally been limited to the offspring of well-established families.

With separate metropolitan editions since 1888, and a single national edition in recent years, the *Social Register* has long been the accepted arbiter of established status. It constitutes, in Digby Baltzell's (1966) phrasing, a definitive "metropolitan upper class index." According to Baltzell, appearance in the Social Register is largely inherited and cannot be attained simply through sheer wealth or achievement. The inclusion of a manager in the 1978 or 1979 editions of the national *Social Register* is taken to constitute an indicator of a senior manager's upper-class origin.

The second indicator is attendance at one of the nation's exclusive preparatory schools. Following Baltzell (1958), Domhoff (1970), and Levine (1980), fourteen of the most exclusive boarding institutions are used here: Choate, Deerfield, Groton, Hill, Hotchkiss, Kent, Lawrenceville, Middlesex, Milton, Portsmouth Priory, St. George's, St. Mark's, St. Paul's, and Taft. The appearance of a manager in the alumni directories of any of these schools constitutes the other measure of upper-class origin.[10]

These two indicators of high social origins are combined into a single rough measure. A senior manager is deemed to be or upper-class origin if the manager graduated from one of the fourteen exclusive schools *or* is included in contemporary editions of the *Social Register*. By these criteria, one in six of the senior managers (16.2 percent) originate in upper-class families.

SCHOLASTIC CAPITAL AND CAREER ADVANCEMENT

To examine the influence of university credentials on corporate careers, we examine the probability that senior managers with varying types of "scholastic capital" will advance to the very highest positions in the corporate community. We identify as especially successful those senior managers who are (in ascending order): (1) currently holding the position of chief executive officer, (2) serving on two or more corporate boards, and (3) active in one or more of the four main business associations.

It is essential to keep in mind that we are comparing the experiences of senior managers whose careers have been highly successful. All have become at least vice-presidents or outside directors of major corporations. They are holding highly paid and responsible positions toward which many strive and few reach. We are therefore focusing on the difference that university credentials make among these relatively successful corporate executives. We are concerned *not* with whether aspiring middle manager with top university credentials will reach the senior level of a firm, but rather with those factors that increase the probability that senior managers already there will reach even higher levels of power and responsibility within the corporate world.

To highlight the difference that education makes, and to economize on space, we initially focus on four university backgrounds out of the nine in which the managers have been grouped (as classified in Table 8.1). These four backgrounds represent the broadest diversity in university experience, and they display some of the sharpest differences in subsequent career experiences among the senior managers. The four groups are (1) those who did not attend a college; (2) those who graduated from a lesser-ranked college (and received no postgraduate training); (3) those who received a bachelor's degree from a highly ranked college (with no post-graduate education); and (4) those who received an MBA degree from a top program.

In all three areas of attainment within the senior management level, scholastic capital makes a considerable difference. Those senior managers who complete an undergraduate education at a lesser institution fare better than those without a higher education, but earning a top level BA is even better for further upward movement at the senior level (Table 8.2). Of those senior managers with no university schooling, about one in four (26.5 percent) reached the chief executive office: but of those with bachelor's degrees from lesser ranked colleges, more than one in three (36.4 percent) reached it, and the senior managers with college degrees from elite institutions, more than one in two (51.6 percent) became chief executive. One way to summarize the difference that education makes is to calculate odds ratios for successful upward movement of senior managers with higher education compared to those who did not attend college. Compared to senior managers holding no college degree, the ratio of those with a less BA is 1.37 to 1 for becoming a CEO; of those with a top BA, the ratio is 1.94.[12]

TABLE 8.2
Percentage of Senior Corporate Managers Who Serve as Chief Executive Officer,
Multiple Corporate Director, and Leader of a Major Business Association,
by Educational Background

Educational Background	Chief Executives	Multiple Directors	Business Association Leaders	Number of Managers
All managers	38.9%	25.9%	18.4%	(2,729)
No college	26.5%	9.6%	4.5%	(291)
BA only, unranked college	36.4	20.5	14.9	(753)
BA only, top college	51.6	37.9	22.5	(306)
MBA, top program	44.9	29.6	23.4	(385)
Significance*	<.001	<.001	<.001	

*Based on analysis of variance F-test comparing the proportions with high attainment among the groups with varying educational backgrounds.

Similar credential differences are evident between senior managers who do and managers who do not become directors of several large corporations or leaders of the major business associations (Table 8.2). Of those with no university experience, 9.6 percent become active in the Business Roundtable and other associations. Of those with a bachelor's degree from one of the top eleven institutions, by contrast, 37.9 percent become multiple directors (on odds ratio of 3.95) and 22.5 percent come to take an active role in the business associations (a ratio of 5.00)

Receiving an MBA from a top program, however, does not materially improve the senior manager's prospects for achieving a chief executiveship above the prospects of those who have already earned a BA degree from a top-ranked university. Of the managers holding MBA degress, 44.9 percent became chief executives, but of those with only the top BA degrees, 51.6 percent reached the same office. The differences in becoming a multiple director show a similar reverse disparity, and the differences are negligible for becoming a participant in a major business association.

The incremental value of a top MBA degree for upward movement within senior management may only be evident, these data seem to suggest, for senior managers who do not already possess an elite BA degree. Evidence confirms this supposition if we compare the achievements of those holding different combinations of undergraduate and graduate business credentials. Among senior managers holding the lesser-ranked BA degree, the percentages who reach CEO status, become multiple directors, and become business association leaders are found to be sharply higher if they subsequently obtain a top MBA degree. Among those senior managers holding the top BA degree, however, the percentages achieving these ranks are not enhanced if they go on to acquire a top MBA degree. In the case of CEO status, for instance, among those with a lesser-ranked BA degree and no subsequent MBA degree, 36.4 percent became chief executives; of those with the lesser BA degree and who went on to earn a top MBA, 46.9 percent reached CEO status. By contrast, of those with a top B.A., the proportions who reached the chief executive suite were virtually identical whether they earned a top MBA or not (51.6 versus 51.5 percent). Similar percentage differences characterize the multiple-directorship and business-association statuses.

It is possibe, of course, that the general findings on the importance of the educational credential are a partial artifact of the varying ages of senior managers. Compared to managers over the age of 61, for instance, managers under the age of 55 are modestly more likely to have received a top MBA degree (18.9 percent versus 9.2 percent) and less likely to have received a top BA only (10.1 percent versus 14.7 percent), though the proportions receiving a BA from a lesser institution show little secular change (27.5 percent versus 25.6 percent). The relationship between age and reaching the chief executive status is also relatively modest. Of those under 55, 38.2 percent had become CEO's, while among those over 62, the percentage is 45.1. These limited age differences reflect the restricted age range of the senior managers who are the focus of the analysis; indeed, about one-third are in the 55 to 61 age range, with one-third over 61 and one-third under 55.

Limiting the analysis to only those senior managers who are age 55 to 61, approximately the middle third of the executives, we find that the relationship between educational credentials and the achievement of the CEO status parallels the overall patterns reported in Table 8.2. Of those who did not attend a university, 35.8 percent had reached the CEO position: of those holding a lesser BA, a top BA, and a top MBA, the respective percentages are 46.5, 64.6, and 62.6 (p < .001). As is the case for all senior managers, then, even among this age restricted group the holders of lesser BAs do significantly better than those who received no higher education, and the holders of top BAs and top MBAs do considerably better still and about as well as one another.

UPPER-CLASS ORIGINS, SCHOLASTIC CAPITAL, AND CAREER ADVANCEMENT

The results of the previous section reveal that, for all companies combined, senior managers with only a BA from a top institution generally do as well as or even slightly better than managers who acquire the quintessential professional management degree, an MBA from a top-rated school. This can be most sharply demonstrated if we compare the managerial careers of those who completed undergraduate degrees at one of three leading universities—Harvard, Yale and Princeton—and who received no post-graduate education thereafter, with those members of our corporate sample who obtained MBA degrees from the nation's preeminant post-graduate business program, Harvard's Graduate School of Business.

Senior career experiences among senior managers with these distinctive backgrounds are shown in Table 9.3. The differences in the rates of high achievement are virtually indistinguishable. Those holding only baccalaureate degrees from Harvard, Yale or Princeton are about as likely to become chief executives (40.3 percent did) as those who hold MBA degrees from Harvard (41.4 percent). Similarly, 33.6 percent of the Harvard, Yale and Princeton BA recipients became multiple directors, and 31.3 percent of the Harvard MBA recipients did so; the corresonding figures for serving in the major business associations are 21.6 percent and 23.3 percent.[13]

TABLE 8.3
Percentage of Senior Corporate Managers Achieving High Corporate Position,
for Graduates of Harvard, Yale, and Princeton Universities

Educational Background	Chief Executive	Multiple Director	Business Association	Number of Managers
BA only from Harvard, Yale or Princeton	40.3%	33.6%	21.6%	(268)
MBA from Harvard	41.4	31.3	23.3	(227)
Significance*	n.s.	n.s.	n.s.	

*Based on a t-test comparing the BA graduates of Harvard, Yale and Princeton with the graduates of the Harvard Business School.

Senior managers who have acquired what is reputed to be best technical training for a management career, the Harvard MBA, are no more successful, our results reveal, in pursuing that career to its heights than are senior managers who received a BA from Harvard, Yale or Princeton and received no specific training in management. Since earning a Harvard MBA degree should presumably offer some tangible advantage for a career in business, this finding suggests that senior managers who only completed an undergraduate degree at a top institution may possess forms of capital, other than educational credentials, that facilitate their advancement in the corporate world. An upper-class social origin is one of those possibilities.

Consistent with this expectation, we find that the proportion of senior managers with upper social origins varies considerably by educational category. Among senior managers who did not attend college, 10.3 percent were descendants of upper-class families; similarly, only 8.6 percent of those who received BAs from non-elite colleges were of upper social origin. Among the graduates of the top eleven undergraduate institutions, however, 38.9 percent shared this origin. Among alumni of Harvard, Yale and Princeton, the proportion reached 49.6 percent.[14] Graduates of the top MBA programs are, however, of more modest origins on average, with only 20.8 percent coming from established backgrounds. A slightly larger proportion—26.4 percent—of the Harvard MBA graduates were of patrician background, but this is still just over half the proportion of the Harvard, Yale and Princeton BA holders from such families.

Because top educational credentials are, as the above figures demonstrate, strongly correlated with coming from an upper-class background, specification of any independent effect of scholastic capital or senior managers' careers requires the introduction of family background into the analysis. Accordingly, we divide the managers into those of upper-class origins and those without such backgrounds, and examine the association between university credentials and position within the stratified ranks of senior managers; the results are displayed in Table 8.4.

TABLE 8.4
Percentage of Senior Corporate Managers Achieving High Corporate Position,
by Social Origin and Educational Background

University Background	Chief Executive		Multiple Director		Business Association		Number of Managers	
	Other Origin	Upper Origin	Other Origin	Upper Origin	Other Origin	Upper Origin	Other Origin	Upper Origin
No university	26.4%	26.7%	6.9%	33.3%	3.8%	10.0%	(261)	(30)
BA only, unranked college	34.6	55.4	18.0	46.2	13.7	27.7	(688)	(65)
BA only, top college	51.9	51.3	32.6	46.2	14.4	35.3	(187)	(119)
MBA, top program	44.9	45.0	25.9	43.8	22.0	38.8	(305)	(80)
All educational-background groups	37.3	47.3	22.2	44.8	15.7	32.4	(2287)	(442)
Significance*								
Education	<.001	.053	<.001	.003	<.001	.056		
Social origin	<.001		<.001		<.001			

*Based on analysis of variance F-tests; the social origin significance level compares the two origin groups for managers of all educational backgrounds.

Whatever the social background of the senior managers, we see that stronger educational credentials generally enhance the probability of upward ascent within senior management ranks. The increase in probability with rising credentials is, however, steadier among those of non-upper than upper social origins. Of those with non-upper origins, for instance, 7 percent of the managers without college experience were serving on two or more corporate boards: 18 percent of those with a top BA were so located: and among top MBA holders, the proportion stood at 25 percent. Among multiple directors with upper-class backgrounds, however, there were no notable differences among those who had attended college.

Among senior managers from patrician families, higher credentials are also generally associated with reaching higher positions within senior management, but the upward progression is less steady. The gap between the probability of high achievement for the upper-origin managers holding the two types of undergraduate degrees is small. There is virtually no difference, for instance, in the likelihood of reaching the chief executiveship of a corporation or of becoming a director of several companies between those possessing the top and the lesser BA credentials. Thus, an upper-class origin provides a kind of career insurance within the senior ranks if the manager attended a lesser undergraduate institution rather than one of the leading eleven. Possessing superior social and perhaps economic capital, these upper-class individuals are, as Bourdieu's framework suggests, less dependent on the acquisition of rare forms of scholastic capital.

The patterns in Table 8.4 also reveal that the probability of joining the ranks of senior managers is, even controlling for educational credential, in many instances substantially higher for upper-class individuals than for the others. In some cases, however, there is no difference; there is no gap, for example, between the proportions of upper- and non-upper class top MBA graduates who become chief executives (the percentage for both cases is 45). In most of the cases, however, class background makes a considerable difference. The largest gap is in the proportion obtaining multiple directorships among those holding BAs from non-elite institutions: 18.0 percent of the non-patrician managers had so succeeded, compared to 46.2 percent of the managers from upper-class backgrounds.

In sum, these figures reveal that upper-class origins confer a significant advantage on the career prospects of senior managers with the same educational credentials. Credentials also make a substantial independent difference in the careers of senior managers, though less so for the minority of managers from upper-class backgrounds than for the majority who are not. The effects of social origin, though present inside the firm, are considerably more powerful in the external corporate world—a point to which we shall return later. Whereas senior managers of upper-class origins are 1.27 times more likely (47.3 percent versus

37.3 percent) to become CEO than their non-patrician counterparts, they are 2.02 times more likely to become multiple directors, and 2.06 times more likely to become representatives of key business associations.

COMBINATION OF CAPITAL AND ADVANCEMENT BEYOND THE CORPORATION

The greater influence of upper-class background on advancement outside the firm suggests that a somewhat different set of attributes may facilitate movement into the highest circles of business leadership. The kinds of qualities rewarded inside the company may not be the same as those that provide access to the more diffuse and "political" positions involving the management of relations among firms and between business and government. Senior managers with characteristics appropriate for the first may lack some of the less tangible qualities that would enable them to move easily into the second.

Moving outside the firm is, however, to a considerable extent contingent on proven success within the firm. Senior managers often move well beyond the corporation if they have already reached the top within it. This is evident if we compare the outside success of the senior managers who have reached the chief executive suite with those who have not. Among those who are not chief executives, 35.5 percent have become multiple directors; among the chief executives, 65.6 percent are serving on the boards of several other major firms. Similarly, among the non-CEOs, only 11.6 percent take an active role in a major business association, while 29.6 percent of the CEOs have assumed this leadership role.

Successful movement into the informally structured networks among large corporations depends, however, on more than positional location within one. It calls upon a set of attributes not necessarily acquired on the way up the corporate ladder: a capacity to understand problems facing companies operating in entirely different markets; an ability to develop broadly conceived and long-range political strategies for businesses as a whole; a facility in mixing with established families that are still a force in the life of some corporations; and a capacity to work with a range of conflicting and sometimes hostile groups and constituencies, ranging from federal officials to leaders of the environmental and labor movements. Some managers develop such qualities during their long career climb into their company's senior executive ranks (Useem, 1985). Others may, by virtue of educational and/or social background, already possess many of the attributes that facilitate ascent within inter-corporate circles long before reaching the firm's apex.

To explore the special value of educational and background advantages for moving beyond the corporation, we contrast the experiences of four groups of senior managers towards the extremes of the distribution of scholastic and social capital. These are senior managers with (1) low education and low background; (2) low education and high background; (3) high education and low background; and (4)high education and high background. "Low" (or nonelite) education is here defined broadly to include graduation from a non-elite college, attending but not completing college, or never attending college; "low" background is defined to be of non-upper-class origin. High education is defined as graduating from a leading MBA program, the training most technically relevant to a career in management; high background is defined to be of upper-class origin. The percentages and probabilities of the latter three groups succeeding outside the firm compared to the percentages and probabilities of the senior managers with neither educational nor origin advantages are displayed in Table 8.5.

TABLE 8.5
Ratios of Percentages of Senior Corporate Managers Advantaged
by Education and Background Who Become Chief Executives,
Multiple Corporate Directors, and Business Association Leaders,
Compared to Percentages of Non-Advantaged Senior Managers Who Achieve These Positions

Senior Managers	Chief Executives	Multiple Directors	Business Association Leaders	Number of Managers
Low education, low background*	1.00 (34.0%)	1.00 (15.0%)	1.00 (11.3%)	(1086)
High education, low background	1.37 (47.6%)	1.90 (28.5%)	1.69 (19.1%)	(492)
Low education, high background	1.45 (50.4%)	2.63 (39.5%)	1.86 (21.0%)	(119)
High education, high background	1.40 (48.7%)	3.01 (45.2%)	2.98 (33.7%)	(199)

*The low education group comprises managers who never attended college, failed to graduate, or who graduated from a lesser university; high education consists of managers who received an MBA degree from one of the top-ranked programs.

Using the second column of the table as a baseline, the figures indicate that 15.0 percent of the senior managers with non-elite educational and social backgrounds became a multiple director. If a senior manager had no family advantage but earned an MBA degree from a top program, the probability of reaching this status is 1.90 times higher than that of the group with neither (28.5 percent versus 15.0 percent). Conversely, if the manager had low educational credentials but a high origin, the probability ratio is 2.63 (39.5 percent versus 15.0 percent). Finally, if the manager were advantaged in both areas, the probability ratio for achieving several major corporate directorship is 3.01 (45.2 percent versus 15.0 percent). The latter ratio implies that a senior manager with an upper-class origin and an MBA degree from a leading program is three times as likely as a senior manager with neither to be invited to join the board of several major corporations. Trends in the same direction if not the same magnitude are found for achieving the chief executiveship of a major firm and business leadership of a major association.

The probabilty ratios are larger for multiple directorships and association leadership than for the chief executiveship. Among those advantaged by education but not background, the probabiltity ratio is 1.37 for becoming a chief executive, but 1.90 for becoming a multiple director, and 1.69 for becoming an association leader. In other words, the value of a senior manager's elite business degree, in the absence of an upper-class family background, is somewhat greater for advancement beyond the firm than within it. Similarly, among those advantaged by background but not education, the ratios are also increasing, rising from 1.45 to 2.63 and 1.86. To the extent that an elite educational grounding and an upper-class upbringing impart the kinds of social and cultural capital required for effective movement beyond the corporation, the evidence confirms the importance of each of these capacities for success outside it.

The disparities in the probabilty ratios are even greater for senior managers advantaged by both background and education. The probability ratio is 1.40 for becoming a chief executive, but rises to 3.01 for invitation onto other corporate boards, and to 2.98 for service in the major business associations. The career value of the abilities engendered by both a top MBA education and an upper-class origin is, thus, important for reaching the chief executive suite, but even more critical for reaching beyond it. Movement in the organizationally diverse and politically conflictual world of corporate boards and business associations is, our results reveal, facilitated by the early experiences that come with these backgrounds.

Education and background are of course only two of the many factors that account for managerial advancement in the large corporation. Individual qualities such as personal drive, persuasive skills, intellect or a shrewd sense of the market, and more structural factors such as location in an expanding industry, propel many managers ahead despite the lack of elite educational and social credentials (Kanter, 1977; Squires, 1979).

THE LAW DEGREE AS AN ALTERNATIVE
EDUCATIONAL PATHWAY

One of the most striking findings of our study thus far is that advancement both inside and outside the firm depends to a considerable degree on the possession of characteristics other than the technical or administrative capacities engendered by graduate business programs. The conventional skills of marketing, budgeting, and managing personnel may be important (especially within the firm), but so too may be the capacity to deal with the judicial and executive branches of the state, especially in an era of corporate mergers and government regulation. The data collected in the present study do not allow direct confirmation of this interpretation. If it were true, however, we would expect to find that the possession of a top law degree (LL.B.) confers significant career advantages among senior managers.

Law schools may inculcate the kinds of skills that are especially useful to firms as they attempt to manage uncertainty in difficult, and at times, hostile political and economic environments. While an elite legal education might be helpful for rising within a firm, we anticipate that its impact would be great outside the firm as well. And if there is far more to rising within the corporate world than the possession of the technical and managerial training imparted by business schools, then holders of top-ranked law degrees might fare as well as top MBAs.

To test this possibility, we examine the career advancement of senior managers who held law degrees from nine previously identified, top-ranked programs. Of the 203 senior managers who held a law degree from one of these programs, we compare the proportion who achieved the three levels of career distinction with the proportions who achieved these levels among those holding a BA or MBA degree from one of the top institutions. The proportions are reported in Table 8.6; for a baseline for comparison, we also report the corresponding proportions among those who did not attend a university.

A top-ranked law degree is seen to be as effective a pathway for moving up the corporate ladder as a BA from one of the top eleven universities or a top MBA. Of the top BA holders and MBA holders, 51.6 percent and 44.9 percent, respectively, have become CEO's; of the top law degree holders, 45.3 percent have achieved the same (compared with 26.5 percent of those without a university education). The attributes acquired in a top liberal arts program, top MBA program, or top law school all apparently provided resources that facilitate the final upward climb.

The results in Table 8.6 also confirm our hypothesis that a top law degree is useful for ascent in the broader corporate community. Thirty-six percent of the top law graduates serve on several major boards, compared to 37.9 percent and 29.6 percent of elite BAs and MBAs, respectively (and only 9.6 percent among those with no higher education). For leadership of a major business association, the three groups of elite graduates are also about equally likely to serve (the percentages range from 22.5 to 25.6, compared to 4.5 percent of those without university training).

TABLE 8.6

Percentage of Senior Corporate Managers Who Serve as Chief Executive Officer,
Multiple Corporate Director, and Leader of a Major Business Association,
among Those Holding a Bachelor's, Business or Law Degree from a Top University or Program

Educational Background	Chief Executives	Multiple Directors	Business Association Leaders	Number of Managers
No university	26.5%	9.6%	4.5%	(291)
BA only, top college	51.6	37.9	22.5	(306)
MBA, top program	44.9	29.6	23.4	(385)
Law, top program	45.3	36.0	25.6	(203)

Though top law programs offer no explicit training in management, we see that their graduates do at least as well as top MBA graduates in becoming CEOs and in moving beyond the firm. In the contemporary corporate environment, the legal and political capacities developed in law school may be as useful as the managerial skills stressed in business schools. But whatever the reason, graduation from a top law school provides an alternative pathway that is apparently as smooth as the more familiar route traveled by holders of top MBAs.

PATTERNS OF ASCENT AMONG SENIOR CORPORATE MANAGERS

Having established that there are a variety of pathways to the corporate elite and that both educational and class background affect the likelihood of ascent from within the ranks of senior managers, we now turn to a simultaneous analysis of the advantaging effects of the educational and background variables. Analyses of the impact of these on each of the study's three main dependent variables— becoming a CEO, joining the board of directors of more than one firm, and participation in the leadership of a major business association—are conducted separately to allow for the possibility of distinct dynamics of advancement.

To undertake these analyses, we create seven predictor variables, including four to represent the senior manager's educational background:

(1) holding a bachelor's degree from a non-elite institution (and no post-graduate training); (2) possessing a BA degree from a top institution (with no post-graduate education); (3) receiving an MBA degree from a top program; and (4) holding a law degree from a top school. Social origin is introduced as a binary variable distinguishing between (5) senior managers with upper-class origins and those with non-upper-class origins. Two additional predictor variables are introduced to represent the two major sources of interaction that we have implicitly described in earlier results. These are dichotomous variables representing those who (6) hold a lesser BA degree (and no post-graduate training) and are of upper-class origins, and those who (7) hold a non-elite BA and a top MBA degree.

Three multiple regressions are performed.[16] The first is with service as a chief executive officer as the outcome variable and the above factors as predictor variables. The second regression is with service as a member of the board of directors of several major corporations as the outcome variable. For this regression, the senior manager's position in the firm is introduced as a predictor variable, for we have previously seen that appointment to several boards of directors is significantly enhanced if the manager holds the chief executive position. The third regression is with business association leadership as the outcome variable, and for this analysis we introduce both the managerial position and multiple directorship position as predictor variables. Entry into the business association leadership is partially contingent on previously reaching each (see Useem, 1984). We therefore also create binary variables representing those who (8) serve as chief executive, and those who (9) serve on two or more corporate boards. The results of all three regression analyses are presented in Table 8.7.

The multiple regression for service on the board of directors of several major corporations reveals that nearly all of the factors independently increase the prediction of movement into this highest circle of the business community (Table 8.7). Compared to those without the benefit of a university education, and controlling for other factors, a senior manager is .07 more likely to serve on several major boards if a BA is held from a lesser-ranked university (drawing on the unstandardized coefficients). If a BA from a top-ranked university is held, the probability is increased to .17; if an MBA from a top-ranked program, by .11; and if a law degree from a top school, by .23. An upper-class origin independently advantages a senior manager by .17. Neither of the interaction effects yields significant coefficients, but reaching the chief executive suite does, with an unstandardized coefficient of .22.

TABLE 8.7

Regression of Senior Managers' Service as Chief Executive, on Several Corporate Boards, and as Business Association Leader: with Educational Background, Social Origins, and Company Position

Independent Variables	Chief Executive			Multiple Director			Business Association		
	b	beta	p	b	beta	p	b	beta	p
Educational background									
BA only, unranked college	.084	.084	<.05	.072	.080	<.05	.054	.068	n.s.
BA only, top college	.249	.184	<.01	.167	.138	<.01	.048	.045	n.s.
MBA, top program	.148	.120	<.01	.110	.099	<.01	.084	.086	<.05
Law, top program	.101	.072	<.01	.232	.183	<.01	.134	.121	<.01
Upper social origins	.016	.012	n.s.	.166	.143	<.01	.088	.086	<.01
Interaction factors									
Unranked BA, top MBA	.051	.034	n.s.	.018	.014	n.s.	.011	.009	n.s.
Unranked BA, top family	.191	.070	<.01	.067	.028	n.s.	−.032	−.015	n.s.
Business position									
Chief executive	—	—	—	.217	.243	<.01	.118	.150	<.01
Multiple director	—	—	—	—	—	—	.211	.240	<.01
Multiple correlation coefficients	.175		<.01	.365		<.01	.372		<.01
Multiple R squared	.031			.133			.138		
(Number of senior managers=1,993)									

The regression coefficients are generally smaller in predicting ascent into the chief executiveship but larger in predicting movement into the leadership of the major business associations. All of the education coefficients are significant for predicting the chief executiveship, but the social origins factor is not. For predicting business association leadership, the two BA coefficients are not significant predictors, but holding a top MBA or top law degree, and upper-class origins are. The only significant independent interaction effect among the three regressions is observed for those of upper-class origins holding a non-elite BA, where the combination does advantage the holder for becoming a chief executive.

Scholastic capital thus makes a continuing difference in the careers of those at the highest levels of corporate management. It helps distinguish those who will become chief executives from those who will not. Among those who do reach the top office of the corporation, it further distinguishes those who will join the governing board of several other corporations and enter the leadership of the major business associations. The educational credential need not, however, be an elite MBA. Indeed, for ascent outside the firm, a top law degree confers an even greater advantage than the top MBA (the regression coefficients are larger for multiple directorships and business association leadership than for chief executiveship).

Finally, originating in an upper-class family has a positive effect on the careers of senior managers independent of all other variables. This effect is not statistically significant for ascent within the firm to the status of CEO, but coming from a patrician background does confer important advantages in gaining access to positions of leadership outside the firm. Of the five background variables, upper-class origin is second only to a top law degree in affecting the likelihood of participating in a leading business association. Thus, although family capitalism may be on the decline, as Bell (1960) argued more than a quarter of a century ago, coming from an upper-class background remains an important resource in gaining access to the highest rungs of the corporate world.

DISCUSSION

Our results reveal that, first, even among senior corporate managers, continued upward career mobility is enhanced by the possession of prestigious educational credentials. Among this highly select group of late-career individuals, scholastic capital still makes a difference, as anticipated by Bourdieu, Collins, and others. Compared, for example, to a senior manager without a college education, a senior manager holding a bachelor's degree from one of the nation's top undergraduate institutions is twice as likely to be chosen to be a CEO. Compared to a senior manager holding a BA degree from a non-elite institution, the holder of the top BA is 42 percent more likely to reach the chief executive suite. Similarly, the top BA holder has a 51 percent higher probability than the lesser BA holder of moving into the leadership of key business associations, and an 85 percent greater likelihood of joining several corporate boards of directors.

Our findings also demonstrate that there are a variety of educational pathways to top corporate management, and that the MBA is but one among many. Elite business schools are quite successful in placing their graduates in the ranks of top senior management, but so too, our findings demonstrate, are institutions that do not even purport to train their students in the science of management. Indeed, by the late 1970s lawyers were represented among the ranks of top senior managers in numbers roughly equal to MBA holders. The prominence of attorneys in our sample may, we suspect, represent a shift in activities of senior managers away from the traditional tasks of producing and marketing a product to the more externally oriented tasks of trying to manage an increasingly complex political and economic environment.

Scholastic capital is by no means the only form of capital that facilitates success in the higher reaches of the corporate world. Social capital— defined in our study as originating in an upper-class family—has positive effects on the careers of corporate managers with identical educational credentials, especially outside the firm. More than twice as many managers from patrician backgrounds served as directors on several corporate boards and were members of leading business associations than their counterparts from non-upper-class backgrounds.

While our data do not permit us to specify the precise mechanisms that advantage those who come from upper-class families, it seems likely that their superior social capital gives them greater access to strategic elite networks. One piece of evidence that is consistent with this hypothesis is Barton's (1985) finding that upper-class members of the business elite were more involved in inter-elite sociometric networks. These contacts promoted participation in the kinds of policy-planning organizations that we have referred to as major business associations. Such contacts—whether based on the "old school tie," membership in exclusive social clubs, or other characteristic means of upper-class linkage— would also facilitate invitation onto corporate boards.

The study's principal hypothesis—that those individuals who possess the greatest amount of scholastic *and* social capital will be most likely to gain access to the core of the American business elite—is also confirmed. The data do not permit us to test directly why this is so, but some of our results would seem to cast doubt on explanations stressing the superior technical expertise of the managers who are most successful. For example, an elite MBA offers technical training most directly relevant to life as a corporate executive, yet those members of our sample who possess a top BA degree were found to be equally successful.

If the greater success of those of superior educational and social background is not largely a product of technical expertise, it is less clear what does explain it. One possibility is, as Collins (1971, 1979) has suggested, that individuals with top educational and social credentials tend to differ from their less advantaged counterparts in personality and style in ways that prove advantageous in the corporate world. Since uncertainty is, as Kanter (1977) and other analysts of organizations have noted, most pronounced at the highest levels of management, trust is critical. And one of the simplest ways for organizations to entrust decisions to the "trustworthy" is for the already powerful to promote people most similar to themselves educationally and socially.

Yet if our findings indicate that both social and scholastic capital facilitate ascent into the highest levels of the corporate world, there is nothing in our results to suggest that a social or academic elite monopolizes such positions. Few of the "non-upper-class" members of our sample, are, to be sure, likely to be the children of manual workers.[17] Moreover, well over 80 percent of our sample graduated from college at a time when no more than 15 percent of their cohorts even entered higher education. Nonetheless, if top corporate management reflects a socially and educationally privileged segment of its generation, it also includes a significant number of individuals of non-elite origins. Over 10 percent of the corporate elite, for example, did not attend college at all and an additional 6 percent failed to complete a bachelor's degree.

Such figures on educational background could not, it is worth noting, be found in any of the high-status professions, for such professions are far more credentialized than the world of business. Medicine, law, and other prestigious professions are often viewed as the embodiments of industrial society's inherent trend towards "universalism" (Parsons, 1951, 1971). Yet as neo-Weberians (Parkin, 1979) have argued, these professions may be seen as exhibiting exceptionally high rates of intergenerational immobility. The world of corporate management is, to be sure, becoming increasingly credentialized, and social background continued to play an important role within it.[18] Nonetheless, the world of business, by virtue of its relative openness to market innovation, may be more permeable to upward mobility than highly credentialized professions that implicitly require heavy concentrations of cultural capital.[19]

A final implication of our study is that it suggests that a theoretical framework, such as that proposed by Bourdieu, which stresses the impact of different forms of "capital"—social, economic, cultural, and scholastic—on the career trajectories of elites, is likely to be a fruitful one. Though we were not able in this study to include measures of all the relevant types of capital, we were able to establish that differences in the amounts of both scholastic and social capital possessed by senior corporate managers powerfully affected their positions *within* the stratified ranks of corporate management. Interestingly, the impact of possessing both is greatest where it arguably matters most—in gaining access to the highest levels of power and responsibility in the corporate world and in taking on leadership roles in those organizations that claim to speak for the interests of business as a whole.

NOTES

*The research reported here has been supported by grants from the National Science Foundation (SOC77-06658, SES-80-25542 and SES-83-19986), and this article is a fully collaborative effort by the two authors. We would like to acknowledge helpful comments on an earlier draft by Richard Alba, Paul J. DiMaggio, Caroline H. Persell, David Swartz, and several anonymous reviewers.

1. In his essay on bureaucracy in the *Economy and Society*, Max Weber noted the crucial role education has come to play in the distribution of privilege: "The role played in former days by 'proof of ancestry'," wrote Weber, "is nowadays taken by the patent of education." "The elaboration of the diplomas from universities, business and engineering colleges, and the universal clamor for the creation of further educational certificates in all fields," he observed, "serve the formation of a privileged stratum in bureaus and in offices." "Such certificates," Weber concluded, "support their holders' claims . . . to the monopolization of socially and economically advantageous positions" (Weber, 1978:1000).

2. Though the line separating a firm's senior managers from others is imprecise, for purposes of analysis we adopted a widely used definition of top management as the seniormost six to ten managers of the firm. A survey by the Conference Board of the chief executives of 432 large companies in 1981, for instance, reports that "top management" is generally considered to include the highest ranking six to ten executives, with a median near eight (Shaeffer and Janger, 1982). Our definition of senior management is, thus, consistent with that used within most large companies, and our procedure is similar to that used by other researchers studying top company management. It is similar, for instance, to that used by Wagner et al. (1984) in their analysis of the determinants of turnover among senior corporate management.

3. The standard reference sources included Dun and Bradstreet's *Reference Book of Corporate Management*; Standard and Poor's *Register of Corporations, Directors, and Executives*; Marquis' *Who's Who in America* (several editions), *Who's Who in Finance and Industry, Who's Who in the World, Who's Who in the East, Who's Who in the West, Who's Who in the Midwest, Who's Who in the South, Who's Who in Law*, and *Who's Who in Government*. For more details on the sources used, as well as a list of the names of the firms studied, see Useem (1984).

4. The exclusion of the 376 managers may bias the results, and this possibility can be examined by comparing the "respondents" and "non-respondents." We have collected complete information on which members of both groups have attended three leading private universities, Harvard, Yale, and Princeton. This was done through direct consultation of the alumni directories of the three institutions, thereby avoiding the non-response problem that biographical directories face in depending on managers' cooperation for the compilation of alumni information. Comparing the proportions of the two groups which had received bachelor's degrees from the three universities (including those who went on to earn post-graduate degrees), the proportions are found to be modestly greater for respondents than non-respondents. Of the respondents, 15.4 percent had graduated from one of the three schools; of the non-respondents, 11.4 percent

had graduated. The exclusion of the non-respondents from the ensuing analysis thus creates a modest upward bias in the distribution of educational credentials. Comparisons on other dimensions reveal similar upward skews: respondents are more likely to be associated with large than middle-sized manufacturing firms than are non-respondents (32.3 versus 16.8 percent); affiliated with the Business Roundtable and three other major business associations (18.5 versus 1.8 percent); and listed in the 1978 or 1979 editions of the *Social Register* (11.0 versus 7.0 percent). There is no difference, however, in the extent to which they are drawn from the financial sector. On most dimensions, then, there is a general upward response bias. The relatively small proportion of non-respondents—12.1 percent—does not, however, seriously distort the analyses' estimates.

5. The composition and general characteristics of boards of directors of large U.S. corporations are described in Bacon (1973), Pfeffer and Salancik (1978), Aldrich (1979), Pennings (1980), and Harris and Associates (1977).

6. Descriptions of the role organization and role of these associations are contained in Domhoff (1979), McQuaid (1980), and Burch (1983). For a discussion of the choice of these particular four organizations, see Useem (1984).

7. The year of Coleman's rating of undergraduate institutions, 1940, is ideal for the period when the largest number of the managers in our study were enrolled in higher education. In that year, the average age of the individuals in our study was 19. In 1977, the year for which much of the information on their current position was collected, the average age was 56, a figure nearly identical to those recorded in other studies of senior management (Burck, 1976; Bonfield, 1980).

8. These eleven institutions were selected because they were the only colleges to appear in the top four of Coleman's 33 prestige categories and in Pierson's (1969) list, based on his synthesis of numerous studies, of the 20 institutions that, historically, have educated the largest number of corporate executives.

9. These eleven business schools are the only institutions to appear on a list of the top dozen institutions in *MBA Magazine* (1974) and on Pierson's 1969 list cited above in note 8. The sole institution excluded on the basis of Pierson's findings was Carnegie Mellon.

10. Two of the better known boarding schools, Exeter and Andover, are not included because they support numbers of students on scholarships and their admissions policies have historically been less socially exclusive than the other fourteen schools (Baltzell, 1964; Domhoff, 1967; Levine, 1980). Had Exeter and Andover been included, the number of senior managers attending major prep schools would have increased from 267 (9.8 percent) to 353 (12 percent).

11. Of the 442 managers who are identified as being of upper-class origin, 30.3 percent (134) are included because they graduated from one of the preparatory schools; 39.6 percent (175) are included because they appear in the *Social*

Register; and 30.1 percent (133) are included because of both. It should be noted that our measure almost certainly *underestimates* the proportion of our sample that is of upper-class origin. Many individuals from high-status families, especially from smaller towns and cities in the South and West, appear neither in the *Social Register* nor among the alumni of the prominent preparatory schools in the Northeast. This measure also excluded individuals from affluent upper-middle-class families, many of whom may possess special capacities by virtue of their backgrounds which advantage them in corporate careers as well.

12. As would be expected, senior managers holding lesser MBA degrees do less well than those with top MBA degrees. Indeed, lesser MBA recipients achieve at rates similar to those of lesser BA recipients. The likelihood of a lesser MBA holder achieving the chief executiveship, for instance, is .358, virtually the same as the .364 probability for the lesser BA holder.

13. While the two groups display nearly identical upward movement within the ranks of senior management, the BA-only graduates of Harvard, Yale and Princeton arrived in the senior ranks more quickly. Among the Harvard, Yale and Princeton graduates, 39 percent reached a vice-presidency of a major company (among the nation's 1,300 largest firms) before the age of 40, while only 32 percent of the Harvard MBA recipients did so. These undergraduate degrees did not advantage them over Harvard MBA holders within the senior management hierarchy, but they did more often place them on the fast track into senior management.

14. For an analysis of the forces shaping the admissions policies of Harvard, Yale, and Princeton during the years before World War II, as well as additional evidence on the social origins of students at these institutions during this period, see Karabel (1984).

15. Since our measure of upper-class origin was based on two separate factors, it may be useful to disaggregate the effects of preparatory school attendance from those of inclusion in the *Social Register*. Cookson and Persell's (1985) study of elite boarding schools reveals a self-conscious socialization for future leadership in these schools' curricula. It might be argued, then, that the preparatory school experience may be more important for managerial advancement than inclusion in the *Social Register*, for the latter is more of a sign of family lineage than anything else. To examining this possibility, we compare the careers of the senior managers with one, both, or neither of the two measures of upper-class origins. We find that having either or both factors significantly increases ascent in the corporate world, but that there is relatively little difference between the factors, either singly or in combination. Thus, while 37.3 percent of the managers with neither characteristics had become a chief executive officer (Table 8.4), 49.2 percent of the preparatory school graduates, 42.3 percent of *Social Register* members, and 51.9 percent of those with both had reached this position. The corresponding percentages for becoming a multiple director are 22.0, 37.3, 50.9, and 44.4; and for business association leadership they are 15.7, 27.6,

33.1, and 36.1. It would appear that high social origins can be an enduring asset in a business career, regardless of how they are defined or refined.

16. Because of the dichotomous structure of the outcome variables and their skewed distribution, particularly for business association leadership, we also performed a logistic regression. The relative magnitudes of the coefficients were virtually identical to those reported for the multiple regressions above.

17. Studies of the social background of top corporate managers, cited earlier, typically find relatively low proportions with blue-collar origins. In a study sponsored by *Fortune* magazine, for example, Diamond (1970) reported that only 16 percent of a sample of chief executives were sons of manual workers or farmers, while 45 percent had fathers who had been company founders, corporate presidents, or self-employed businessmen. "American lore is filled with tales of the up-from-nowhere achiever," he concluded, but "the reality is that most chief executives grew up in comfortable middle- and upper-middle-class surroundings."

18. The rising importance of the educational credential in business can be seen in trends in the number of students pursuing the MBA degree. In 1955-56, only 3,280 MBA degrees were awarded nationally, but by 1978-79 the number had increased more than tenfold to 50,506 (National Center for Educational Statistics, 1981: 129).

19. For evidence that the high-status professions may be less open to upward mobility than business management, see Marceau's (1977) study of class and status in France, and Brint's (1981) analysis of patterns of recruitment into six high-status occupations, including business management, in the United States.

REFERENCES

Aldrich, Howard. 1979. *Organizations and Environments,* Englewood Cliffs, NJ: Prentice-Hall.

Bacon, Jeremy. 1973. *Corporate Directorship Practices: Membership and Committees of the Board.* New York: Conference Board.

Baltzell, E. Digby. 1958. *Philadephia Gentlemen: The Making of a National Upper Class.* New York: Free Press.

_____. 1964. *The Protestant Establishment: Aristocracy and Caste in America.* New York: Random House.

_____. 1966. " 'Who's Who in America' and 'The Social Register: Elite and Upper Class Indexes in Metropolitan America." Pp. 266-75 in *Class, Status, and Power,* edited by Reinhard Bendix and Seymour Martin Lipset. 2nd Edition. New York: Free Press.

Barton, Allen. 1985. "Determinants of Economics Attitudes in the American Business Elite." *American Journal of Sociology* 91:54-87.

Bell, Daniel. 1960, *The End of Ideology.* New York: Free Press.

Blau, Peter M., and Rebecca Zames Margulies. 1974-75. "A Research Replication: The Reputations of American Professional Schools." *Change* 6:42-47.

Bonfield, Patricia. 1980. *U.S. Business Leaders: A Study of Opinions and Characteristics.* New York: Conference Board.

Bourdieu, Pierre. 1973. "Cultural Reproduction and Social Reproduction." In *Knowledge, Education and Cultural Change,* edited by Richard Brown. London: Tavistock. (Reprinted on pp. 487-511 in *Power and Ideology in Education,* edited by Jerome Karabel and A. H. Halsey. New York: Oxford University Press, 1977).

———. 1984. *Distinction: A Social Critique of the Judgment of Taste.* Cambridge: Harvard University Press.

Bourdieu, Pierre, and Luc Boltanski. 1978. "Changes in Social Structure and Changes in the Demand for Education." Pp. 197-227 in *Contemporary Europe: Social Structure and Cultural Patterns,* edited by Salvador Giner and Margaret Scotford Archer. London: Routledge & Kegan Paul.

Bourdieu, Pierre, and Jean-Claude Passeron. 1977. *Reproduction in Education, Society and Culture.* London: Sage Publications.

Brint, Steven. 1981. "Intra-Occupational Stratification in Six High-Status Occupations." Unpublished manuscript. Cambridge, MA: Huron Institute.

Burch, Philip H., Jr. 1983. "The American Establishment: Its Historical Development and Major Economic Components." *Research in Political Economy* 6:83-156.

Burck, Charles G. 1976. "A Group Profile of the Fortune 500 Chief Executive." *Fortune,* May, pp. 173ff.

Coleman, Richard. 1973. "Report on College Characteristics." Cambridge MA: Harvard-MIT Joint Center for Urban Affairs.

Collins, Randall. 1971. "Functional and Conflict Theories of Educational Stratification." *American Sociological Review* 36:1002-19.

———. 1979. *The Credential Society: An Historical Sociology of Education and Stratification.* New York: Academic Press.

Cookson, Peter W., Jr., and Caroline Hodges Persell. 1985. *Preparing for Power: America's Elite Boarding Schools.* New York: Basic Books.

Diamond, Robert S. 1970. "A Self-Portrait of the Chief Executive." *Fortune* 81 (May):181, 320, 328.

Domhoff, G. William. 1967. *Who Rules America?* Englewood Cliffs, NJ: Prentice-Hall.

————. 1970. *The Higher Circles: The Governing Class in America.* New York: Random House.

————. 1979. *The Powers That Be.* New York: Random House.

Fortune. 1978. *The Fortune 1978 Double 500 Directory.* New York: Fortune Magazine.

Harris, Louis and Associates. 1977. *A Survey of Outside Directors of Major Publicly Owned Corporations.* New York: Conference Board.

Kanter, Rosabeth Moss. 1977. *Men and Women of the Corporation.* New York: Basic Books.

Karabel, Jerome. 1972. "Community Colleges and Social Stratification." *Harvard Educational Review* 42:521-62.

————. 1984. "Status-Group Struggle, Organizational Interests, and the Limits of Institutional Autonomy: The Transformation of Harvard, Yale, and Princeton, 1918-1940." *Theory and Society 13:1-40.*

Karabel, Jerome, and Alexander W. Astin. 1975. "Social Class, Academic Ability, and College 'Quality'." *Social Forces* 53:381-98.

Keller, Suzanne. 1963. *Beyond the Ruling Class.* New York: Random House.

Levine, Steven B. 1980. "The Rise of American Boarding Schools and the Development of a National Upper Class." *Social Problems* 28:63-94.

Lipset, S. M., and Reinhard Bendix. 1959. *Social Mobility in Industrial Society.* Berkeley, CA: University of California Press.

Marceau, Jane. 1977. *Class and Status in France: Economic Change and Social Immobility,* 1945-75. New York: Oxford University Press.

MBA. 1974. "The 15 Top-Ranked Graduate Business Scools in the United States." *MBA* 8:21-25.

McLachlan, J. 1970. *American Boarding Schools: A Historical Study.* New York: Scribners.

McQuaid, Kim. 1980. "Big Business and Public Policy in Contemporary United States." *Quarterly Review of Economics and Business* 20:57-68.

Merton, Robert K. 1968. "The Matthew Effect in Science." *Science* 3810:56-63.

Miller, William (ed.). 1952. *Men in Business: Essays in Entrepreneurship.* Cambridge: Harvard University Press.

Mills, C. Wright. 1956. *The Power Elite.* New York: Oxford University Press.

Moore, Gwen, and Richard D. Alba. 1982. "Class and Prestige Origins in the American Elite." Pp. 36-60 in *Social Structure and Network Analysis,* edited by Peter V. Marsden and Nan Lin. Beverly Hills, CA: Sage Publications.

National Center for Educational Statistics. 1981. *Digest of Educational Statistics.* Washington, DC: Government Printing Office.

Newcomer, Mabel. 1955. *The Big Business Executive: The Factors That Made Him: 1900-1950.* New York: Columbia University Press.

Parkin, Frank. 1979. *Marxism and Class Theory: A Bourgeois Critique.* New York: Columbia University Press.

Parsons, Talcott. 1951. *The Social System.* New York: Free Press.

———. 1971. *The System of Modern Societies.* Cambridge: Harvard University Press.

Pennings, Johannes H. 1980. *The Interlocking Directorates.* San Francisco: Jossey-Bass.

Pfeffer, Jeffrey, and Gerald R. Salancik. 1978. *The External Control of Organizations: A Resource Dependence Perspective.* New York: Harper and Row.

Pierson, George W. 1969. *The Education of American Leaders.* New York: Praeger.

Schaeffer, Ruth G., and Allen R. Janger. 1982. *Who Is The Top Management?* New York: Conference Board.

Scientific American. 1965. *The Big Business Executive, 1964: A Study of His Social and Educational Background.* New York: *Scientific American.*

Squires, Gregory D. 1979. *Education and Jobs: The Imbalancing of the Social Machinery.* New Brunswick, NJ: Transaction Books.

Swinyard, Alfred W., and Floyd A. Bond. 1980. "Who Gets Promoted?" *Harvard Business Review.* pp. 5ff (September/October).

Taubman, Paul, and Terence Wales. 1974. *Higher Education and Earnings.* New York: Carnegie Commission.

Taussig, F. W., and C. S. Joslyn. 1932. *American Business Leaders.* New York: MacMillan.

Useem, Michael. 1979. "The Social Organization of the American Business Elite and Participation of Corporation Directors in the Governance of American Institutions." *American Sociological Review* 44:553-72.

_____. 1982. "Classwide Rationality in the Politics of Managers and Directors of Large American Corporations in the United States and Great Britain." *Administrative Science Quarterly* 27:199-226.

_____. 1984. *The Inner Circle: Large Corporations and the Rise of Business Political Activity in the U.S. and U.K.* New York: Oxford University Press.

_____. 1985. "The Rise of the Political Manager." *Sloan Management Review* 27:15-26.

Useem, Michael, and S. M. Miller. 1975. "Privilege and Domination: The Role of the Upper Class in American Higher Education." *Social Science Information* 14:115-45.

Wagner, W. Gary, Jeffrey Pfeffer, and Charles A. O'Reilly, Ill. 1984. "Organizational Demography and Turnover in Top-Management Groups." *Administrative Science Quarterly* 29:74-92.

Warner,W. Lloyd and James C. Abegglen. 1955. *Big Business Leaders in America.* New York: Harper and Row.

Weber, Max. [1920] 1978. *Economy and Society.* Berkeley, CA: University of California Press.

Zuckerman, Harriet. 1977. *A Scientific Elite: Nobel Laureates in the United States.* New York: Macmillan.

Part III

Professional Schools

INTRODUCTION

Increasingly, to be a financial success in our "credential society" (Randall Collins's apt term), high-income aspirants must pass through the right academic stations. Not only are the lucrative professions of law and medicine closed to those without the required credentials, but "fast track" positions in corporate business are often quasi-professional, almost requiring an M.B.A. for career advancement. Indeed, these elite professionals in law, medicine, and business have come to account for a larger proportion of all high-income earners.[1]

Yet if the "professionalization of everyone" has become a commonplace observation, the connection between professional credentials and the stratification system has been only minimally probed. Who gains these credentials? On what basis are people admitted to programs? What affects success within professions? All these questions are far from being adequately answered. To this list we should add: how are the elite professional schools distinctly connected to the stratification system? Much of the evidence on this latter question is impressionistic and anecdotal, but the very prominence of the graduates from elite schools in top law firms and corporate positions suggests the value of more detailed study.

In Chapter 9, "The Inside Tracks: Status Distinctions in Allocations to Elite Law Schools," Charles L. Cappell and Ronald M. Pipkin analyze how academic and social factors affect placement within the hierarchy of law schools. Their detailed statistical analysis is well suited to show how these factors *interact* to create wide variations in chances of admission to the elite law schools. Much like Hearn's analysis (Chapter 6) of undergraduate admissions, they show that meritocratic principles have a critical though far from complete role in the admissions process.

In Chapter 10, "Getting on the Fast Track: Recruitment at an Elite Business School," Paul William Kingston and James G. Clawson consider why the graduates of elite business programs are so assiduously courted by corporate recruiters. Their case study, based on intensive interviews and questionnaires, addresses the larger issues of "credentialism" and makes the case for taking a disaggregated approach in analyzing the connection between education and careers.

NOTE

1. For documentation of this point, see Paul William Kingston, "The Credntial Elite and the Credential Route to Success" *Teachers College Record*, 1981 (82:589-600).

CHARLES L. CAPPELL
RONALD M. PIPKIN

Chapter Nine

The Inside Tracks: Status Distinctions in Allocations to Elite Law Schools

Ever since the 1921 Carnegie Foundation's Reed report first characterized the American legal profession as consisting of separate and unequal segments, many scholars have recognized the disparity between the bar's public claim of an open, democratic, egalitarian, and representative legal profession and the empirical facts. The failure of the profession to constitute itself according to these legitimating tenets may well have contributed not only to the decrease in the public's regard for the profession, but also to the waning respect for the formal rule of law (Auerbach, 1976). This tension quite likely contributed to the increased admission of women and racial minorities to law schools which began in the early 1970s (Cappell, 1985, 1986; Epstein, 1983).

Professional degrees and credentials awarded by university-based professional schools are the ticket to lucrative occupational statuses (Bledstein, 1976; Collins, 1979; Cullen, 1978; Jencks, 1979; Larson, 1977). However, a focus on the role of professional education in stratifying the labor force overlooks the significant diversity within a single profession. The practice of law has an especially marked degree of internal stratification (Heinz and Laumann, 1982: Ch. 3), and particularly relevant to the concerns of this analysis, the quality of the law school at which a lawyer received legal training is significantly linked to subsequent statuses within the profession.

LEGAL EDUCATION AND STRATIFICATION WITHIN THE BAR

The important connection between the status of law schools and the status hierarchy within the profession was consciously fashioned by some of the largest firms. The Cravath firm in New York, circa 1916, instituted recruitment criteria that required membership in Phi Beta Kappa and law review at the best schools, high social status indicated by a family listing in the *Social Register,* and strength of personality (Swaine, 1948: Ch. 7; Smigel, 1964).

Studies of the legal profession have elaborated the processes allocating individuals first to law schools and subsequently to different positions within the legal system. In the Chicago area, while attendance at elite schools increased the likelihood of large firm practice in general, attendance at an Ivy League law school increased the likelihood of large firm practice even more, almost three times so (Cappell, 1982:72; see also Zemans and Rosenblum, 1981). Similarly, in the Detroit area during an earlier period, attendance at a quality law school significantly increased the chances of working in a large law firm (Ladinsky, 1963). Attendance at quality law schools was also found to be correlated with large firm practice within a national sample of private practitioners (Erlanger, 1980).

Attendance at elite law schools also has been linked to the attainment of direct professional power. Leadership positions within the Chicago Bar Association (CBA), a local bar association a thousand miles from Boston, were held disproportionately by lawyers from Ivy League law schools: nearly a third of the past chairmen of CBA substantive law committees had attended an Ivy League law school (Cappell, 1982: 58). Furthermore, approximately a fifth of the members elected to serve on the CBA Board of Managers during the 1955-74 period had graduated from an Ivy League law school (Cappell, 1982: 90), and that percentage increases to nearly 40 percent when one includes graduates from the University of Chicago. This pattern of leadership attainment within the CBA deviated only slightly from that reported for an earlier period (Carlin, 1962). Thus, a number of studies share the conclusion that graduation from an elite law school is a crucial gateway to elite standing within the practicing bar. Crucial to consider, then, are the factors that influence allocation to these most prestigious institutions.

SOCIAL STATUS AND LAW SCHOOL ATTENDANCE

The findings from previous studies do not always lead to the same conclusion about the allocation process to elite law schools. As an illustration, four often cited studies reached four separate inferences regarding the effect of paternal occupation on law school attended: (1) that it had a simple and direct positive effect on the quality of law school attended (Ladinsky, 1963); (2) that it had a curvilinear effect: children of high-status fathers were more likely to attend the highest- and the lowest-status law schools (Zemans and Rosenblum, 1982); (3) that it interacted with academic achievement to influence the law school attended (Warkov and Zelan, 1965); and (4) that it had no effect on the quality of law school attended (Erlanger, 1980).

How can we explain these different conclusions? One major reason is that the studies were based upon different populations. Ladinsky sampled practicing attorneys in the Detroit area; Warkov and Zelan used a national sample of college seniors and then first-year law students; Erlanger analyzed a national sample of practicing attorneys; and Zemans and Rosenblum estimated the effects from a sample of Chicago lawyers. Second, the classification of law schools differed from study to study. Third, the methods used to predict law school distributions varied across studies, from regression and path analysis to cross-tabulations of, at most, three variates. Fourth, the studies varied in their ability to control for pre-law school academic achievement. None of the studies to date has optimally combined appropriate sample frames and appropriate statistical methods to generate the proper inferences about the process of allocation to law schools.

Law school allocation processes, or law school markets, are best studied region by region. Ideally, the sample should be drawn from the total applicant pool so that both those accepted and those rejected by law schools are included in the study. Given the near impossibility of independent researchers obtaining this type of sample, the next best sample frame consists of law students, not practitioners. The methods of multivariate contingency table analysis are better suited than other techniques because law schools can be grouped into discrete categories or even treated individually. These techniques also allow for the routine study of the more complex interactions between background variables, indicators of academic achievement, and law school attendance patterns. By incorporating these features, our study overcomes many of the deficiencies present in earlier studies of the status effects on the allocation of students to law schools of different quality. In addition, our study includes the sex of the respondent, providing for the first time evidence of how women's increased interest in law careers is being organized in the marketplace of legal education.

Our research answers the following specific questions: what are the relative weights of pre-law school academic performance, parental occupational and income status, religious background, and sex in explaining the observed distribution of students among elite and other types of law schools? Do class and status attributes persist beyond objective meritocratic criteria in the allocation of students to law schools, or are these effects mediated by variables measuring academic achievement? Is there any evidence of a direct religious or socioeconomic status related bias in the allocation of students to different law schools? Are women at a disadvantage when it comes to gaining admission to the best law schools?

STUDY DESIGN

Our analysis of law school attendance patterns was based on data collected by questionnaire for a larger study of legal education.[1] Students in seven law schools were surveyed during the 1975-76 academic year. The total sample size from the seven schools combined was 1,370. The response rate for the sample as a whole averaged 70 percent. but the rate varied across schools from a high of 81 percent to a low of 64 percent. Nonwhite respondents and respondents for whom we had no information about racial identity were excluded. With these deletions, and by estimating some background information from highly correlated extraneous variables, we were able to make available for analysis a sample of 1,221 respondents. Of this total, 72.2 percent were male, and 27.8 percent were female.

The seven participating law schools were classified into three strata: (1) at the lowest status were two schools (one public and one private nonsectarian) identified here as local schools; (2) two other law schools (one public and one Catholic) were classified as regional schools; and (3) three schools with reputations as being among the most prestigious in the nation were grouped as elite. The distinction between the two lower-status categories was based on the presence in the local schools of part-time divisions, which among law schools has long been a basis of status distinction (Kelso, 1972; Fossum, 1978). The sample, however, was taken from the full-time divisions in these schools.[2] The distribution of students across these law school types was fixed by the sampling design, so the percentages that were attending each of the schools does not reflect the overall likelihood of attendance at schools of various types.

Respondents were classified according to the religious preference of their parents when both parents were of similar religions, or according to their own preference when only one of the parents shared that preference. By using this scheme, we were able to derive a very good estimate of the respondent's family religion.[3] Students were broadly categorized as having Catholic (34.3 percent), Protestant (37.1 percent), or Jewish (28.6 percent) backgrounds.

We created an index of socioeconomic status (SES) using father's and mother's education, father's occupation, and family income.[4] Respondents were classified into one of four SES groups:

LOW-MIDDLE (I):
> A group composed of those with parents having high school educations, with fathers who worked in nonprofessional occupations, and with family incomes reported to be less than $20,000. These students are homogeneous with respect to all of the criteria and constituted about 36 percent of the total.

MIDDLE (II):
> A group composed of those with at least one parent with a college degree with fathers who worked in nonprofessional occupations, and with family incomes reported to range from the lower-middle levels to more than $40,000. These students are most homogeneous with respect to the nonprofessional occupations of their fathers. Although there is variability in their family incomes, nearly half come from families with incomes greater than $40 000. These students constituted about 20 percent of the total.

MID-UPPER (III):
> A group composed of those with fathers who earned college degrees or graduate or professional degrees, with mothers who were less likely to have earned college degrees than high school diplomas, with fathers who worked in professional occupations, and with family incomes reported to be above $20,000 but less than $40,000. These students are most homogeneous with respect to the professional occupations of their fathers. They are also more likely to have fathers with more education than the students in the Middle level (II) SES category. These students constituted roughly 13 percent of the total.

UPPER (IV):
> A group composed of those with fathers who earned graduate degrees, with mothers also more highly educated (a third of them also had earned graduate degrees), with a father who worked in a professional occupation, and with family incomes greater than $40,000. This group of students is homogeneous with respect to the high levels of their fathers educations and family incomes and constituted about 30 percent of the total.

To place these profiles of socioeconomic status in context, we note that in 1974 the median family income in the region under study was $13,800 and that only 12.4 percent of the families earned income exceeding $25,000 (U.S. Bureau of the Census, 1975 : 393). In 1974, only 14 percent of the population had completed four or more years of college

(U.S. Bureau of the Census, 1975:118). Thus, students classified in our SES II group, for the most part, come from families that would rank in the top fifth of families in the United States; our SES IV group easily ranks within the top 5 percent of all families. We are clearly dealing with status allocations at the high end of the socioeconomic spectrum.

We also created an index of pre-law school academic achievement and credentials using the type of the undergraduate college attended, the student's undergraduate grade point average (GPA), and the self-reported Law School Aptitude Test (LSAT) score.[5] Respondents were classified into one of three groups:

> LOW ACADEMIC CREDENTIALS
> A group who scored relatively low on the LSAT, most certainly below 700 and more often below 650: who earned GPAs above 3.00, with half having earned a GPA above 3.50; and who most likely graduated from public colleges, but some of whom graduated from private non-sectarian colleges. This group constituted 42 percent of the total.
> MEDIUM ACADEMIC CREDENTIALS
> A group with middle-level LSAT scores, most falling within the 650-750 range; who earned low to medium GPAs, generally falling in the 3.00-3.50 range; and who nearly always graduated from private non-sectarian colleges. This group constituted 17.8 percent of the total.
> HIGH ACADEMIC CREDENTIALS
> A group with high and middle levels of LSAT scores, most commonly above 700; who uniformly earned GPAs above 3.5; and who graduated most frequently from private nonsectarian colleges and less frequently from public colleges. This group constituted 40.2 percent of the total.

As a first step in the analysis, we examined the simple relationships between each of the background variables and the type of law school attended. In these simple bivariate analyses, each of the background variables was found to be statistically associated with the chances of a student attending an elite, regional, or local law school. The strongest association was found, not unexpectedly, between the levels of academic performance and the quality of law school attended. Of those with low academic performance, most (55.9 percent) were attending local law schools; an additional 35.1 percent were attending regional law schools; and 9 percent were attending elite law schools (see first panel in Table 9.1). Students with medium academic achievement were fairly evenly distributed across all three types of law school. For those with the highest levels of academic performance, the vast majority (88.4 percent) were attending elite schools.

TABLE 9.1
Percentage Distributions of Student Background
Characteristics across Law School Types

Independent Variables	School Type: Local	Regional	Elite	Percent of Total (N)	
Academic Credentials					
Low	55.9	35.1	9.0	42.0	(513)
Medium	34.6	35.5	30.0	17.8	(217)
High	2.6	9.0	88.4	40.2	(491)
(Chi-square = 682.65 with 4 d.f.; p-value < .0001)					
Religious Background					
Catholic	45.6	28.9	25.5	34.3	(419)
Protestant	24.9	23.4	51.7	37.1	(453)
Jewish	20.3	21.2	58.5	28.6	(349)
(Chi-square = 106.48 with 4 d.f.; p-value < .0001)					
Socioeconomic Status					
I. Low-Middle	34.3	29.0	36.6	35.6	(434)
II. Middle	34.5	24.5	41.0	21.4	(261)
III. Middle-Upper	27.2	20.9	51.9	12.9	(158)
IV. Upper	25.3	21.2	53.5	30.1	(368)
(Chi-square = 28.7 with 6 d.f.; p-value < .001)					
Gender					
Male	29.5	23.3	47.2	72.2	(881)
Female	33.8	28.2	37.9	27.8	(340)
(Chi-square = 8.67 with 2 d.f.; p-value < .05)					
Percent of Total in Each Law School Type	30.7	24.7	44.6	1221	

Religious background was associated with the prestige of the law school attended (see second panel, Table 9.1). The striking finding here reverses the stereotypical image of the elite law school student commonly found in commentary about the profession more than twenty years ago. Jewish students had higher attendance rates at the elite law schools than Protestants: 58.5 percent versus 51.7 percent, respectively. Students with Catholic backgrounds were disproportionately underrepresented in the elite schools: only 25.5 percent were attending the elite law schools.

We found a weaker yet still significant association between SES levels and type of law school attended. With similar rates, students from SES Levels I and II, the lower levels, disproportionately attended local and regional law schools. Their patterns of attendance were very similar. Students from SES Levels III and IV, the upper two levels, disproportionately attended the elite schools, 51.9 percent and 53.5 percent, respectively. Given this simple analysis, the SES effect would seem to differentiate the upper two levels from the lower two levels. Recall that the difference in father's occupational status, nonprofessional versus professional, was a major factor that differentiated SES Levels I and II from Levels III and IV. Looked at from the perspective of the elite schools' composition, these distributions mean that more than half of the elite school attenders were raised in affluent professional families, and another fifth were raised in nonprofessional families near the top of the income distribution.

The students' gender also was associated with the type of law school attended. Males were more likely to attend the elite law schools (47.2 percent versus 37.9 percent); females, the local and regional schools.

These simple tabulations give some indication of the status factors that influence the distribution of students across law school types, but more conclusive evidence for the independent effects of each background variable requires a multivariate analysis.

THE SPECIFICATION OF A MODEL FOR
LAW SCHOOL ATTENDANCE PATTERNS

Log-linear statistical techniques were used to ascertain the independent effects of each of the background variables, controlling for each of the other variables and for all of the indirect effects of social status on academic achievement.[6] We begin with the joint distribution of law school attended (L) (three levels), gender (G) (two levels), parents' SES (S) (four levels), religion (R) (three levels), and academic credentials (A) (three levels). A recursive model was fit: that is, various models of the effects of each of the background variables on law school attended were tested with each model including the full interaction: the complete cross-classification, among gender, religion, SES, and academic credentials. Thus, all of the indirect effects of the status variables on academic achievement are taken into account. We learn the size of the remaining *direct* effects by hypothesizing various relationships, such as a gender effect on law school attended (GL) and observing whether including such a term makes the prediction of cell frequencies appreciably closer to the observed frequencies. The size of the chi-square statistic is used as a measure of the goodness of fit of the model. In this way various models can be tested and compared.

We were first interested in testing for the adequacy of the meritocratic model. This model hypothesizes that the only influential factor affecting the type of law school attended is the level of academic credentials. This is accomplished by fitting only one interaction (AL), besides the full interaction of the background variables. The results of this test appear as Hypothesis 2 in Table 9.2. The very high chi-square value

(207.08) with its corresponding low significance level, or p-value, indicates that this model does not fit the observed frequencies well enough. It does substantially better than the model which hypothesizes that the law school attended is independent of all background factors, Hypothesis 1 in Table 9.2.

TABLE 9.2
Tests of Models Relating to Academic Credentials,
Gender, Religion, and SES to Law School Attainment

Margins Fit under Null Hypothesis					d.f.	X^2	L.R. X^2	p-value
H1.	(AGRS)	(L)			142	825.78	992.93	.000
H2.	(AGRS)	(AL)			138	225.15	207.08	.000
H3.	(AGRS)		(GL)		140	817.70	984.21	.000
H4.	(AGRS)			(RL)	138	782.82	883.76	.000
H5.	(AGRS)				(SL)	136	818.73	964.21	.000
H6.	(AGRS)	(AL)	(GL)	(RL)	(SL)	126	152.42	139.41	.196
H7.	(AGRS)		(GL)	(RL)	(SL)	130	761.86	858.97	.000
H8.	(AGRS)	(AL)		(RL)	(SL)	128	156.75	146.97	.121
H9.	(AGRS)	(AL)	(GL)		(SL)	130	201.74	175.62	.005
H10.	(AGRS)	(AL)	(GL)	(RL)		132	162.17	157.11	.067
H11.	(AGRS)			(RL)	(SL)	132	772.28	869.91	.000
H12.	(AGRS)		(GL)		(SL)	134	807.10	953.16	.000
H13.	(AGRS)		(GL)	(RL)		136	774.72	874.26	.000
H14.	(AGRS)	(AL)			(SL)	132	204.50	183.26	.002
H15.	(AGRS)	(AL)		(RL)		134	172.36	163.52	.042
H16.	(AGRS)	(AL)	(GL)			136	215.31	201.04	.000
H17.	(AGRS)	(AGL)		(RL)	(SL)	122	131.44	131.78	.257
H18.	(AGRS)	(ARL)		(GL)	(SL)	118	149.03	137.54	.106
H19.	(AGRS)	(ASL)		(RL)	(GL)	114	146.70	131.68	.123
H20.	(AGRS)	(GRL)		(AL)	(SL)	122	151.29	138.37	.148
H21.	(AGRS)	(GSL)		(AL)	(RL)	120	156.17	133.65	.186
H22.	(AGRS)	(RSL)		(AL)	(GL)	114	146.23	130.10	.144

A = academic credentials (3 levels).
G = gender (2 levels).
R = religious background (3 levels).
S = socioeconomic status (4 levels).
L = law school type (3 levels).

Results for the tests of models which hypothesized a solitary background effect of academic achievement (AL), gender (GL), religion (RL), and SES (SL) are listed as Hypotheses 2 through 5, respectively, in Table 9.2. These results reveal that relatively simple models hypothesizing only one effect on law school attended are inadequate. However, it is also apparent that previous academic achievement accounts for an overwhelming proportion of reduction in the unexplained chi-square.

We explicitly tested the statistical significance of additional terms by comparing the models, including a given background effect to the model of independence. Panel A in Table 9.3 presents the reduction of unexplained chi-square caused by including the effects of the academic variable (AL), of gender (GL), of religion (RL), and of SES (SL) on law school attended. As can be seen, including the term which takes into account the relationship between academic credentials and law school attended reduces the unexplained chi-square from 992.93 to 207.08 (see Table 9.2), a difference of 785.85. The second most important factor in reducing the unexplained chi-square (see Table 9.3) is the religious background of the student (109.17); the third most important factor is SES (28.72); and although still statistically relevant, the respondent's gender is the least important (8.72).

TABLE 9.3
Likelihood Ratio Tests of Casual Parameters Needed
to Predict Law School Attended

Hypotheses Compared		Parameters Tested 0	Difference in L.R. X^2	Difference in d.f.	p-value
A.	H1 : H2	(AL) = 0	785.85	4	.000
	H1 : H3	(GL) = 0	8.72	2	.020
	H1 : H4	(RL) = 0	109.17	4	.000
	H1 : H5	(SL) = 0	28.72	6	.000
	H1 : H4	(RL) = 0	109.17		
B.	H6 : H17	(AGL) = 0	7.63	4	.112
	H6 : H18	(ARL) = 0	1.87	8	> .500
	H6 : H19	(ASL) = 0	7.73	12	> .500
	H6 : H20	(GRL) = 0	1.04	4	> .500
	H6 : H21	(GSL) = 0	5.76	6	> .500
	H6 : H22	(RSL) = 0	9.31	12	> .500

A sense of the relative importance of factor in explaining the pattern of law school attendance is obtained by computing the ratio of the reduction in unexplained chi-square to the degrees of freedom associated with each factor, since a larger proportion of the chi-square is usually associated with variables having more categories. These ratios are as follows: academic credentials, 196.4; religion. 27.3; SES, 4.8; and gender 4.4. It is clear that the right combination of academic credentials is by far the most important factor in accounting for the observed pattern of law school attendance. But it is not the sole basis of allocation. Status variables have an additional and independent effect.

A model that includes an effect for *all* of the background variables on law school attended (H6 in Table 9.2) fits the data much better than the one incorporating only the academic performance measure (H2 in Table 9.2) or ones excluding any single background factor. The contribution of each effect can be assessed by comparing the results from fitting H6 to the results from testing H7-H10, which exclude one of the effects in turn. The model that excludes the effect of the respondent's gender on law school attended (H8) shows the least reduction in unexplained chi-square, yet this effect should not be assumed to equal zero. These various tests force us to conclude that none of the background variables should be excluded from the model predicting law school attendance patterns. Academic merit along with social status determines the type of law school attended.

Furthermore, tests for the importance of higher-order terms that take into account a possible three-way interaction among academic credentials, gender, and law school attended produced a better fit to the observed frequencies (H17 in Table 9.2). Tests of whether this term as well as the other three-way terms should be included in the model are presented in Panel B of Table 9.3. When we set our critical p-value level at $p = .10$, only the three-way interaction among gender, academic achievement, and law school attended approaches statistical significance. This term indicates that the advantage gained by having high academic credentials acts upon the chances for elite law school attendance differently for men than it does for women.[7] Having established the best-fitting model to explain the pattern of law school attendance — a crucial analytical step, though one that may seem arcane to many readers — we can now offer a substantively interpretable summary of these effects. This translation involves the use of intuitively understandable odds ratios: the chances one group of students has of attending a more prestigious law school versus the chances of another group.

SUBSTANTIVE SIGNIFICANCE OF THE BACKGROUND VARIABLES ON LAW SCHOOL ATTENDED

By making use of the log-linear parameters estimated from fitting H17 in Table 9.2, it is possible to see the effects of one of the variables on the odds of attending an elite versus a regional school, and its effects on the odds of attending a regional versus local law school taking into account the effects of all the other variables.[8] Estimated odds were calculated for several particularly interesting combinations of the independent variables in order to clearly present the relative importance of each of the variables (see Table 9.4).

We have used as a basis of comparison the odds of attending an elite versus a regional law school (and the odds of attending a regional versus a local law school) for Protestant males with the highest SES and academic credentials. We expected that such a constellation of factors would give a student the inside track to the most elite law schools. These odds are recorded in Row 1, Column 1.[9] For this category of respondents, the odds of attending an elite versus a regional law school are roughly 24 to 1; and the odds for attending a regional versus a local school, 6 to 1 (Row 1, Column 3). The odds drop to 1.3 and 1.2 respectively, when this same social group possesses only medium academic credentials (Row 2). The odds are quite low that respondents in this social group with relatively low academic records would enter an elite law school versus a regional school, 0.5, or a regional versus a local school, 0.7 (see Row 3).

TABLE 9.4

Odds of Attending Elite versus Regional and Regional versus Local Law Schools
for Various Combinations of Independent Attributes
(Estimated Using Model in Hypothesis 17)

Academic Performance	Gender	Religion	SES	(1) Est. Odds: Elite v. Reg.	(2)[e] Ratio: Row 1 to Row i	(3) Est. Odds: Reg. V. Loc.	(4) Ratio: Row 1 to Row i
1. High	Male	Prot.	Upper	23.895	1.000	6.188	1.000
2. Medium	Male	Prot.	Upper	1.332	17.939[a]	1.165	5.312[c]
3. Low	Male	Prot.	Upper	.496	48.175	.705	8.777
4. High	Female	Prot.	Upper	9.974	2.396[b]	2.552	2.425[d]
5. High	Male	Cath.	Upper	12.295	1.943	4.403	1.405
6. High	Male	Jewish	Upper	34.329	.696	7.318	.846
7. High	Male	Prot.	M. Upp.	13.831	1.728	4.938	1.253
8. High	Male	Prot.	Middle	13.862	1.724	5.061	1.223
9. High	Male	Prot.	Mid-Low	10.087	2.369	6.827	.906

[a]The difference in the elite versus regional odds for different levels of academic achievement (17.939) comes from two sources: one effect is from the differences due to academic achievement alone (86.5%); the second source is due to the interaction effect between gender and academic achievement (13.5% of the difference).

[b]The difference in the elite versus regional odds for men and women (2.396) comes from two sources: one effect is from being male versus female (46.9% of the difference); the second effect comes from the interaction term between gender and academic credentials (53.1% of the difference).

[c]The difference in the regional versus local odds for different levels of academic achievement (5.312) comes from two sources: one effect is from the differences due to academic achievement alone (74.3% of the difference); the second source is due to the interaction effect between gender and academic achievement (25.7% of the difference).

[d]The difference in the regional versus local odds for men and women (2.425) comes from two sources: one effect is from being male versus female (29.4% of the difference); the second effect comes from the interaction term between gender and academic credentials (70.6% of the difference).

[e]The ratio in columns 2 and 4, technically defined as odds ratios, are the ratios obtained by dividing the estimated odds in Row 1 by the estimated odds that appear in each of the subsequent rows. Substantively, this expresses the magnitude of the advantage (disadvantage) individuals with the social characteristics defined in Row 1 enjoy over their counterparts.

The impact of different levels of academic performance within the ranks of affluent Protestant males can be seen in Columns 2 and 4 of Table 9.4. For students with this set of social characteristics, moving from the middle to the highest levels of academic achievement increases the odds of attending an elite versus a regional law school by a factor of 17.9. Such an improvement in the level of academic achievement increases the odds of attending a regional versus a local law school by a factor of 5.3.

The remaining entries in Table 9.4 refer to the odds of attending an elite versus a regional law school (Columns 1 and 2) and to the odds of attending a regional versus a local law school (Columns 3 and 4) for groups with high academic performance levels and with only one attribute different from the comparison group reported in Row 1. Column 2 in Table 9.4 is the ratio to Row 1 of the odds of attending an elite versus a regional law school for groups identified in each of the subsequent rows. Similarly, Column 4 shows the ratio to Row 1 of the odds of attending a regional versus a local law school for each group. These comparisons identify the relative degree of disadvantage encountered in attending an elite law school for groups with differing social status.

The estimated odds for Protestant females with the highest SES and academic credentials attending an elite rather than a regional law school is 9.97 (Row 4, Column 1). This value is well over one, but not equal to the odds for males, 23.9. In other words, compared with women of similar academic merit and social background, men have a 2.4 greater chance of attending an elite school (Row 4, Column 2). Although highly qualified women from high-status families have greater odds of attending an elite law school than men with similar backgrounds but poorer academic records, these women clearly suffer a disadvantage when compared to their equally qualified male peers. (See also Spangler et al., 1978.)

Somewhat surprisingly, male Jewish respondents with the highest levels of SES and academic performance are estimated to have the best odds of attending an elite law school in the region studied (Row 6). They are on the inside track. This finding negates the speculation derived from earlier studies of attorneys that Protestants have an advantage over their Jewish colleagues in attending elite law schools (e.g., Smigel, 1964; Carlin, 1962). That generalization needs to be reinterpreted in the light of these data. Apparently, some unmeasured labor market effects existed which influenced the patterns reported in those studies, quite likely a bias against Jewish practitioners working in large central city law firms (Smigel, 1964).

Consistent with other studies is the notable disadvantage Catholics seem to have relative to those from other religious backgrounds in reaching the elite schools (Row 5). For Catholic males with the highest levels of SES and academic performance, the odds of attending an elite versus a regional law school are estimated to be 12.30. Although this is a favorable odds ratio, Protestants with the same constellation of factors are nearly twice as likely to attend an elite versus a regional law school. It could be argued that this is the result of self-selection on the part of Catholics, reflecting in part the Catholic educational system, which includes some well-respected law schools. However, that argument is questionable because Catholics were 30 percent more likely than Protestants and 39 percent more likely than Jews, with other attributes held constant, to attend a local rather than regional school, when the latter category contained a Catholic law school.

By looking at Rows 7-9, we can also see the effect of having less than the highest family SES on chances of attending an elite law school among highly qualified Protestant males. The largest increment to the likelihood of attending an elite versus a regional law school is produced by the combination of the factors that assigned respondents to the highest SES group. The odds for the highly qualified male Protestants from the highest SES category are nearly twice as great as those for their academic peers from the SES II and SES III categories and more than twice as great as those from the lowest SES category. Students from the SES IV category have a nearly uniform advantage over their academic peers in each of the other three SES categories. Although SES III and IV students were both characterized by the presence of professional fathers, all SES IV students were from families with relatively high incomes and exceptionally highly educated parents. This bundle of extremely high-status characteristics translates into likelihoods of elite law school attendance that are twice the likelihoods experienced by students from lower-income professional families, similar to the advantage they had over students from non-professional families.

Recall that we also found an interaction among gender, academic achievement, and law school attended. The meaning of this term is that males with the highest levels of academic achievement had an extra advantage in the odds of elite school attendance over women with equally high qualifications. This increment to the chances of males, estimated to be 1.26, is in addition to the increment already obtained for being male and for having the highest academic performance. For women with the highest academic credentials, the interaction term adjusts the odds downward by a factor of 0.79.

The design of our study does not permit us to state definitively that these differences in the chances of men and women are evidence of sex discrimination, just as we cannot conclude that there is evidence of discrimination against students from the middle and working classes. The patterns of law school attendance could result from self-selection as well as from lower rates of admission. When we looked closely at some specific cases of highly qualified women who were enrolled at regional and local law schools, we found some evidence of self-selection. These students mentioned that a need to live close to home and other family considerations influenced their choice of schools. These could be rationalizations or masks of more influential factors, especially since we studied a relatively circumscribed geographical region. But Epstein, in her study of women lawyers, reported that 90 percent of the women lawyers she interviewed in 1965-66 chose to attend a law school on the basis of nonprofessional criteria, primarily family proximity (Epstein, 1983:35). The SES factor which showed that the disparity occurred between the highest group and the remaining three does suggest that economic factors are likely to influence the rates of attendance at the elite law schools, which generally have higher tuition costs.

CONCLUSIONS

The allocation of students to law schools is not simply a function of aptitude test scores and previous academic performance. We explicitly tested and rejected the meritocratic model of elite law school attainment. At least for the schools in the region we studied, gender, religious background, and SES all influence patterns of law school attendance. Academic credentials are by far the most important factor in establishing the odds of attending an elite law school, but given an excellent academic record, a Jewish or Protestant background, high socioeconomic status, and being male put one on the inside track in the competition to enroll at an elite law school. Women, Catholics, and all those not from the highest SES category are in the outside tracks. Those without high academic credentials are hardly in the race.

Our discussion has emphasized the *direct* effects of gender, religion, and SES upon law school allocation patterns after taking into account the substantial effects of academic performance. We have not discussed the *indirect* effects of the status variables which operate through their effect on pre-law school academic achievement. However, it is clear that measures of social background have substantial indirect effects as well. In our analysis of LSAT scores, the most significant component of our academic credentials variable, we found that women, Catholics, graduates of sectarian colleges, and those with lower undergraduate GPAs had lower LSAT scores. Thus, the background characteristics that directly affect LSAT performance continue to influence directly the allocation to law school. The import of these characteristics on the later stages of the allocation process reinforces their effects on LSAT performance. Status advantages are thereby multiplied throughout the process.

Elite law schools draw from a national pool of law school aspirants and therefore have a very high ratio of applicants to available positions. Among this pool, applicants are not likely to be distinguished on the basis of academic credentials alone. Judgments concerning admissions that are necessarily discretionary, involving applicants with comparable high academic records, have worked to reproduce an existing social, academic, and cultural elite. Admission decisions certainly do not diminish the disadvantage of those who have already overcome substantial odds in order to be in the competition at all. Perhaps their academic effort is not accorded the same credibility as the effort of those for whom excellence is expected.

Of course, we are not arguing that self-selection may not be a factor here, but the very strong relationship between academic credentials and law school allocation patterns suggests that law students have a rather good sense of law school status differences and their own potential in the competition for admission. Elite schools are inundated with applications each year, indicating a market knowledge of the importance of an elite law school education. Nor are we arguing that well-qualified students who have apparently suffered from a status disadvantage were not able to attend a good law school. But given the close link between law schools and the profession's status hierarchy, those who suffer status disadvantages have fewer professional opportunities that an elite law school education, and the resulting networks of friends, can provide. Finally, it is important to note that in this period of increased reliance on standardized and objective procedures for admission to law schools, as late as 1976 elite sectors of society had no difficulty in reproducing their elite status within the legal profession. This study provides at least one point of reference by which subsequent research will be able to record a movement toward or away from equal opportunity in law school attendance.

NOTES

1. The study, the Law Student Activity Patterns Project, was directed by Ronald M. Pipkin. For other details on the sample, see Pipkin, 1976 and 1979. The project was advised by the American Bar Association's Special Committee for a Study of Legal Education, Ronald J. Foulis, chairman.

2. Random samples were drawn at each of the seven law schools, but the seven law schools do not represent the true population distribution of law schools. Thus, these marginal distributions cannot be generalized; nor can the actual estimated or observed odds of attending elite schools versus the other categories. Those odds have been fixed by the nonrandom choice of law schools. This paper focusses on the relative effects of each of the independent variables chosen for study, and these findings are generalizable since they are estimated independently of the marginal distribution. In this respect our study resembles what have been called "retrospective epidemiological studies." See Fienberg, 1977: 105-7.

3. A log-linear analysis of the contingency table of father's religion by mother's religion by respondent's religion was used to develop an assignment rule. Respondents who failed to report a religion or reported none were thus able to be assigned a religious background.

4. The assignment of individuals to one of four SES classes was made on the basis of a latent structure analysis of the joint distribution of father's education, mother's education, family income, and father's occupation (Clogg, 1977). The results of this analysis and the assignment rules are available upon request.

5. The same procedure of latent structure analysis was used to assign respondents to one of three classes on the basis of their joint levels of college attended, grade point averages, and LSAT scores. The results of this analysis are available upon request.

6. Computations and hypothesis testing were performed using LOGLINEAR, an algorithm written by S. Haberman, but parameter estimates were transformed and are presented according to Goodman's (1973) notation according to a scheme suggested by Haberman (1979:398-411). We should also like to note that a fully saturated model was necessary to explain the effects of background on academic credentials.

7. We chose to discuss the more complicated model, H17, in this paper. The major contribution of this term in reducing the unexplained chi-square results from a reduced likelihood of women in the category of highest academic credentials attending the elite category of law schools compared with that of men. This difference is illustrated well enough in our substantive discussion of the impact each factor has on the odds of having attended a school in the elite category and suggests that women with high academic credentials are not benefitting from affirmative action. See Table 9.4.

8. The log-linear model represented in H17 implies that the observed odds can be adequately estimated as the product of certain parameters estimated in the log-linear procedure. Thus, for example, the odds of attending an elite rather than regional law school for various combinations of the background variables are obtained by inserting the appropriate values in the following equation:

$$\frac{F^{LAGRS}_{1jklm}}{F^{LAGRS}_{2jklm}} = \frac{\tau^{L}_{1}}{\tau^{L}_{2}} \cdot \frac{\tau^{LA}_{1j}}{\tau^{LA}_{2j}} \cdot \frac{\tau^{LG}_{1k}}{\tau^{LG}_{2k}} \cdot \frac{\tau^{LR}_{1l}}{\tau^{LR}_{2l}} \cdot \frac{\tau^{LS}_{1m}}{\tau^{LS}_{2m}} \cdot \frac{\tau^{LAG}_{1jk}}{\tau^{LAG}_{2jk}}$$

The term on the left-hand side of the equation refers to the estimated odds of attendance, which are, of course, a reasonable approximation of the observed odds. The terms on the right-hand side of the equation decompose the overall odds into the constituent parts that are due to the various background factors. The first term on the right takes into account the overall marginal distribution of attendance at elite versus regional law schools. The size of this parameter was, in fact, determined by our sampling frame. The second term refers to the adjustment one needs to make in estimating the odds for the various levels of academic achievement. If we take the highest level of academic achievement as an example, the term in the numerator refers to the impact of attaining this highest level on the frequency of attendance at an elite law school. This parameter was estimated to be 7.55. The denominator contains a comparable term for attendance at a second level law school.

9. For a model that hypothesizes only two-way effects from each independent variable on law school attended, the ratios indicating the effect of a given variable would be the same for any combination of the other variables. But since our model requires a three-way interaction between academic achievement, gender, and law school attended, ratios which highlight the difference between men and women include two sources of difference, that due directly to gender and that due to the interaction of academic achievement and gender. Similarly, the ratios which highlight the difference due to academic achievement contain some variability due to the interaction. We chose the group characterized by the attributes in Row 1 as the comparison group because of its obvious stereotypical significance.

REFERENCES

Auerbach, Jerold L. (1976) *Unequal Justice: Lawyers and Social Change in Modern America*. New York: Oxford University Press.

Bledstein, B. (1976) *The Culture of Professionalism*. New York: W.W. Norton.

Cappell, Charles L. (1982) Professional Projects and the Private Production of Law. Ph.D. Dissertation, University of Chicago.

———. (1985) "The Status of Black Lawyers." Paper read at the Law and Society Meetings, San Diego, 1985.

_____. (1986) "Minorities and Women in Law School: New Status Classes?" Paper read at the Law and Society Meeting, Chicago, 1986.

Carlin, Jerome (1962) *Lawyer's Ethics*. New York: Russell Sage Foundation.

Clogg, Clifford (1977) "Unrestricted and Restricted Maximum Likelihood Latent Structure Analysis: A Manual for Users." University Park, Penn.: Population Issues Research Office.

Collins, Randall (1979) *The Credential Society: An Historical Sociology of Education and Stratification*. New York: Academic Press.

Cullen, J. (1978) *The Structure of Professionalism*. New York: Petrocelli.

Epstein, Cynthia Fuchs (1983) *Women in Law*. New York: Anchor Press/ Doubleday.

Erlanger, Howard (1980) "The Allocation of Status within Occupations: The Case of the Legal Profession." 58 *Social Forces* 882-903.

Fienberg, Stephen (1977) *The Analysis of Cross-Classified Data*. Cambridge, Mass.: MIT Press.

Fossum, Donna (1978) "Law School Accreditation Standards and the Structure of American Legal Education." *American Bar Foundation Research Journal* 515-543.

Goodman, Leo (1973) "Causal Analysis of Data from Panel Studies and Other Kinds of Surveys." 78 *American Journal of Sociology* 1135-1191.

Haberman, Shelby (1979) *The Analysis of Qualitative Data*, 2 vols. New York: Academic Press.

Heinz, John, and Edward Laumann (1982) *Chicago Lawyers: The Social Structure of the Bar*. Chicago: American Bar Foundation; Beverly Hills: Russell Sage Foundation.

Jencks, Christopher et al. (1979) *Who Gets Ahead? The Determinants of Economic Success in America*. New York: Basic Books.

Kelso, C. (1972) *The AALS Study of Part-Time Legal Education*. Washington, D.C.: Association of American Law Schools.

Ladinsky, Jack (1963) "Careers of Lawyers, Law Practice, and Legal Institutions." 28 *American Sociological Review* 47-54.

Larson, M. (1977) *The Rise of Professionalism: A Sociological Analysis*. Berkeley, Calif.: University of California Press.

Pipkin, Ronald (1976) "Legal Education: the Consumers' Perspective." *American Bar Foundation Research Journal* 1161-1192.

——— (1979) "Law School Instruction in Professional Responsibility: a Curricular Paradox." *American Bar Foundation Research Journal* 247-275.

Smigel, Edwin (1964) *The Wall Street Lawyer: Professional or Organizational Man?*" New York: Free Press.

Spangler, E., Gordon, M., and R. Pipkin (1978) "Token Women: an Empirical Test of Kanter's Hypothesis." 84 *American Journal of Sociology* 160-170.

Swaine, Robert (1948) *The Cravath Firm*, 2 vols. New York: Ad Press Ltd.

U.S. Bureau of the Census (1975) *Statistical Abstract of the United States 1975*. Washington D.C.: U.S. Govt. Printing Office.

Warkov, S., and J. Zelan (1965) *Lawyers in the Making*. Chicago: Aldine.

Zemans, Francis, and Victor Rosenblum (1981) *The Making of a Public Profession*. Chicago: American Bar Foundation.

PAUL WILLIAM KINGSTON
JAMES G. CLAWSON

Chapter Ten

Getting on the Fast Track: Recruitment at an Elite Business School

The ongoing rush of students to graduate schools of business administration attests to the importance of the Masters in Business Administration (MBA) in American corporate business. These students correctly perceive that an MBA enhances chances of getting on the corporate "fast track," a career ladder promising quick advancement and great reward.

MBAs are increasingly responsible for top corporate decisions. A *Forbes* (1974) survey of chief executive officers shows that one-third have an MBA, but the proportion under 45 with this degree is almost twice that for executives in the 56-65 range. A study of 12,000 top-level executives (vice presidents and above) indicates that the precentage with MBAs had tripled from 10 per cent in 1967 to 30 per cent in 1980 (*Time* 1982). And, in line with the recent prominence of MBAs at the highest corporate levels, many firms are willing to pay their new business school recruits—in effect, the prime candidates for future top management positions—extraordinary starting salaries. Average starting salaries of those graduating from the most prestigious schools now are well in excess of $30,000 and range up to $90,000. Despite criticism within and outside of business about the value of the degree (*Time* 1982, Behrman and Levin 1984), overall enrollments have remained strong (60,000 + degrees in 1983), and graduates of the "name" schools continue to command impressive starting offers and relatively great prospects for career advancement.

The prominence of these professionally-trained managers in the corporate sector is a quite recent development. As recently as the late fifties, a Ford Foundation study of corporate hiring practices indicated little interest in MBAs except in certain areas of a few companies (cited in Pearson 1959). Many companies actually reported that they preferred applicants without advanced business degrees. In sharp contrast, the College Placement Council reported a few years ago that in critical organizational areas of corporations, "all recruiting is at the MBA level" (cited in Freeman 1976, p.132).

To the extent that corporations look forward to MBAs for management trainees, what we have witnessed, in a short time, is a significant movement toward the "quasi-professionalization" of American corporate management. Holders of this degree are educationally certified to have acquired specialized, job-related competencies through formal training, and entry to many of the best entry-level positions is in effect restricted to MBAs. Obviously the MBA is not now, nor is it likely to become, a formal license required for the "practice" of business management. The "professionalization" of management is not as complete as, say, law. Nonetheless, at a rapid rate, the MBA has become a widely accepted credential linking professional educational training to lucrative careers[1].

We seek to analyse the nature of this link by studying corporate recruitment at a nationally esteemed business school. Our main purpose is to describe how this recruitment process works. This particular linkage between school and career is important to understand because of the critical societal role of MBAs, but we are further concerned to relate our analysis to more general perspectives on the education-job connection. More specifically, we see this analysis as a revealing case for researchers seeking to develop theoretical explanations as to *why* and *how* education "pays off" in various sectors of the occupational world.

THEORETICAL CONTEXT

The question "who gets ahead?" has a thoroughly documented answer: the relatively well-educated (e.g., Jencks et al. 1979, Featherman and Hauser 1978). As a broad descriptive fact, this answer is unassailable, but social scientists have made much less progress in specifiying the reasons why education is financially rewarded. To be sure, there are competing theoretical explanations of this connection, but the issue remains unresolved.

In brief, the theoretical debate is defined by two general perspectives: the"socialisation model" (which explicitly or implicitly has more commonly infused empirical research) and the "allocation model" (Kerckhoff 1976, Kamens 1981). The "socialization model" emphasises how schools transform the capacities of *individuals*, making them better able to compete in the labor market. In focusing on individual change, this model incorporates both the learning of skills (technical capacities) and the development of particular values and personality traits (social capacities). There are differing emphases as to the relative importance of these capacities, but the common presumption is that school changes people in economically desired ways. This argument has been most directly expressed in "human capital theory": education enhances productivity and since people are paid in accord with their marginal productivity, the well-educated enjoy greater prospects (e.g., Becker 1964, Mincer 1974). Underlying this line of reasoning is a view that occupational attainment reflects a generally open societal competition in which the winners are determined by the individual capacities of the contestants.

In contrast, the common thread in the somewhat diverse arguments which make up the "allocation model" is that education has been used to ". . . identify, select, process, classify and assign individuals according to externally imposed criteria" (Kerckhoff 1976, p. 369). Thus the focus is on the structural conditions which impinge on careers (i.e., the organization of labor markets) and how education is used as a "sorting device." In this light, education is a "credential," creating opportunities for the *group* which has a particular degree. That is, it is used as a "screen" to identify the desired group and exclude others (Collins 1979, Thurow 1975). Some proponents of this view further contend that the criteria of desirability are unrelated or only indirectly related to productivity. For example, different sorts of degrees have been portrayed as symbolizing variations in "cultural capital," markers of certain social status and cultural outlook, which are used to designate individuals as "socially suitable" for particular positions in the economic hierarchy (Bourdieu and Passeron 1977). Within this model as well there are significant differences in emphasis, but the unifying assumption is that education is economically rewarded because of how it is socially used, not because of its effects on individuals' capacities.

The large literature related to this controversy cannot be reviewed here, yet to establish the context of this analysis, it is worth highlighting certain difficulties with each general explanation. The most damning criticism of the socialization or human captial approach is that evidence linking education and productivity is so sparse (Berg 1970, Collins 1979). Moreover, the human capital theorists' view of the labor market, with rational, profit-maximising employers seeking out the most productive workers, is derived from postulates of microeconomic theory. Some empirical results may appear to "fit" with these postulates, but the actual operations of labor markets are not directly examined. Critics have justifiably charged that this perspective unduly neglects structured differences in the labor markets associated with various sectors of the economy, as well as the internal organization of firms. Such factors seem to condition the economic returns to education (Beck *et al.* 1978, Rosenbaum 1979, Tinto 1981).

By the same token, however, the evidence cited in support of "credentialism" is generally indirect. It is possible to show that economic sector affects the economic "return" of eduation or that, net of a large set of "human capital" variables, degree completion (Jencks *et al.* 1979) or degree prestige (Foster and Rogers 1979, Kingston 1980, Tinto 1980) is related to career attainment. Such findings are difficult to interpret in accord with the human capital perspective, but while one may infer that some sort of allocation process is operative, the findings are still open to diverse interpretations. Furthermore, while some historical evidence does suggest that certain status groups at times successfully imposed credential requirements for particular jobs as a way to protect their "occupational property" (Collins 1979), the general significance of this process in the current operation of labor markets is indeterminate.

A common deficiency in these competing explanations is that analyses generally neglect the actual operations of the labor markets in which people with varying educational attainments acquire jobs. To understand why education has a pay-off, it seems essential to examine the outlooks and actions of those who do the hiring. That is, the "demand side" of the "matching process" is crucial here (Granovetter 1981).

At the same time, research increasingly suggests the need to take a disaggregated approach to the connection between education and job. The "arrow" in our models between education and job usually refers to the average impact of education (the coefficient for years of education, sometimes with a separate coefficient for degree completion) on career attainment. However, as the previously cited literature suggests, different sorts of education may have different impacts in different contexts— and, by implication, may do so for different reasons. A sociologically informed understanding of the labor market must recognize its organizational diversity and keep open the possibility that education may have different roles in various segments.

Our study of recruitment at an elite business school represents such a disaggregated approach. We analyze: 1) characteristics of the corporate recruiters, 2) the selection criteria which they employ, as well as their reasons for seeking out MBAs in general, and 3) the nature of the recruitment "pool" from which corporations hire future top-level managers. By considering these matters, we will be able to assess the extent to which socialization and allocation processes are involved in this small but consequential segment of the labor market.

Before turning to the interview and survey data, we should briefly outline the process in which these corporate recruiters are involved.

THE RECRUITMENT PROCESS

Corporate recruiting at the top echelon business schools follows fairly standard procedures. The linkage between school and job is usually both routinized and direct.

First, after selecting schools at which they will recruit, corporations send job descriptions and literature about their company to the placement offices of these schools and choose people to conduct the "initial screening" interview. These executives make appointments to visit the selected schools during a designated interviewing season. (Students are interviewed after the holiday season of their second year for jobs to begin the following summer.) During their one or two day stay, corporate recruiters face a strenuous task. Each interviews a dozen or so job candidates, with one following the other in a tiring barrage of thirty-minute sessions interrupted only by coffee breaks and lunch. While firms often send several recruiters, the initial on-campus interviews are one-on-one.[2] In a few cases, a firm may have established some prior contacts with a candidate, perhaps at an "informational reception" at the school or through correspondence, and some are chosen for interviews after review of the school's résumé book. Even so, the handshake at the door of the interviewing room is usually the first contact between candidate and company. Recruiters are supplied with the résumés of the candidates on their schedule but seldom have more information about candidates than conveyed by the telegraphic phrases of these short forms. At this and other elite schools the recruiters do not have prior access to transcripts, faculty recommendations or other supporting materials. In effect, with very little advance information, recruiters have less than a half hour to determine which few will be invited to the firm for a second round of interviews. Recruiters must also sell the candidate on the firm in this brief period.

The impressions created in this first session are fateful; these on-campus recruiters are "gatekeepers." Even if they themselves do not decide which candidates to invite back to the firm, their judgments are the crucial factor in any collective decisions made at headquarters. Without a favorable evaluation in this initial screening, a candidate is virtually precluded from further consideration.[3]

Companies follow somewhat different procedures in the "second round," but generally it involves a day-long visit to the firm with numerous individual and group interviews, in offices and over meals. At most firms being "called back" implies that the candidate has a good chance of receiving an offer, though some firms prefer to consider a relatively large number and offer jobs only to a few. Companies also vary as to where in the organization the "hire" decision is made, but, in any case the evaluations of the on-campus screeners restrict the competition for a position to a select few.

While our study is limited in focusing on the characteristics and perspectives of these initial gatekeepers, they are key actors whose views play a crucial role in the outcome of the process. At the same time, their views are likely to be expressive of their corporate culture. They have incentive to establish a record of "calling back" candidates who meet the approval of others (especially their supervisors) for it is a sign of their own "good judgment."

Clearly not all companies hire exclusively in this way. Some consider MBAs (and others) who directly apply to the firm. Some firms may turn to an executive placement office to identify suitable candidates, often with an MBA, among the currently employed. Nonetheless, the fact that in 1984 some 75 per cent of the graduates of this school got their job through on-campus recruitment points to the centrality of this process in linking the MBA degree to one's first job. So, although we cannot get a complete picture of this education-job linkage by examining the behavior of on-campus recruiters, they do provide an illuminating and accessible vantage point from which to examine the process.

Data

Our analysis is based on a series of informal, qualitative interviews and a short questionnaire given to corporate recruiters at the Colgate Darden Graduate School of Business Administration, University of Virginia.

Preliminary to the design of the questionnaire, in the 1983 "interviewing season" the first author met with recruiters at breakfast for informal discussions about the recruitment process. These thirteen interviews generally lasted a half hour or slightly longer; six involved more than one recruiter, while the others were personal. Notes from these interviews were made immediately afterward; quotations in the text are therefore subject to the normal inaccuracies of memory.

In the 1984 interviewing season all recruiting firms either received a short questionnaire within an information package on arrival at Darden or were sent this questionnaire in a follow-up mailing from the Placement Office. (We do not know how well the distribution worked for the questionnaires which were sent to the firms.)

We received 100 completed questionnaires. The total included multiple responses from 13 companies, and thus recruiters from 84 companies responded. Given the corporations' control over distribution of the mailing, we cannot calculate precisely the response rate from those who actually received a questionnaire. However, assuming that the total number of recruiters is the relevant base for this calculation, the response rate is 25 per cent. We received some response from 46 per cent of the recruiting companies. Questions about response bias obviously arise. We cannot dispatch these concerns fully, but the respondents are very similar to the total population of recruiters in their industry background and the location of their firm. Furthermore, it is difficult to think of sources of serious systematic response bias other than perhaps some greater cooperation among Darden graduates who feel some desire to help out their school. Unfortunately, in any case, the small response precludes detailed analyses of difference in recruitment procedures by industry, function, region, and other relevant dimensions.

A complementary concern relates to the representativeness of our "case." To what extent is the process at the Darden School representative of that at graduate business schools generally and, more particularly, at the other elite schools? In the absence of systematic data, the question is hard to answer. Informed sources within business schools and in the corporate world appear to believe, however, that the process operates in a very similar way at the other elite schools. Indeed, as we will indicate, the elite schools seem enmeshed in a rather tightly restricted labor market. By the accounts of our respondents, many firms recruit only or primarily at elite schools; our respondents themselves were often sent to these schools as recruiters.

We believe that the "Darden case" is illustrative of the general process involved in recruitment at elite schools even if differences in regional "connections" or reputations for curriculum type and functional strength may lead to some distinctive features at individual schools. Even so, we must caution that these data are only suggestive and point to the need of a larger study incorporating a range of schools and firms.

THE GATEKEEPERS

In educational background, the initial corporate gatekeepers are often very similar to the people whom they are recruiting, though the task of conducting the first round of interviews is not exclusively assigned to MBAs. Of our 100 respondents, 59 had earned an MBA, another 16 had some other advanced degree, and 25 had a bachelor's degree. Yet the number of MBAs does not reveal the full extent of shared educational background. Corporations frequently send graduates of *elite* business schools to interview students at this elite school. Indeed, 27 actually graduated themselves from this school, and another 15 graduated from a set of twelve nationally distinguished schools. In short, almost half of the recruiters had an elite business school education. This vantage point, as some claimed, may provide some distinctive, discriminating insight in evaluating candidates from elite schools, and it may also create some personal interest in having such degrees accorded value in corporate hiring.

Most commonly, corporations send recruiters from the functional area within their firm where the hired business school graduates will work. Seventy per cent of the recruiters had a staff or line position other than personnel or human resources. While the large majority of firms prefer this "look for yourself" strategy, they also provide little formal training in personnel selection. Overall, only 30 percent reported having "extended training" in recruitment interviewing, while 43 per cent had a "few sessions or less" and a quarter had no training whatsoever. Recruiters who were not from the personnel department were especially likely to rely on their interviewing instincts: 55 per cent had no more than a few sessions of training, and 34 per cent had no training at all. As one young executive remarked, "I guess they [his superiors] just assumed that I'd know who the 'right' people are." Another said that he and a fellow recruiter had "talked informally" on the day before the visit but was essentially left to rely on "my gut feelings." However, some firms provided evaluation forms to be completed on each interviewed student, and these may have provided some guidance.

Some recruiters brought great experience to this assignment, though many firms were willing to send relative newcomers. The average number of years with their present firm was 7.6, but a quarter of the recruiters had been employed at the firm for two years or less and another 30 per cent for three to five years. Moreover, 41 per cent had made at least ten recruiting trips to business schools, but an even greater number (45%) had made five or fewer. Sixty-two per cent were at least vice presidents or directors; the rest were lower level managment.

Apparently, then, neither long immersion in a particular corporate culture nor particularly high rank nor great interviewing experience are essential qualifications for becoming a gatekeeper. Corporations pursue a variety of strategies, but there is a general tendency to send executives within a functional area, often with an elite MBA themselves, to seek out those whom they would like to employ.

SELECTION CRITERIA

What are these recruiters looking for as they consider candidates? "The best. The most qualified, those who can really excel in our company." "A few good men and women." "Students with the qualifications, interests and personality to fit the needs of our organization." "I don't know what we're looking for."

As all of these respondents recognized, such general statements hardly advance the practical task of selecting specific people for further consideration at a firm. We were struck by the the interviewers' willingness to readily acknowledge the ambiguities and uncertainties of the selection process. One managment consultant related, "Maybe we should take a 'random walk' approach to MBA recruiting. I don't know if we'd do any worse or better. We like to think we're doing better, but I don't know. . . . It's more art than science. We're troubled by this." Troubled or not, none of the recruiters pointed to an operational formula which they used to define the "desirable" candidate. Nor did they believe that a specific set of operationally-defined criteria was possible or desirable. Nonetheless, they made choices, and explicitly or implicitly, certain considerations were relatively important in their evaluation of candidates.

To get some rough sense of what defined a desirable MBA candidate, we asked on the questionnaire, "How important were the following to *you* in evaluating the candidates?" and provided a list of thirteen criteria (and an "other" category). Results are presented in Table 10.1 which indicates the distribution of responses for each criterion and rank order of importance. (Scores were tabulated for each criterion assuming that the responses "a crucial factor" through "irrelevant" represented a five-point scale.)

We should first note that all of these criteria are important to at least some firms. Having a "technical-scientific BA/BS," for example, is generally not an important consideration, yet for some firms it is critical. A manager at a chemicals company said, "We favor those with a scientific or engineering background because they can talk with the scientists at our company easier and they're important to what happens." On the other hand, a recruiter from sales said flatly, "Undergraduate background doesn't matter at all in sales."

TABLE 10.1

Importance of Selection Criteria to Recruiters
(Criteria Are Listed in Rank Order*)

	A Crucial Factor	A Significant Consideration	Of Some Concern	Largely Inconsequential	Irrelevant	N
Ability to communicate in the interview	76%	24	1	0	0	(100)
Apparent personal fit with people in your firm	74%	19	7	0	0	(99)
Clarity of career goals	35%	46	16	2	1	(100)
Quality of job experience (pre Darden)	19%	48	31	3	0	(99)
Darden academic performance	12%	36	42	9	1	(100)
Knowledge of your firm	10%	38	40	12	1	(99)
Darden course concentration	6%	37	44	12	1	(100)
Extra-curricular activities	3%	41	32	20	4	(100)
Experience within specific functional area	5%	28	40	22	5	(100)
Relevance of last summer's work experience	2%	25	49	16	8	(98)
Faculty recommendations	8%	24	29	29	11	(100)
Experience within your industry	3%	17	36	34	10	(100)
Technical-scientific BA/BS	6%	13	28	29	24	(100)

*Scores were tabulated for each criterion assuming that the responses represented a five-point interval scale.

Yet the aggregate patterns do reveal marked emphases. Quite clearly, personal characteristics are accorded greater importance than work experience and academic preparation. The strong emphasis on personal characteristics is certainly sensible in light of the important role of personality for successfully operating in a bureaucratic organisation. However, the much lesser concern for academic training and performance does little to legitimate graduate business schools' own claims that their education enhances the productive skills of their students.

Academic Performance

The fact that not even half of the recruiters rated Darden academic performance as "crucial" or "significant" points to the modest concern for academic considerations. Presumably the courses are intended to teach valuable professional skills, and grades should indicate at least the *relative* skill levels of the students; but these grades are not generally used to distinguish the candidates. Indeed, less than a tenth (8 per cent) of the recruiters even asked students for copies of their transcripts. Of course, grades may not be considered a valid indicator of analytical ability, but most recruiters also did not turn to faculty recommendations as a potentially more discriminating source of evaluation. Not even a third rated them as "significant" or "crucial," and only just more than a third (38%) contacted any members of the faculty for evaluations of students, either before or after the interviews.

Moreover, the recruiters generally had relatively little concern for what the students studied while at business school. At the Darden school, all students take a common "core" of basic courses and then are allowed a maximum of four courses in a particular area (e.g., finance or marketing) to develop specialized skills. (This policy is in keeping with the school's avowed general management perspective.) Just 37 per cent of the recruiters viewed this specialization as "significant" and only 6 per cent as "critical." Although the overwhelming number of students will have first, post-MBA jobs within a particular functional area, these recruiters (mostly from the functional areas themselves) remain generally unconcerned about the depth of specialized training. Indeed, they accord almost as much significance to the students' extra-curricular activities as to their course of study.

These results do not imply, however, that "personality is everything" or that analytical ability or the intrinsic value of an MBA education is deemed largely irrelevant in the business world. Indeed, general intellectual ability is assumed. As one recruiter noted, "I know that from going here that everyone is smart, at least bright enough. . . . Getting in here is the intellectual hurdle. Then if they survive it, I don't have to worry." In a similar vein, another related, "grades are the lowest priority to me. Really I think the admissions process has done the screening for us on that." Moreover, it seems assumed that all students acquire sufficient "analytical tools" to perform competently. "They all know accounting," one said. Another suggested, "I don't really care if they know the in's and out's of some financial model, but I do know they have had some exposure and they can pick up from there." In short, these recruiters presume that a degree from this elite school certifies an acceptably high level of general intelligence and technical training, but they see little value in attempting to make further distinctions among the candidates on these matters.[4]

Personality

The recruiters overwhelmingly rated "ability to communicate in an interview" and "apparent personal fit with people in your firm" as the most important considerations. About three quarters of the recruiters rated each of these as "critical." No other considerations are even remotely close in importance. The distinctions among candidates are thus most fundamentally based on assessments of personal style and oral facility, in effect the candidates' ability to create quickly a favorable impression of savvy, drive, and affability. Looking over the responses to the open-ended question, "What personality characteristics do you look for in the interviews?", we find frequent mention of such traits as "aggressiveness," "self-confidence," "maturity," "outgoing personality," "enjoys contact with others," "ambition," "assertiveness," "poise," "articulate," "mental alertness," "team orientation," and "positive attitude." Notably, in light of some popular criticism that MBAs are inclined to be amoral careerists, there was little concern for matters such as integrity, honesty and loyalty. Of course, this lack of explicit attention may reflect the recruiters' assumption of generally acceptable integrity rather than a lack of concern for it.

To be sure, recruiters place different emphases—one, for example, being especially impressed with a self-confident, aggressive style and another with a warm, sociable style. And yet it seems possible to discern a common concern for "presence"—a "buzzword," one recruiter related, which means "an ability to articulate a point of view, to be convincing, to seem on top of things." As many recruiters explicitly recognized, having "presence" mostly involves having social skills which fit the culture of top corporate managment. A half hour interview affords little opportunity to probe analytical ability or personal character, and so they are left to rely on what one called "gut level feel." This recruiter looked for someone who seemed "lively and bright" and whom "I would want to work with on a day to day basis." A recruiter from a management consultant firm looked for "self assurance" and a "sense of what questions to answer concisely and what ones to be expansive on because that is critical in dealing with clients." He added, "Back at the firm, if they 'pass' this, we do try to see how well they can think." Perhaps as an unusually unqualified example of this orientation to social compatibility, one recruiter commented: "If the interview seems like it lasts only five minutes, then I figure the person must be pretty good. At least they're interesting. If it drags, if they don't have much to say, I don't usually invite them back. If you're going to pick someone, you might as well pick someone who seems interesting."

Career Goals

Besides these personality factors, the recruiters place a strong emphasis on clarity of career goals. Thirty-five per cent rated this factor as "crucial" and 46 per cent as "significant," the third highest rating. To outsiders, this emphasis is hard to fathom because one would expect that most business students would share a strong concern to be high level business executives. However, since success can be achieved by different routes and in different realms, the recruiters apparently look for particular expressions of this goal. Some coursework at business school is intended to help students develop their goals, or at least learn what are deemed the appropriate expressions on the matter.

Work Experience

The concern for work experience before business school also exceeds that for performance at business school. Note that "quality of job experience" was considered a crucial factor by 19 per cent and a significant consideration by another 48 per cent. All factors related to business school experience—academic performance, course concentration, faculty recommendations, extra-curricular activities—are accorded lesser significance. At the same time, these recruiters attached relatively little significance to having experience within a particular industry or functional area. Apparently, these recruiters were not looking for job experience which was immediately transferable to the positions for which they were recruiting so much as some exposure entailing responsibility.

THE RECRUITMENT POOL

We further asked these gatekeepers about the scope of their corporation's recruitment efforts. In effect we sought to find out who the

Darden graduates are in competition with, thus delineating some main features of the labor market segment in which the graduates of elite business schools are involved. Some of these recruiters are not likely to be fully apprised of the entire scope of their firm's recruiting efforts, but allowing for inaccuracy in detail, their responses point to important, broad structural characteristics of this market segment.

More specifically, we asked the recruiters, "For the position(s) for which you interviewed at Darden at what other graduate business schools did or will your company recruit?" We thus acquired lists of the "competing" schools.[5]

We classified the lists of schools visited into four mutually exclusive categories and present the distribution below:

Elite Only; All schools on the list are among the highest eleven ranked schools (plus the Tuck School at Dartmouth) in the Cartter Report rankings (Change 1977): 26%.[6]

Elite Emphasis; Half or more of the schools on the list were among the twelve schools listed above: 51%.[7]

Diverse Pool; More than half of the schools are not designated as "elite": 14%.

Regional Approach; All the schools on the list are Southern schools: 8%.[8]

This information does not reveal, however, the full scope of the "recruitment pool" because many corporations do not restrict their recruitment efforts to candidates from graduate schools which they visit. Responses to a further question indicate the significance of these on-campus visits in the recruitment process. These gatekeepers indicated that recruitment for these positions will:

- be largely confined to candidates from these schools: 35%.

- will focus on candidates from these schools and may *secondarily* consider candidates from other MBA programs: 25%.

- will focus on candidates from these schools but *actively* consider candidates from other MBA programs: 21%.

- consider BA/BSs: 6%.

- other: 13%.

Plainly, these response categories require the respondents to make subjective judgments about recruitment policies, and similar responses may reflect different operational efforts. The responses should therefore be viewed as only a crude indicator of the extent to which on-campus recruitment delimits the recruitment pool.

An obvious point to be drawn from these data is that the students at Darden School are primarily competing with fellow MBAs for positions. Few companies consider recent bachelor degree holders or the currently employed with experience for the same positions. Especially at the larger companies, the policy is to bring in each year, at the same time, a new crop of recently minted MBAs to replenish their managerial ranks.

Attendance at one of the schools visited by recruiters seems to significantly enhance chances in the recruitment process at that company. Just more than a third of the firms "largely" confine their recruitment efforts to the set of visited schools, while another quarter focus their efforts on candidates from these schools though "secondarily" considering others. Our impression is that some of the firms (21%) which report "actively" considering candidates from other programs may do little more than remain receptive to particularly persuasive, unsolicited letters which may make their way onto some executive's desk. In short, among the set of firms involved in on-campus recruitment at this elite school, the "competition" is mostly with fellow MBA students at other schools which those firms visit.

Furthermore, these firms highly concentrate their recruitment efforts at the nationally esteemed schools. About a quarter (26%) make recruitment visits only to elite schools, and at another 51 per cent of the companies, at least half of the visits are to elite schools. By a wide margin, the most commonly cited "competitors" were other elite schools—a geographically diverse group—and two regionally esteemed schools. The presence of "second tier" schools on individual lists seemed largely to reflect "localistic considerations"—that is, firms turning to schools located near their own operations. The corporations' on-campus recruitment efforts are thus nationwide, though often restricted to a small set of schools. Corporations based in the South pursuing a "regional approach" account for a small proportion (8%) of the firms recruiting at this elite school.

In Table 10.2, we cross tabulate this classification of schools with the variable relating to the significance of these on-campus visits. The cell percentages in the table refer to the percentage of the total (84). (This total refers to the number of separate *firms* represented by the recruiters in the sample.)

This analysis indicates that the Darden students are not enmeshed in a labor market segment which strictly limits competition to the elite business schools. Only 12 per cent of the firms in this sample report that they visited just at the elite schools *and* largely confine their recruitment efforts to candidates from these schools. Nonetheless, at the firms in this

Professional Schools

TABLE 10.2
The Recruitment Pool for Firms in the Darden School Study*

| Scope of Recruitment Effort | Type of Business Schools Visited | | | |
	Elite Only	Elite Emphasis	Diverse Pool	Regional Approach
Largely confined to candidates from these schools	12%	17%	2%	4%
Focus on these and secondarily consider other MBAs	6%	11%	4%	1%
Focus on these and actively consider other MBAs	5%	17%	2%	1%
Consider BA/BSs	0	2%	1%	2%
Other	1%	6%	5%	1%

*Cell percentages are of the total (84).

sample, students from elite schools have a decided, institutionalized advantage in the recruitment process. Note that half of the firms make at least half of their on-campus visits to elite schools *and* make only secondary efforts or less to include others in the recruitment process. Thus, among this set of firms seeking MBA students, the decision of where to recruit does not in general rigidly delimit the recruitment pool yet often strongly affects the "odds" of being included in the competition.

On what basis is this corporate decision actually made? In light of the preponderance of elite schools, considerations of degree prestige seem involved. And, indeed, by the accounts of the recruiters we talked to at length, some vague sense of degree "prestige" or "quality" and personal ties, not a systematic assessment of recruitment strategies and goals, usually is decisive. One said, "We just look at the rankings and go to all of the best." Another related that the cost of recruitment limited his firm's search to three or four schools, institutions where they have "built up contacts" and seemed to have had "good success" in the past. Why these schools in the first place? That he did not know, though all were in our "elite" category. A larger firm visited "six schools or so which have a good reputation" yet, according to this recruiter, "We change around depending on where we have luck. We have a lot from [names an elite school], and I think people from there like to go back." Others straightforwardly said that they came to Darden because that is where they went: "I like the place, and I know what to expect out of the students."

As many validly recognized, recruitment is expensive, and it is only economically rational to limit the pool of applicants so as to avoid prohibitive information processing costs. All schools cannot be visited, nor can all applicants who would like to apply directly to the firm be thoroughly evaluated. Yet however rational some restriction of the pool may be, it seems much more guided by a very general sense of a school's prestige or overall quality rather than the distinctive strengths and emphases of particular programs. Schools with reputations for quite different curricular emphases and pedagogical styles appear on the same lists. Of course, these schools may not create distinct "products," but the corporate recruiters seem to have little concern for this matter, even if they do recognize the schools' claims of particular strength.

In short, these firms tend to recruit primarily and very disproportionately at elite schools, concentrate their hiring among candidates from these schools, and select schools for inclusion in the pool primarily on the basis of somewhat vague notions of "prestige" (and local connections). Besides the obvious limitations of examining recruitment at one graduate business school, we should stress that these results are necessarily more suggestive of the management recruitment pool of firms which have made *some* commitment to recruitment at an elite school than the pool at all firms. While our sample includes a diverse "mix" by industry, size, and region, it is necessary to sample *firms* (not schools) to assess fully the prominence of elite schools in the labor market for management executives.

Why Seek Out MBAs?

In the preceding section we examined the relative weight recruiters give to various factors in evaluating candidates at the business school. However, the fact that pre-graduate school experience and such "personality" matters as "ability to communicate in an interview" and "personal fit" with the firm are accorded such significance raises the issue of why seek out MBAs in the first place? After all, these candidates had their job experience before enrolling in school, and while business school may directly sharpen a student's sense of what image to convey and how to convey it, fundamental personal orientations and styles are largely set by this time in a person's life. Those matters on which business school should have the most direct effect—the acquisition of technical skills and analytical abilities which are relevant to business—are considered less important. One might therefore ask: why don't corporations simply seek out experienced lower-level executives who have demonstrated the "right" personality and sufficient intellectual capability on the job and in undergraduate education?

Clearly the responses of a few corporate recruiters cannot reflect the full range of structural forces which give rise to the significance of the elite MBA degree, but they may at least suggest some of the reasons why the elite schools are so central to corporate recruitment efforts. As one recruiter maintained, "What we do by going here is up the odds of finding the right people. Others could do it, even those without the degree, but there's a real high concentration here. It's pretty hard to miss." Others had similar responses alluding to the high concentration of the "right" sorts—people described as having "analytical ability," a "feeling for the big picture," a "commitment to business," and a "sense of how to dress and act." In effect, they are saying that recruiting at an elite business school reduces their recruitment costs. Rather than consider a great number of candidates from many different sources, an effort requiring considerable organizational expense, the firms concentrate efforts where they believe they will get the greatest "return" for their investment in recruiting. This policy excludes both outstanding and undesirable candidates without the graduate degree, but it conveniently includes a sufficient number of very desirable candidates. One remarked, "Just about all of them [referring to Darden students] would fit in and do a pretty good job."

The economic "rationality" of concentrating recruitment efforts certainly entails the reduction of recruitment costs, but whether MBAs are "worth" the extra cost in terms of enhanced productivity on the job seems to be an open question. Several recruiters expressed ambivalence about the value of an MBA. However, with varying degrees of conviction, recruiters did seem to believe that there was some "value added" to the students by virtue of having completed the graduate business program. One alluded to "awareness of analytical tools" and "more maturity and judgment." Yet he added, "Hey, they're older," and went on to say he did not know if greater maturity was just a natural phenomenon or could be attributed to the schooling. A graduate of the school talked about his own education as reason for recruiting MBAs: "I can embrace the whole of a problem, see how the marketing and financial sides fit together. The cases we did here really did that for me. You get a model [of how to think]." Another recruiter valued the fact that they "bring in new ideas" because of their "exposure to diverse perspectives." And yet not even the most enthusiastic boosters of the intrinsic value of the degree saw it as necessary or even signficant for effective job performance. The general sentiment seemed to be that the school enrolled desirable candidates and may have marginally enhanced their desirability.

DISCUSSION

At the risk of some oversimplification, we can point to a recruitment process in which the recruiters tend to look at people much like themselves, proceed with an uncertain feel for what defines a desirable candidate while emphasizing considerations of personal style over indicators of analytical-technical competence, and concentrate their efforts among those who have received the imprimatur of a prestigious degree. Simply by being admitted to this school, students ensure themselves of the opportunity of being considered for many "fast track" positions in the corporate world; but once entered in the contest, largely because of demonstrated prior academic and job achievements, they compete among themselves on the basis of their ability to convey a personal style which comports with the prevailing norms of "executive" behavior at particular companies.

The results of this study do not provide a direct test for the competing socialization and allocation theories which relate to the education-job connection, even for this small segment of the labor market—in part because of the limited scope of the investigation but perhaps more critically because these theories are not formulated in falsifiable terms. Indeed, there may be some truth in both perspectives, but even so, we can only consider how our findings are loosely "consistent" with each general point of view.

Perhaps the best point of departure for this discussion is to look at this recruitment process in light of the argument of human capital theory. Recall that human capital theorists argue that workers are paid a (real) wage rate proportional to their marginal product (subtracting costs for general training); since better educated workers are more productive (and are in short supply), they receive a positive return for their investment in education. Presumably, then, MBAs are rewarded so well because their schooling has provided them with productive abilities which few others without this training possess.

Two years of business school experience likely does have some productivity-enhancing impact, but the recruiters do not *act* in ways consistent with the notion that education is being rewarded *because* it augments job performance. First of all, they give precedence in the selection process to those factors which business school could have relatively little or no effect on—personality factors and prior job experience. The socialization experience of business school may have some impact on personal characteristics, but the effect is likely to be marginal, and it is certainly quite removed from the business schools' own claims of providing distinctly "professional" managerial competencies. Moreover, if a particular type of schooling does enhance a person's productive potential, the better students in the program should be presumed to have acquired greater endowments of the desired competencies. Even if the relationship between grades and job performance is not tight, the logic of the school-enhances-productivity argument would suggest that recruiters should attempt to discern which candidates performed relatively well in the program. Yet, the accounts and activities of the recruiters point to a minor concern in most cases. In comparison to the selection process which many law school and medical school graduates go through, the corporate business concern for achievement in the academic program dedicated to professional training seems slight.

We do not mean to imply that the corporate recruiters are imposing irrelevant selection criteria. Many observers of corporate life attest to the importance of particular social abilities and styles (e.g., Kanter 1977 and Jackall 1983), and virtually all would agree that successful management involves an "art" which can be acquired only by the "hands on learning" of a job. Nonetheless, to the extent that these concerns are emphasized in the selection process, business schools function, in the words of Richard West, former dean of Dartmouth's Tuck School, as "bottling plants." That is, the MBA is a credential signalling desirable qualities, not necessarily related to the content of the education: "The product is about 90 per cent done before we ever get it. We put it in a bottle and we label it" (*Time* 1982).

We are not in a position to debate the size of the business school impact, but the comments and activities of the recruiters in this study do point to such an "allocation" process. As a group, the graduates of this elite business school benefit from their degree because it is presumed that they have the desired qualities, even if these cannot be primarily attributed to the educational program. To an extent, recruiters seem attracted to these students because they are all presumed to have acquired business-related analytic tools by going through the program. Yet, more fundamentally, the degree seems to signal a combination of an acceptable level of general analytical ability, a personal commitment to a business career, and a social style and cultural outlook which will "fit" the corporate world. The signals, then, primarily point to both "intellectual" and "cultural" capital, not "professional" job skills in the sense of special, distinctive knowledge-based competencies.[9]

The allocative aspect of an elite business school degree is further evidenced by the organization of the labor market in which Darden graduates are involved. Entry into the fast track positions at the firms in this study is not "open" so that the most productive workers among all potential employees are hired. The concentration of recruitment efforts at elite schools means that job candidates with the "right degrees" gain a large edge over those without the desired academic certification, even those who may have greater individual capacity to be productive than the beneficiaries of the screening process. Those with the academic certification of such a degree have a strongly enhanced chance of getting in the running at these firms.

This considerable restriction of the "fast track" competition to MBA candidates from a relatively small set of schools approximates what Rosenbaum (1979) has labelled a "tournament mobility" model.[10] The job candidates from the elite business programs have "won" previous academic and job "contests," and as winners, they have the opportunity to continue competing for higher positions, though they have no assurance of further success. On the other hand, the "losers"—those not admitted to the "right" schools—are excluded from further competition or compete with a severe handicap. To be sure, few of the prestigiously credentialled are likely to lose out entirely, but after proving their intellectual and practical mettle in previous contests, they now compete primarily in terms of their ability to interview well and personally "fit" with the styles of line managers who serve briefly as critical recruiting gatekeepers.

As we suggested, this restriction of the recruitment pool may be rational in reducing information processing costs on the assumption that the graduates of these schools are relatively likely to have the greatest potential for "productivity," significantly including the "contributions" of social and personal disposition. Yet the process continues without evidence of a larger rationality connecting the sought out attributes and actual productivity. Perhaps no such evidence can be forthcoming because, as one of the recruiters with a sociological bent speculated, "We're involved in a self-fulfilling prophecy; we say they're (MBAs) going to be successful." Only a fine-grained analysis of corporate operations can tell us whether there is merit to this view.

NOTES

1. MBA degree programs have differential "pay-off," and schools at different levels of the hierarchy may be valued for different reasons. In other fields as well, the prestige of the degree does seem to count, but the importance of school prestige seems particularly pronounced for MBAs.

2. Students indicate their preferences for firms through a variety of "bidding systems" and are assigned by their placement office to the interviewing schedules of individual recruiters. Firms may purchase a "résumé book" of the class and pre-select candidates to invite for interviews, though much more generally they rely on the students' expression of interest.

3. Before deciding whom to invite back, firms have the opportunity to request from students their transcripts and recommendations, though as we indicate later, few do so.

4. This presumption about a generally high level of academic ability is warranted. In the class of 1983 the G.P.A. range for the mid 80 per cent of the accepted applicants was 2.67-3.67; the GMAT range for the mid 80 per cent was 550-680. The admission committee considers records of achievement and leadership in jobs and extracurricular activities.

5. We have responses from two recruiters at 12 firms and from three recruiters at another firm. Recruiters from the same firm listed remarkably similar sets of schools, thus enhancing our general confidence in the responses of other respondents. We combined all school names on the recruiters' lists before classifying the set. There was more disagreement between recruiters as to how significant the on-campus visits were to their firm's overall recruitment effort. In the seven cases of disagreement, the responses differed between either "largely confined" and "focus but secondarily" or "focus but secondarily" and "focus actively." That is, none of the differences points to fundamentally different perceptions of corporate policy. In the cases of disagreement, we coded corporate policy as the response which indicated a more *open* recruitment process. Thus, the unit of analysis in this section is the firm, not the individual recruiter.

6. These "top dozen" schools are: Harvard, Stanford, Carnegie Mellon, Columbia, U.C.L.A, U. of California-Berkeley, Wharton (Pennsylvania), Sloan (M.I.T.), N.Y.U., Cornell, Tuck (Dartmouth), Northwestern.

We recognize that any list is inevitably arbitrary. Most observers of graduate business schools would recognize these schools as among the most "prestigious" or "highest quality," but a handful or so of other schools could probably lay claim with some validity to at least equal stature. Indeed, some of the most frequently cited "non-elite" schools in our study (Duke, Michigan, Indiana, and U.N.C.) have impressive reputations. If we had enlarged our "elite" category to include these schools, the proportion of companies following an "elite only" strategy would be somewhat greater. One irony of using this list is that the Darden School is not considered an "elite" school. However, its present elite status seems definite in that its 1983 graduates enjoyed the third highest average starting salary of all graduate business programs.

7. In making this classification, we included the Darden School in the base and designated it as an "elite" school.

8. If the only school visited was Darden, we classified the corporate recruiting efforts as "elite only."

9. While we have suggested that the business school socialization is not likely to have much direct impact on matters of personal style, the allocative functions of an elite business degree may have indirect socialization effects. As Kamens (1981) has argued, students entering a particular type of school recognize its "charter," its allocative function, and may adopt in advance the self-definitions and outlooks which fit the roles which they will go on to fill. Thus MBA students may enter the program with a reinforced sense of the importance of an "executive bearing."

10. Rosenbaum's (1979) explicit point of contrast is Turner's (1960) famous distinction between 1) contest mobility systems, in which selection for desired positions is delayed as long as possible and individuals compete in a relatively open arena on the basis of individual attributes, and 2) sponsored mobility systems, in which existing elites select individuals early in their lives for their ultimate positions. In this latter system, individuals do not "win" positions so much as are inducted into them. Clearly, the recruitment process described here lacks the openness of the contest sytem, but neither does early "success" guarantee the top position as implied in the sponsored system. An ongoing series of successes, in competitions with somewhat changing rules, is essential.

REFERENCES

Beck, E.M., Patrick Horan and Charles Tolbert II. 1978. "Stratification in a Dual Economy: A Sectoral Model of Earnings Determination." *American Sociological Review*. 43: 704-720.

Becker, Gary. 1964. *Human Capital: A Theoretical and Empirical Analysis with Special Reference to Education*. New York: Columbia University Press.

Behrman, Jack and Richard Levin. 1984. "Are Business Schools Doing Their Job?" *Harvard Business Review*. January-February, 140-147.

Berg, Ivar. 1970. *Education and Jobs: The Great Training Robbery*. New York: Praeger.

Bourdieu, Pierre and J.C. Passeron. 1977. *Reproduction*. Beverly Hills, CA: Sage Publications.

Change. 1977. "The Cartter Report on the Leading Schools of Education, Law, and Business." *Change* 9 (February): 44-48.

Collins, Randall. 1979. *The Credential Society*. New York: Academic Press.

Featherman, David and Robert Hauser. 1978. *Opportunity and Change*. New York: Academic Press.

Forbes. 1974. "Stereotypes, Statistics and Some Surprises." *Forbes*. 113: 119-124.

Foster, Edward and Jack Rogers. 1979. "Quality of Education and Student Earnings" *Higher Education*. 8: 21-37.

Freeman, Richard. 1976. *The Overeducated American.76. The Overeducated American*. New York: Academic Press.

Granovetter, Mark. 1981. "Toward a Sociological Theory of Income Differences." In I. Berg (ed.), *Sociological Perspectives on Labor Markets*. New York: Academic Press.

Jackall, Robert. 1983. "Moral Mazes: Bureaucracy and Managerial Work." *Harvard Business Review.* 83: 118-130.

Jencks, Christopher *et al.* 1979. *Who Gets Ahead?* New York: Basic Books.

Kamens, David, 1981. "Organizational and Institutional Socialization in Education." *Research in Sociology of Education and Socialization.* 2: 111-126.

Kanter, Rosabeth Moss. 1977. *Men and Women of the Corporation.* New York: Basic Books.

Kerckhoff, Alan. 1976. "The Status Attainment Process: Socialization or Allocation?" *Social Forces.* 55: 369-381.

Kingston, Paul. 1980. *The High Income Track.* Unpublished Ph.D. dissertation, Columbia University.

Mincer, Jacob. 1974. *Schooling, Experience and Earnings.* New York: Columbia University Press.

Pearson, George. 1959. *The Education of American Businessmen.* New York: McGraw-Hill.

Rosenbaum, James. 1979. "Tournament Mobility: Career Patterns in a Corporation" *Administrative Science Quarterly.* 24: 220-240.

Thurow, Lester. 1975. *Generating Inequality.* Washington D.C.: Brookings Institute.

Time. 1982. "The Money Chase." *Time,* May 4: 58-64.

Tinto, Vincent. 1980. "College Origins and Patterns of Status Attainment: Schooling among Professional and Business Managerial Occupations." *Sociology of Work and Occupations.* 7: 458-486.

———, 1981. "Higher Education and Occupational Attainment in Segmented Labor Markets: Recent Evidence from the United States." *Higher Education, 10:499-516.*

Turner, Ralph. 1960. "Sponsored and Contest Mobility and the School System." *American Sociological Review.* 25: 855-867.

Index of Authors

Subject Index

Achievement (academic): education as, xxviii; influence or college attendance, 105, 119, 122-123, 130-128; influence on law school attendance, 213, 216-226; role in corporate recruiting, 241-242

Admissions policies: at undergraduate institutions, 105-106, 117, 119, 122; historical changes, 125-126; favored treatment of private schools, 35-40; at Columbia, 78-81; at Penn, 84-86; at Harvard, Yale, Princeton, 91-93; effects of ascription, 122-123; effects of achievement 122-123; at law schools, 212-214, 225-226

Allocation models (of education), xxviii, xxix, 26, 170-171, 232-234, 249-250, 252

Ascription (social): education as, xxvii-xxviii; influence on college attendance, 69, 122, 126, 130-135; influence on law school attendance, 213, 216-226

Baltimore: upper class education, 64-66; role of Johns Hopkins, 65

Bancroft, George, 5

Bartering: defined, 29, 35; role of college advisors, 35-41; process, 37-41

Boston: upper class education, 54, 55-61; special role of Harvard, 57-8

Boyden, Frank, 10, 11-13, 16

Business executives: class background, 175-176; education of, 175-176, 181-182; effects of education on careers 183-199; effects of undergraduate prestige, 184-192, 194-199; effects of upper class origins, 187-192, 194-199; recruitment of, 231-251.

Business schools: prestigious degrees, 166-168, 180-181, 252; "top dozen," 252; recruitment procedures at, 235-237; characteristics of recruiters, 237-239; how recruiters evaluate stu-

dents, 239-243; as part of executive recruitment pools, 243-247; effects of undergraduate prestige on attendance, 166-168. *See also* Masters of Business Administration

Cambridge University, xviii, 27

Charters (of schools), 26, 27, 42, 154, 252

Choate School, xiv, 29, 183

Cogswell, Joseph, 5

Coit, Henry, 7-8

College advisors, 35-41

Columbia University: role in New York upper class education, 59-60; historical perspective on prestige, 78-84, 93-96; "Jewish problem," 80, 82-84, 94. *See also* Prestigious degrees: definitions of

Contest mobility, xxx, 253

Credential cronyism, xxvii, xxviii, 171, 173

Credentialism, xviii-xxix, 25, 148, 158, 234, 250. *See also* Screening and allocation theory

Cultural capital, xxviii, 123, 138, 177, 199, 233

Darden School, 236, 237, 241, 244, 245, 246, 248, 250, 252

Deerfield Academy, xix, 12-13, 29, 183

Drury, Samuel, 10

Duke University, xx. *See also* Prestigious degrees: definitions of

Education. *See* achievement, education as; ascription, education as

Eliot, Charles, 58

Elite schools: general definition of, xvi-xxi; imprecise designation, xvii-xviii; continuity, xx, usual rankings, xx; consistency of rankings, xx. *See also* Select 16, Little Three, Ivy League, Seven Sisters, Prestigious degrees